METAMORPHOSOS

A Proposed Path
to Independent Living

ESTON ROBERTS

ISBN 978-1-959895-73-2 (paperback)
ISBN 978-1-959895-74-9 (hardcover)
ISBN 978-1-959895-72-5 (eBook)

Printed in the United States of America

WESTPOINT
PRINT AND MEDIA

For Preston Roberts:
Metaphor Made Actual

CONTENTS

INTRODUCTION

There are as many roads to the "perfect" therapy as there are paths to heaven, and it is presumptuous to suggest yet another. Still, there are new concepts afloat in the world today, and the approach proposed here—under the cognomen of comparison psychology—attempts to give expression to some of these ideas.

Briefly stated, comparison psychology derives from the assumption that the psychoanalytic notion of drive motivation—that behavior may be occasioned by subconscious impulses—has been too easily discarded, and that survival drive—not Oedipal drives—is at the root of everything.

What I will be saying in this proposal is based on the following convictions: There is indeed more mystery in this world than is dreamed of in any philosophy, and we now know that things once held in perfect confidence were guesses from the start, and that comparison is at the root of every naturally, and unnaturally, occurring system.

Acceptance of the ineluctable uncertainty—the quantum wobble—of the universe, along with an honest commitment to the search for a realistic mode of living, would go a long way toward reducing the insanity on this planet, as well as the need for much human therapy.

With this in mind, the first step on this proposed path to independent living would be to recognize that the world we perceive is a product of the process of survival-based comparison, a process here referred to as metaphor.

The very words in this document are metaphor, from the individual letters that make them up to the individual words that form the sentences we read—extending, even, to the novels, poems, and treatises we write; the pictures we paint; the sculptures we sculpt; the experiments we run; and the dreams of happiness we pursue.

We may each have our individual metaphorical systems—although the many similarities everyone utilizes are worth recognizing—but the method we use is the same: the *s*'s in this paragraph resemble snakes; the *d*'s are backward *b*'s; the difference between *will and well* lies in the difference between the letters *i* and *e*.

Negative is the other side of positive; our apprehension of colors is a consequence of comparison, as are our senses of smell, taste, touch, and hearing. Nothing, it can be said, exists in our heads (or in the world) except for the agglutinating power of comparison.

Furthermore, phonology is a comparison of sounds; etymology is the study of related lexical variations; numbers compare by how they precede or follow zero; we identify the objects we see by relating them to others with similar or differentiating characteristics; the subjects we draw, or the pictures we paint, are versions of mental perceptions transcribed to paper or to canvas; and we travel from a geographical *here* to a geographical *there* based on guidelines of comparison.

Let us not, then, be naive. Just because the *equals* mark is not apparent in all equations; just because the *as* or *like* is missing from our clauses; just because the brain doesn't inform us at its every step of the difference in temperature that justifies hot or cold (neuroscientists inform us the brain makes a thousand daily decisions without consulting us); just because we've learned the process so well—or so early—that we are not aware of its happening does not mean we are not comparing.

To my knowledge, no one has pointed in detail to the agglutinating function of comparison, its pervasiveness in our universe, or, most importantly, to that most powerful product of comparison—the human self-concept.

Metaphor—the engrained formula at the root of life—is the source of everything on the planet—even, I will argue, the production of matter.

Granted the premise, then, that everything conceived in the brain and in nature is metaphorical, the second concept I will be arguing for is that all metaphors derive from the drive to survive.

The desire to avoid the charge of an enraged bull differs from the desire to escape the presence of a boring acquaintance only in the degree to which adrenaline surges. Both are variations on identical themes of survival—the one being physical, the other psychological.

Survival drive is seen here as that propulsive force born of comparison; it was metaphor at inception. When, I will argue, in that post "big bang" moment; two subatomic particles discovered affinity and merged, these particles experienced an early form of consciousness, something like that emotion we have come to verbalize as the *aha!* response.

This initial moment of awareness—and recognition of any affinity would not be possible without some degree of awareness!—was subject, as was everything in nature, to evolutionary adaptations important to survival efficiency. Over time, this initial awareness came to be associated in the mind with pleasure, the search for it becoming the driving force behind all forms of consummation.

Thus, it was that metaphor came to be. It was the first instance of unity—the creation of substance (be it gas, energy, matter, or idea)—out of apparent nothingness; and, coincidental though it was, it is to this cosmic coupling that I trace the first instance of consciousness and the birth of survival drive, the comparison force behind the creation of everything known and yet to be known in the universe.

The way metaphor secures survival in the physical world is through aggrandizing. One physical particle identifies affinity in—similitude in aspects of constituents—and then combines with another particle. The process might be better characterized as absorption, for the end effect is one of growth through assimilation.

This differs, somewhat, from the metaphorical process involved in survival of biological forms. In protoplasmic materials, physical survival is accomplished through ingestion—a process based not so much on affinity as on compatibility. Here, survival is accomplished by recognition of edibility—a variation on absorption, yes, but one that extends the recognition of affinity to another level.

The processes are similar, but there are differences. In the second instance, the metaphor that is survival allows for matter to move beyond the mineral to the biological—from the solid to the flexible, from the inanimate to the animate.

This progression is a lesson in metaphor and the way it can take one affinity and build upon it in a new and unexpected way, never leaving its base entirely behind. Metaphor is indeed at the root of everything.

Matter, while a product of metaphor, is something else in addition. Created in the mind that is nature, matter is no less a metaphor than any idea, but it is also an object possessing mass, as opposed to the metaphorical equivalent of mass, idea—an immanence of the brain based, like all metaphors, on survival.

It follows, then, that man-made objects—pharmaceuticals, laser beams, political treatises, poems, even this theory of metaphor—are metaphorical products (objects) that use matter to give substance to ideas.

This is an important concept, for in the world of mind-held metaphor, objects like poems and other works of art are held to be as real as granite—just formed from immaterial materials—and, in the way of physical objects, they may be employed in the making of other objects.

Be it rock, then, or poem, macroeconomics or quantum computer, the thing is an object. Whether held in the hands or in the mind, these metaphors are objects given form at the behest of survival drive.

Metaphor, then, is not only the idea of bones in the skeleton; it is the skeleton as well. Nothing—maker or product, action or idea—exists except through the agency of metaphor. An idea framed in nature—the making of an atom, for instance—is no less an idea than one formed in the brain; both, though we tend not to see it as such, are formed in nature.

Impelled by the original metaphor, survival drive, a seed will grow from sand lodged in the crevice of a sidewalk, a house cat will beard a pit bull terrier when her kittens are threatened, and salmon will challenge a waterfall to return to their spawning spot.

As it is with the pollination of flowers, so is it with the mating of fireflies; the courtship of swans and humans, the fusion of particles, rocks, and chemicals. All is about fertilization (fusion), about the stratagems employed in nature to the end of continuation of the species, to survival!

This urge to survive—my term for it is "survival drive"—is the original, first-cause metaphor. It can be seen as an appetite coursing beneath the surface of all existence.

Time, to survival drive, is meaningless; its probing fingers seep into every crack and crevice of potentiality. That which works, works; that which does not work survives to fuel other experiments. Survival drive is the idea (metaphor) of eating made possible by the act of eating.

Survival is its business, its only business.

Since, from the perspective of this argument, the metaphor that is survival drive can be shown to be at the root of everything in nature, it should not surprise that language too is metaphorical—to its very core!

As sounds are assigned meaning, as dictionaries are created to standardize spellings and definitions, as rules of syntax are established, and as sentences are ended with periods, so does the brain—the ultimate survival organ—using the same patterns and methods as those utilized in nature—turn language into the most effective survival tool ever invented.

On one level, language is a device for asking for food, warning of predation, for seduction—a tool, in other words, for physical survival.

On another level, one more important to our humanness, language functions as an expression of the need for companionship and communication—a tool, ultimately, used for securing social and psychological survival.

Hunger pangs remind us of the need for food, and food is required for survival. Even so, it is a short leap from the need for food to the desire for money; and the distance between an infant's cry for food and a grown man's sorrow for an unrequited love is not as long a journey as we have been led to believe.

The brain, it goes without saying, is a complex organ. In fact, my reading suggests that an event of nearly supernatural proportions occurred with the advent of the modern human brain; and it can be argued that, in this convoluted and complicated cranial production, survival drive has—in a manner of speaking—made itself into a physical object embodying the essence of survival drive.

The brain's primary function in advanced species is replacing certain survival functions in nature, assuming, thereby, important survival drive functions unto itself. Making metaphor of metaphor in a manner of speaking, it gives birth to a new version of genesis: nature recreating the universe and itself in the miracle of the metaphor-making human brain.

The great evil—in this twenty-first century garden is not a wily seducer of apple-tasting maidens, a wearer of horns, or a carrier of heat-tempered pitchforks. Rather, today's evil is seen here as the unwillingness—or inability—of the human animal to accept responsibility for the conscious development of self-concept, thereby forfeiting the opportunity to unbind itself from the chains of mechanized survival.

Let us begin, then, with the recognition that the brain is first and foremost the organ of survival. This is true whether we're discussing the brain equivalent of the simplest protozoan or that presumed acme of evolutionary wizardry—the brain of Homo *sapiens*.

In fact, and this is a point not made enough of, all thought and behavior is survival-based, and survival drive is first brain—in fact, big brain—with the universe as its cranium. The human contribution is psychological survival.

Interestingly, the metaphor that is survival drive works just like that vaunted survival strategy called intelligence; and, in fact, IQ tests measure only the ability to survive in the milieu being tested. Intelligence, then, may be seen as only one of the many instances in nature of metaphor mirroring metaphor.

In the grand mission of survival, the successful metaphorical gambit is retained and expanded to its limit of potentiality; and even failures may serve as reminders of survival tactics gone awry. The higher the IQ, the greater the odds of survival—physically and psychologically.

And so it goes. Everything is metaphor based on the metaphor that is survival drive.

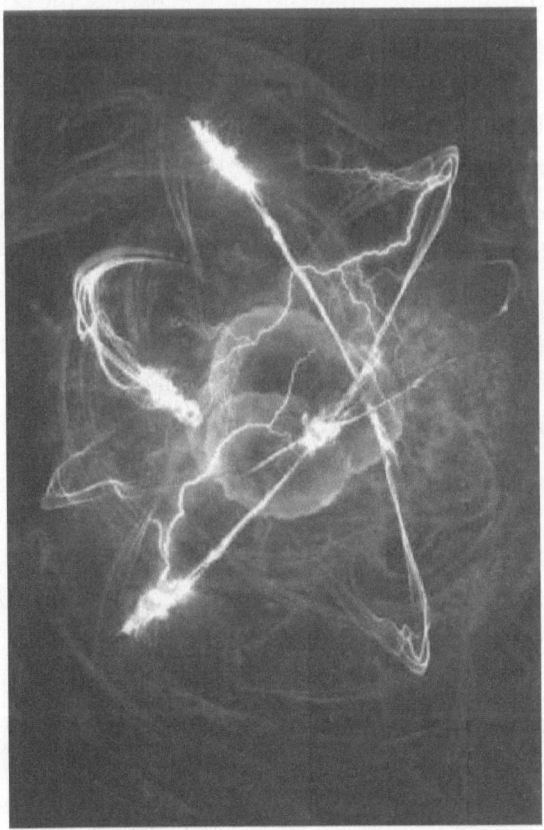

Metaphor in action

Even as the Darwinian concept of evolution may be seen as an extended metaphor of the way life survives, adapts, and develops, so may a similar metaphorical concept be helpful in describing the transition from the world of matter to the world of mind.

To that end, and for ease of discussion, I have invented three types of metaphor, each evolving from its predecessor, and each demonstrating the leap-frog progression that is the footprint of metaphor.

My terms for them are reflexive, hylozoic, and synthetic.

As stated, it is believed that the earliest example of reflexive survival urge occurred in that moment when subatomic particles collided, accidentally discovering affinities and merging. This earliest version of metaphor is aptly illustrated in quantum mechanics, the science of mathematically discovered affinities.

The first of these proposed types of metaphor, reflexive, may be observed in such activities as the autonomic act of breathing, the narrowing of pupils exposed to light, the protozoan's movement around an object, or that act of blinking when eyes are threatened by unexpected movement. Reflexive metaphors exist for the survival of the physical organism.

This suggested form of metaphor is intimated in Murray Cox's quotation of Marion Frank—University of Connecticut—in "A Question of Taste," (**Omni**, February, 1989, 78):

> The old brain is a very primitive region of the human brain, controlling involuntary responses...Hunger, anger, sexuality, emotions—the non-rationalized, pre-programmed responses occur in the limbic system. It's *"hard wired"* to react automatically to a variety of incoming information. (My italics)

Reflexive metaphors, then, are "hardwired" by definition. The "incoming information" (according to my definition) always deals with matters of physical survival.

Later on, Cox is quoted as follows:

> The pleasure (or pain) principle in taste is *reflexive*:
> An infant smiles and sucks when he tastes sweet or
> scowls and spits when he tastes bitter.

On point, a friend recently sent me a video of an infant laughing at the rending of paper by an unidentified male. As the man, presumably a parent figure, continued to rend the paper, the child's laughter increased in intensity, reaching a point approaching delirium.

Initially, my response to the video was one of consternation—how could so young an infant, quite obviously still in the stage of reflexive metaphor, find humor—the product of newly observed incongruity—in such a mundane event?

After much thought and some discussion with a writer friend, it occurred to me that the child, who did not yet possess a concept of self, lived in a world where everything was perceived as a part of everything else.

The act of tearing paper, which illustrated incongruity, evoked the reflexive metaphorical response of laughter. The greater the incongruity and the longer it continued, the greater the laughter.

Along the same line, and with interesting implications for the existence of reflexive metaphors, is a study published in **Scientific American** (Jesse Bering, Special Report, 07/2012) under the title, "The Rat That Laughed."

Bering reports that rats—particularly juvenile rats—laugh, going on to cite Jaak Panksepp's comment that a "primordial form of laughter" serves "an important communicative-affective component…which invigorates social engagement…."

He quotes neuropsychologist Martin Meyer as having suggested that laughter (specifically watching cartoons or listening to jokes) activates evolutionarily ancient structures such as the amygdala and nucleus accumbens.

Based on Bering's article, it is possible to affirm that not only does laughter have primitive roots in animals other than humans, but it has vital survival uses as well. The laughing baby may well have been planting seeds for the eventual flowering of psychological survival.

Reflexive metaphors, then, may be seen as pre-programmed into the system and not "pictured in the mind." They should be viewed, nonetheless, as expressions of survival drive—in the case of the laughing baby, as a reflexive response to incongruity deriving from a conflicted survival drive.

As the earliest form of metaphor, reflexive metaphors are necessarily restricted, in potential for expansion, by neural and cranial limitations (physical space) and by the inability to adapt to circumstances these processes prohibit.

Furthermore, the evident tendency toward increasing survival efficiency, a development found everywhere in nature, doubtlessly contributed to the decreasing employment of reflexive metaphors, as more efficient permutations evolved.

But this is not meant to imply that reflexive metaphors, while unthinking, are insignificant. They perform vital survival functions even today, some of them psychologically pertinent.

As the most primitive expressions of survival drive, reflexive metaphors provide access to the vital (often violent) energies of creation, and it is no coincidence that poetry and the arts—vital expressions of the creative impulse—plunge their roots into them—as do (it must be said) those horrible obituary poems born (even though sometimes provided by funeral home officials) of deep and personal sorrow.

Though obviously advanced in comparison to reflexive metaphors, the next version of metaphor, hylozoic, bears that signature of reflexivity implanted in the first metaphor in that it bears a clear relationship to the drive for physical survival.

Even so, my use of the term hylozoic, is admittedly an arbitrary one, since the line of demarcation between it and its successor cannot be clearly drawn. This said, it is almost certain that the left cranial lobe, with its facility for pragmatic and logical thinking, is involved.

For purposes of discussion, hylozoic metaphors may be differentiated, based on the fact that their referents of comparison are always drawn from objects existing in the physical world. As such, they are seen as metaphors concerned with matters of physical survival.

The difference between them and reflexive metaphors lies in the conscious (rather than pre-programmed or implanted) manipulation of physical constructs in the best interests of survival of the physical self.

In other words, the motive for survival in hylozoic metaphors is shifted from the reflexive to a level where connections between object and purpose are consciously perceived and self-directed.

They derive from the survival urge, yes, but now natural objects can be purposefully manipulated to secure or facilitate physical survival. In this sense, hylozoic metaphors are always transitive.

Hylozoic metaphors range in complexity from a chickadee pecking a sunflower seed against a tree limb to get at the meat inside to an engineer designing and building the Golden Gate Bridge.

Always directed at facilitating the business of physical survival—transportation efficiency being a case in point—hylozoic metaphors, be they bridges or skyscrapers, may be beautiful, but that is a factor owed to a later (or added) function of metaphor.

Products of an evolving brain that is capable of conscious thought and memory, hylozoic metaphors make possible a trial-and-error process of transposition—a shifting of a survival constituent from one slot to another in the comparison equation—as in: I want *food*, I want *meat*, I want *beef.*

The evolution of hylozoic metaphor made for a significant development, in that it either replaced or rendered more efficient that engineered system for survival represented in reflexive metaphors, replacing the engrained and cumbersome process of natural selection—a successful hylozoic strategy obviating the need for a biological one—with the ability to initiate individual survival tactics based on survival necessity.

Finally, hylozoic metaphors make possible the acquiring of skills through practice and the translation of mind-held concepts into action-based gesture—the kinetic imitation of idea—thereby freeing intelligent life forms to get about the business of physical survival with technological efficiency, technology being the adaptation of hylozoic gesture to physical survival.

The development and utilization of tools and machinery are, of course, metaphorical extensions of gesture and retain the hylozoic stamp. They are, in other words, still dedicated to survival of the physical self.

In the final analysis, it is likely this distinction—crafts are dedicated to physical survival—that differentiates them from the fine arts.

Hylozoic metaphors exist in the brain regions where pragmatism and logic prevail, these qualities providing the impetus for many survive-first, survivalist metaphors. Even so, they were seminal to the evolution of synthetic metaphor.

This third level of metaphor, synthetic, is so called because it substitutes symbolic constituents for physical referents, discovering unthought of affinities between ideas and objects in the natural world. Through the use of synthetic metaphor, an idea takes the place of a natural object, establishing a symbolic comparison by saying that an idea is the same as an object—creating, in other words, a synthetic metaphor.

What happened here is not so surprising as it is miraculous, because it is this act of symbolism that made it possible over time to move from a strict concern with survival of the physical self to a concern for survival of a non-physical self—an entity with no existence save a metaphorical one.

This shift (indebted as all metaphors are on their previous incarnation) was, of course, facilitated by hylozoic metaphors in that, through them, individuals could compare their gestural efficiency with that of fellow tribesmen and reach conclusions about their incipient synthetic selves.

Still, it may safely be said that the arrival of synthetic metaphor is the second most important event in the history of the planet, leading eventually to that latest, and most important, permutation of synthetic metaphor, self-concept.

From the point of the arrival of self-concept (and the consequent desire to protect the psychological self), one may deduce the origin of language, the near demise of grunting and pointing, the development of true science (as opposed to technology), and the advent of the first conscious artist and artistry—all dedicated to that new version of survival—the psychological.

Language, because it so clearly evolved from the need for physical survival—"Hand me that apple. Hands off my woman!"—its laws (grammar and syntax) may be seen as applications of a metaphorical system of survival.

As such, it provides us with our best template for study of the metaphor phenomenon.

Not only are all levels of metaphor found in language—the interjection for reflexive, technical writing for hylozoic, and imaginative prose and poetry for synthetic—but a careful analysis of its structure reveals metaphor at work on every level—from the phonetic to the semantic, from the etymological to the grammatical. Language is metaphor to the core.

In much the way it is with language, the study of human psychology may reveal the role of metaphor in our strategies for survival—particularly those relating to survival of the psychological self.

Indeed, underlying the entire argument of this proposal is the conviction that many, if not most, non-genetic psychological disorders may be traced to problems with the perceived state of the psychological self.

This document proposes, then, that the path to independent living begins with the metaphor that is self-concept and with our recognition that self-concept is a structure built consciously or unconsciously by us, and for which we alone are responsible.

As will be shown, self-concept is a metaphor grounded in action—actions and ideas ideally chosen in the interests of a consolidated sense of self.

For obvious reasons, I have called this approach to mind study "comparison psychology."

Summary

The theory of metaphor assumes that all natural phenomena arise from the drive to survive, which is an in-built impetus driving matter and mind to their full potential in a medium where time is irrelevant and survival a consequence of accident allied with opportunity.

There is no inherent meaning in anything. The metaphor that is life is the offspring of happenstance, and its significance is assigned rather than inherent.

It is proposed that life and thought evolve through levels of metaphorical processes called reflexive, hylozoic, and synthetic; that these processes are themselves products of the metaphorical shift that is genesis to everything; and that all planetary problems—be they social, political, or psychological, geographical or environmental—are the consequence of our failure to understand the nature of our responsibility for self-concept and for the opportunities it provides for true freedom and independence.

The purpose of this study is to explore the processes by which self-concept is created and to propose rudimentary guidelines to a system for self-reformation whereby people can learn to practice responsibility for who they choose to be—thereby becoming free in the only sense that is truly possible.

CHAPTER ONE

Self-Concept as Metaphor

It would seem to be self-evident that self-concept is not a tangible entity—no matter that V.S. Ramachandran says it is made up of atoms!—and that it occupies no specific site in body or brain. Indeed, efforts to characterize it elicit words such as *evanescent, immaterial, non-physical,* words that are synthetically metaphoric.

Self-concept, while existent and real, is not made of matter, but of formula, of discovery of the particular affinity that makes physical representation possible. Like all synthetic metaphors, it is one part idea and one part matter. It suggests a solution to the quandry presented by the conflict between Einsteinian relativity and quantum physics—i.e., matter may be altered or destroyed, metaphor cannot.

Still, no one would deny self-concept's existence, as no one will deny its importance. And yet the significance of self-concept as metaphor has nowhere received the discussion it would seem to merit.

Socrates is said to have enjoined his students to "know thyself"—no easier a task in the fourth century before Christ than it is now. Still, the knowledge of self is forerunner to knowledge and ultimately to wisdom itself. To know the self, we must know what the self is.

Without a sense of agency, the industrious pismire, scurrying out in search of sustenance for inhabitants of its hill, would not be capable of pursuing strategies to keep itself alive; the bee could not sting its keeper; and the spider could not spin her sagging silver coronet to swing in morning dew.

The sense of self is necessary to physical survival.

The self and self-concept, however, are different things. The second is a synthetic product—a metaphor—of the first, and, while all life forms possess a rudimentary sense of self, not all life forms possess self-concept.

At the same time, knowledge of one's body occupying and moving in space (see introduction) is a hylozoic awareness, essentially a concern with keeping the physical self alive—a concern shared with viruses, bed bugs, and certain botanical species.

Self, then, should be seen as physical—an object in physical space concerned primarily with reflexive duties.

Self-concept, on the other hand, is a synthetic discovery—the self's awareness of self—and it is this awareness that lays the foundation for that edifice that becomes our life; that we are what we are is a consequence of how we perceive ourselves to be.

Self-concept is a metaphor traceable, as are all metaphors, first to the urge to survive and second to a substance (body) anchored in the physical world. It is, however, a synthetic metaphor as opposed to a reflexive or hylozoic one.

In other words, self-concept is a metaphor originating from the drive to keep the phenomenal self alive, "alive" in this sense meaning intact, content, or self-secure. Its psychological forms are traceable to counterparts in the physical body or the physical world—an aspect of grounded metaphor that will receive considerable emphasis in this document.

In other words, the self-concept metaphor is grounded in its allegiance to objects found in nature and provides, ultimately, the basis for integrity in one's choice of metaphors. Much more on this later!

At this point, it is important to emphasize that synthetic metaphors express themselves through synthetic metaphors, and the closest equivalent of physical survival in the metaphorical world is, by necessity, descriptors such as "intact," "content," and "self-secure."

Adjectival qualities such as low self-esteem, weak self-efficacy, and inadequate self-respect should not be confused with self-concept. They are, as stated, adjectival, qualities that a concept of self may or may not possess. Self-concept is an entity, not a modifier.

Self-concept, then, is a metaphorical construct—likely a holographic one located in different areas throughout the brain—that evolves over time, beginning and evolving, as all metaphors do, from that early awareness of particle affinities, the most primitive form of metaphor.

These cosmic, subatomic particles, geared to merge by the pleasure found in discovering affinities, sought out other particles, formalizing, thereby, the idea of survival as the act of creating (*id est*, orgasm)—as an act forever associated with pleasure.

It was thus that reflexive survival drive and procreation came to be connected and, in terms of outcome, synonymous. In other words, the instinctive drive to survive came to mean, in terms of actual practice, to create, to give birth to.

Survival drive is a self-creating avariciousness exhorted on by that fore-mentioned pleasure found in finding out connections. As it continued to seek out other avenues of expression, it became a making thing, a creator of objects and concepts.

That this progression (Darwin called it evolution), hypothetical though it be, came about as a consequence of trial-and-error methods in the laboratory that is nature, makes it no less a metaphor. It is, in fact, the method of metaphor: Try this. Oh drat! Try this. Eureka!

Thus, an orangutan using a stick to extract termites from deep within their hill is surviving through application of a metaphor, though in this case a hylozoic one. Such is also the case with a dam-creating beaver and a Harvard-educated engineer designing a better structure for the containment of energy.

As the trial-and-error, natural-selection metaphor is exemplified in the movement from reflexive to hylozoic, so did the "idea" of non-physical constructs functioning in the place of physical objects lead eventually to the formulation of synthetic metaphor. It is this synthetic metaphor that is ultimately responsible for the evolution of self-concept, the engine of non-physical (psychological) creations.

In a way of illustrating the process, consider the well-known figure, "The road was a ribbon of moonlight..." (Alfred Noyes, "The Highwayman"). The road (also a hylozoic metaphor facilitating physical survival) is an object in nature and provides the grounding element (the certain indicant of metaphorical effectiveness—see *operant* in dictionary, (Appendix II), page 385.

The road is perceived by the poet as a "ribbon" that ripples in the moonlight, transforming "highway" and "ribbon" into metaphors that remind the highwayman of the ribbon in Bess's black hair; of her standing in the old inn's door; and of his dream of their riding off together, making love, having babies, and enjoying everlasting bliss on the metaphorical road of life.

The metaphor, once it leaves the highway, consists entirely of abstract elements—leading back to and related to the highway, but, unlike it, not made of matter. These abstract elements are synthetic and therefore amenable to utilization by the metaphor that is self-concept—a metaphor restricted in use to synthetic elements.

Like the highway, self-concept is also an object, but its constituents are metaphorical, not tar and gravel. This means that the metaphor that is self-concept is synthetic, yes, but synthetic with a difference.

This difference—made possible by the substitution of idea for matter—means that self-concept is grounded not in nature, but in action, a consequence with far-reaching repercussions, repercussions that will be discussed in greater detail in Chapter 6. For now, the emphasis remains on the evolution of metaphor.

It is hypothesized that the synthetic process went as follows: The agent willing an action and observing its consequence remembers the outcome and attaches a label (a metaphor) to it. The nature of the label is determined by whether the outcome is conducive or aversive to survival—in other words, positive or negative.

Whether the survival consequences are viewed as beneficial or harmful—to the physical body or to the perception of self—those ideations become synthetic metaphors recorded in the history that is self-concept.

Thus, the metaphorical process that is comparison begins. The infant, its puckered mouth spasmodically sucking for sustenance, is a reflexive appetite unleashed into a meaningless void. Its only motive is survival, its piercing scream, a cry for food, for safety, for comfort.

The infant's consciousness of the absence of, or its need for, these essentials is its first comparison, and the consequences to an incipient self-concept are potentially enormous because of the fact that self-concept can only be constructed of materials (experiences) that are available.

For instance, children born under the exegesis of extreme want are forever scarred, and no parents worthy of the name (and not barred by circumstances beyond their control) would suffer this predication to occur, let alone endure.

> *A child conditioned to survival insecurity is very likely the source of evil in the world.*

William James, still inimitably quotable after all these years, describes in **Notes from Psychology: Briefer Course** (p. 16) the newborn's universe:

> The object which the numerous inpouring currents of the baby bring to his consciousness is one big blooming buzzing Confusion. That Confusion is the baby's universe; and the universe of all of us is still to a great extent such a Confusion, potentially

resolvable, and demanding to be resolved, but not yet
actually resolved, into parts.

And it is certainly true that an unsatisfied need for sustenance would
contribute to the "Confusion" that is the baby's universe (the reader is
referred to the episode of the crying baby discussed earlier) and it is evident as well that the source of the infant's confusion is the urgings of
survival drive as suggested by James's phrase "demanding to be resolved."
The "part" not "resolved" is, of course, the concept of self.

That James is aware of this engrained comparison process is apparent. He refers, for instance, to the "law of relativity" (*op. cit.*, p. 25) as
being a product of physiological processes he might well have characterized as reflexive. And on page 290 (*op. cit.*) he writes:

> The machinery of recall is thus the same as the
> machinery of association, and this machinery of asso-
> ciation, as we know, is nothing but the elementary
> law of habit in the nerve-centers.

To James, clearly, the business of association (my term for the
end-product of this being metaphor) was engrained and "habitual," and
it never seems to have occurred to him that this process could itself be
subject to the kind of evolutionary processes suggested in my terms,
hylozoic and synthetic.

What he describes would seem to correspond in every respect to my
concept of reflexive metaphors—which are, indeed, "mechanical."

But the impulse that is metaphor will not abide stagnation, will not
stay "mechanical," and inevitably the exploratory process that characterizes survival drive's quest for efficiency led to the development of the
metaphors here described as hylozoic and synthetic. It is, of course, synthetic metaphor that laid the rails for self-concept, the object of primary
interest here.

It was to the end of firming up my theory of self-concept that over a period of years, during which I taught my theory of self-concept to counselors in the Migrant and Seasonal Farmworkers' Youth Employment and Training Program (YETP) and to disadvantaged students in Wilson, NC, that I set out to determine when students first came to be aware of their consolidated sense of self, it being believed that memories can only be remembered when there exists an agent of self around which to center them.

By requiring students in the Wilson OIC (Opportunities Industrialization Center) program to write down their earliest memory, including a self-portrait from the time of the memory, I was able to determine the average age of self-concept consolidation to be age three. Furthermore, analysis of the drawings—and the fact that none of the drawings was rendered as stick figures—confirmed (in my mind) their possession of a consolidated sense of self.

Of course, James does not perceive the self-concept as a unitary construct, as the addenda he attaches to his title "The Self" (Chapter XII) indicates. There he lists an "*empirical self*," "the *material me*," "the *social me*," and "the *spiritual me*."

But the fact is that, while experiences may well be organized under categories, the concept of self as metaphor mandates that it be a unity, otherwise every effect would have its disparate unity. We would all be libraries without a librarian, warehouses for books without a Dewey Decimal System!

Indeed, there is no reason why the self, like a crafted diamond, should not be a many-faceted though unitary entity: here a splendid shaft of perfect light; there a haunted, pulsating shadow quivering over a mysterious lunar landscape.

And while (as James's earlier citation illustrates) the infant is born without a concept of self, it will inevitably acquire one—as a consequence, very likely, of James's "big blooming buzzing confusion" and the infant's survival-driven need to make sense of the deluge of sensations assaulting her.

The process whereby the many aspects of personality may be consolidated into a unified image of self is suggested in an early introduction to chaos theory by Kathleen McAuliffe in her **Omni** article "Get Smart: Controlling Chaos," (February, 1990, 43ff).

Referring to the work of Paul Rapp of the Medical College of Pennsylvania, she writes: "He is in pursuit of a new cosmology of the mind…revealing a secret inner order to seemingly chaotic phenomena.…" (43)

She goes on to suggest that an entity she calls a "strange attractor" is somehow responsible for assembling neuronal firings into something like a concept of self.

Since Rapp's early investigations, much progress has been made in chaos theory, so much so that many types of attractors have been identified, all revolving around what are called basins of attraction.

Buying into the theory of chaos for a moment, we can see self-concept as a basin of attraction—a product of multitudinous happenings and impressions organized according to the survival principle of affinity and promulgated as a unified sense of self.

Were it possible to reproduce an image of the self-concept through use of electroencephalography (EEG), it is almost certain that what Rapp calls "the thicket of trajectories resulting from the mapping of our multitudinous human experiences" would spin out a pattern with all the wonder of a translucent lunar moth.

In this analogy, self-concept becomes a strange attractor. Not only is it a unitary structure, it also serves as a logical and human replacement for both the homunculus—the little man once thought to live inside our heads and command our behavior—and "that mindless (but so far elusive program)" McAuliffe says modern man has replaced him with.

It is suggested, then, that self-concept, under the auspices of survival drive, is the captain of the unitary ship of mind state, and the history of mankind teaches—subject to certain provisos—that it is a competent skipper indeed.

So it is that our perceived efficiency or inefficiency at securing those things required for physical survival serves as a basis for comparisons having to do with the perceptions of our personal worth and survival of self.

The result is, as stated earlier, the creation of a sense of agency (I-ness) imbued , as all metaphors are, with the drive to survive—in this sense to feel good about the state of one's inner being.

This advanced version of survival drive (self-concept) expresses itself in a thousand different ways—all of them psychological; all of them synthetic; and all of them expressive, each in its own way, of the desire to please, to feel worthwhile, to survive in the realm of self.

(So it is that the infant is driven to smile at its parents in the interest of survival; and so it is that a failure to please becomes a threat to survival and, therefore, a "badness.")

It is for this reason that young children blame themselves, seeing themselves as unworthy of love and never (until their teens!) faulting their parents.

It may be that it is this same unexamined metaphor—the inevitable product of low self-esteem—that is the source of both the abused spouse's continued acceptance of physical and psychological abuse and the abuser's willingness to inflict it.

At the risk of over-extension, it might be said that it is this sense of "badness" that becomes the driving force for evil in the world.

The desire to survive, in the sense of wishing to feel good about the perceived self, is the need that drives creation of self-concept; and as the child's sense of self grows stronger—developing assertiveness in the interest of its own survival—he will venture farther from the security of home and family, daring greater comparisons and risking greater failures in a willed "metaphorization" of the urge to survive.

Driven by the need for self-sufficiency and integrity—necessary elements of a consolidated sense of self—the child will eventually wish to take responsibility for her own metaphors in order to enjoy adult status—that ascendent state seen from the dependent state of childhood as powerful, wise, and free.

This will to independence and the drive for a sense of worth is especially pronounced during adolescence. It is a time decreed by nature and society when all must take, or abdicate, responsibility for their own metaphors.

This drive for independence (often mis-perceived as freedom) expresses itself in terms of specific biological developments—among them the drive for sex. This drive, by the way—despite the primacy mistakenly given it by Freud—is an expression of survival drive, as are—on the psychological level—the crush of peer pressure and the fact of fad, aspects to be discussed below.

Even so, it is important in this context to remember that of all the so-called biological drives, the drive for sex (after the driver's license!) is the one most identified in the mind of adolescents with adulthood and their right to wear the label.

It is at the point of adolescence that the need to like oneself—in this context the desire for the security that derives from psychological equanimity—becomes very nearly manic and obsessive. In fact, as I will document below, most mental illnesses appear during adolescence.

In the following example, names and events have been altered to protect identity: Rob, a young man of my acquaintance, had suffered brutal physical and psychological abuse as a child.

Rob spent most of his pre-adolescent years alone in the woods around his home, bird watching (a more apt metaphor on which to fasten the adolescent search for self is hard to imagine!) or engaging in intensive mock-hunting activities.

His knowledge of birds—he can identify them by song and knows their feeding, migratory habits, and mating practices—is phenomenal. Much of his time not spent in the woods was spent on obsessive fantasizing about peer acceptance or escapist engrossment in classical music.

During adolescence, Rob engaged almost exclusively in one-person games, although he would occasionally go hunting or camping with a reclusive friend, and his introvertive habits became obsessive.

Though exceptionally intelligent, Rob sought (unsuccessfully, during his senior year) peer approval through mockery of teachers and classroom shenanigans. He stayed a loner and continued to immerse himself in classical music, camping, and the memorization of entire sections of *The Encyclopedia Britannica*!

Once in college, Rob quickly allied himself with off-campus fringe populations, people who prided themselves on surviving simply, protecting the environment, and professing strong anti-establishment attitudes. Dumpster diving for food was one of his favorite (and necessary) diversions.

Not surprisingly, he was careless about class attendance and was woefully lacking in academic motivation. He developed a reputation for dare-deviltry and for unconventional behavior—living in a teepee, for instance, during winter blizzards.

Early in his tenure at the university, Rob acquired an interest in folk music, writing songs, playing guitar, and singing in restaurants and coffee houses. He even acquired, over time, a sizable local following. He eventually stopped performing because, as he reported, he was not very good--a faulty judgment, in my opinion.

After years of floating, and showing no interest in completing his degree, he was prodded into action by the registrar's threat of loss of credits; he promptly completed his degree. He is now married with children and is gainfully employed.

While Rob will never be conventional, and he remains suspicious of his material success as he was of his singing, much of the agony of adolescence seems to be behind him.

This said, even when that orgy of comparison madness called adolescence finally subsides, the struggle for concept survival does not end. Not only must adults provide for survival of themselves and family, they must, as Rob has discovered, establish and constantly defend an inner conviction of worth as human beings.

Adults must manage to feel good about themselves in the workplace—a veritable comparison factory based on performance expectation and built deliberately (in capitalist systems) to Machiavellian specifications—something Rob has managed to accomplish.

He was recently promoted to a position of responsibility at his place of employment and, through sheer will, has learned to maneuver competently through the labyrinths of administrative practices. This counts as an unexpected accomplishment, given his typical lost-in-self mindset, and is doubtlessly a tribute to his exceptional intelligence.

This sought-for core of central certainty—this concept of self that constitutes personality and provides the sane among us a modicum of contentment—is a result of actions consciously chosen in the interest of a successful life.

The individual's perception of the relative success or failure of his chosen ventures provides the basic outlines of self into which the metaphorical elements of life are volitionally, or reflexively, poured. Inevitably the goodness or badness of these elements is determined by the quality of self-concept, the evaluative instrument of all human experience.

The resulting image of self, whether it be affirming or denigrating, is a self-derived metaphor and an inevitable consequence of the individual's conscious or unconscious choice of metaphors.

No outside entity requires us to choose a particular idea or actions by pounding on the anvil of our mentality. We build by choice our edifices of self, else it is not possible for our minds to be free. The alternative leaves us a programmed entity with little or no responsibility for its destiny.

I cannot overstress the importance of choice-assuming responsibility for construction of self-concept when it comes to the concept of comparison psychology. Indeed, that no one can coerce another's opinion (metaphor) is basic to the concept being proposed here.

We "buy into" another person's view of ourselves because of inse-curity—either we doubt the worth of our own assessment or because our settling for palatable and pre-digested dogma provides easy access to cheaply bought security.

Victims of physical torture, we are told, must find their suffering intolerable before they give up their secrets and self-respect; and, while our society is more tolerant of confessions obtained through torture than it once was, capitulation to one's enemy is still regarded by many as a conscious act, indicative of cowardice.

While our running from physiological pain may be seen on the reflexive level as the brain's forewarning of an impending threat to phys-ical survival, the pain that accompanies threat to self-worth may be run from as well.

The difference lies in the fact that, because psychological pain is not perceived as life-threatening, our running may take the form of displace-ment or refusal to confront.

This strategy of "mind-blank"—electing to disregard or repress our fears by ignoring them— needs not be a conscious one, but it does, it will be shown, augur very real consequences for prisoners of a different kind of war.

At the risk of waxing moralistic, let it be said: metaphors cheaply bought result in costly consequences. In other words, the simplest way of dealing with problems of personal inadequacy is to use the mind-blank option referred to above.

Unfortunately, because our failures resurrect—through the agency of comparison—memories of past failures, our awareness of inadequacies has a nagging habit of refusing to stay hidden, a fact that intensifies pre-vious inadequacy experiences.

As the catalog of inadequacies accumulates, it becomes increasingly difficult to blank out our sense of failure. Eventually, our perception of worthlessness may become so pervasive that every endeavor is rendered ineffective by self-doubt.

When this occurs, as it inevitably must when the mind-blank option is over-utilized, our failure will have been conditioned beforehand by our cheap and easy choices.

The synthetic metaphor that is self-concept will have been made defective—insecure, inadequate, defensive—because of actions taken or not taken, actions taken on the bases of reflexive or conscious (synthetic) metaphors.

As mentioned, it is basic to the concept of comparison psychology that self-concept is the instrument of evaluation in the phenomenal world, and a direct consequence of this fact is that expectations govern outcome.

If one's frame of reference is dominated by the expectation that the universe will rise up and wreak havoc every time an action is initiated, it is but a matter of time before the expected havoc comes. This happens not so much from cause and effect as from expectation—the numerous generosities life having thrown at our feet not being seen because we were looking in another direction.

We will have conditioned a negative outcome by our expectations, and our expectations are a direct consequence of self-concept—our perception of ourselves as worthy, or not, of luck or justice or happiness.

If, on the other hand, our self-concepts engender expectations of positive outcomes, these are the outcomes we are most likely to see. Our sense of worth will be re-enforced by the good things we discover, and this, in turn, will adduce other positive outcomes. As positive consequences accrue, a presiding sense of competence will ensue.

Even if our positive expectations prove unfounded by outcome, we will still be left in a better position to deal with frustration as a consequence of practiced assertiveness in our own best interest. Empowered by confidence, we will dare to reach outside ourselves to others and to other ventures.

Freed from the fear that is insecurity, we can love, act in the best interests of our fellows, and undertake risks for the sake of discovery. In doing so, we make additional positive investments in our sense of self.

Paula—a freckled, raven-haired, excessively thin young woman—joined a training program for nursing assistants my employer sponsored at a local technical college. She was twenty-three years old but looked seventeen.

Possessed of an exceptional talent for drawing, Paula was abnormally shy—a state of mind owing, doubtlessly, to her having been informed by her high school guidance counselor that she was mentally retarded.

It turned out, though she did not have an easy time with academics, that she was not retarded. As a result of tender support from her instructor and loving encouragement from her classmates, she completed the course and was certified as a nursing assistant.

Regretfully, she was not successful in her first job. In fact, she was seduced shortly after she assumed the position and left the job pregnant and burdened by an overwhelming sense of failure.

She moved back in with her family—an unwholesome environment if ever there was one!—where as a child and young adolescent she had been subjected to dehumanizing sexual abuse by both her father and brother.

Paula and I managed to stay in contact after she completed the training program, and I'll not soon forget the two things she told me:

One was that the doctor had said her stomach was too small to have a baby and that if she had it, delivery would kill her. The second memorable thing she told me, her tone nearly indicating she was discussing a transaction in a pet store, was that a neighbor had told her she would take the baby should Paula decide she didn't want it.

Shortly thereafter I lost touch with Paula, and I'm afraid I assumed the worst.

A year and a half later, though, she showed up in my office, carrying the fattest, most jovial, Buddha-looking infant boy I'd ever seen. She was dressed in a white uniform and had taken a job in a nursing home nearby. Part of her responsibility involved driving a van for day residents.

This was a woman who just two years before had believed she was retarded and had never driven anything more complicated than a bicycle! She radiated a sense of genuine pride in her accomplishments.

Imperfect though Paula's life may yet turn out to be, she has developed significant competencies that her life circumstances would never have predicted. One hopes that confidence achieved through gainful employment and motherhood is transferable!

James (*op. cit.*, p. 458) speaks to the role of effort and will power—in sucessful achievements, elements I will argue that are empowered by a self-concept made strong by significant life accomplishments:

> Of course, we measure ourselves by many standards. Our strength and our intelligence, our wealth and even our good luck, are things which warm our heart and make us feel ourselves a match for life. But deeper than all such things, and able to suffice with itself without them, is the sense of the amount of effort which we put forth. Those are, after all, but effects, products and reflections of the outer world within. But the effort seems to belong to an altogether different realm, as if it were the substantive thing which we *are* and those were externals which we *carry*. (His italics)

At the risk of putting words in the mouth of a very wordy gentleman, it seems to me that the "substantive thing" being discussed here is will—what I would call empowered self-concept.

Perhaps an even more telling exposition of the way self-concept can energize life is told by the late Everett S. Allen (***The Raleigh*** [NC] ***News and Observer,*** 2/15/'87, 17D).

Allen recounts, in an article titled "Henry, once a statistic, enjoys a triumph," how a classmate of his had been imprisoned for a minor offense.

He writes, "…everything about his life had been indications of its tragic aimlessness."

According to Allen, Henry blamed his getting in trouble on the fact that he couldn't read, but it is the fact of Henry having been awarded a "class-work certificate" on which the story turns.

Allen writes: "I dare say [it was] the first record of achievement he ever had." He ends his story quoting Henry:

> "Now I can read and write pretty good," he said. "I got me a job when I get out of here…There's a old man I know runs a little store. I can sleep in the back. This old man can't see good no more. Needs help in the store. Needs somebody that can read and write," said Henry, with firmness in his voice that I never had heard before.

That "firmness" in Henry's voice is the voice of a strengthened self-concept—a newfound energy grounded in the fact of an accomplishment that was his alone and for which he alone could take credit.

It is, of course, absurd to believe that self-concept can be manufactured by our greeting ourselves each morning in the bathroom mirror repeating, "I'm the greatest!" (Mohammad Ali, by the way, earned right to that appellation by conscious actions taken in his own best interest.)

The kind of confidence being discussed here is a real-world consequence of real-world effort. True confidence is always earned, and its confirmation is the inner approbation, the *aha!* response of metaphor.

Paula's growth in confidence was not the result of her being a mother; it was a consequence of her being a good mother. Henry, through an exercise of will, found much more than a warm room in the back of a store.

This phenomenon, this relationship between what we look for and what we experience, is not a product of magic or even practice.

Rather, it is a consequence of conscious choices over which we alone have control and by which we are conditioned. It is ultimately this condition—the quality of self-concept we have constructed—that we bring to the act of perceiving.

This fact of individual responsibility for self-concept structuring will receive repeated emphases as exposition of the concept of comparison psychology continues. This necessary emphasis grows out of the woeful fact that self-concept can be, and often is, a product of reflexive processes.

Summary

That the awareness of a physical self as a separate and autonomous entity is an aspect of hylozoic knowing entirely different from self-concept—that edifice of assigned merit each of us builds or accretes for ourselves in interest of survival of our psychological selves—is an important distinction.

The physical self needs room to get around in, is distressed by insects and snakes, and is generally concerned with getting food and avoiding pain—issues primarily hylozoic.

Self-concept, on the other hand, is a synthetic metaphor we are aware of by age three, one we have fought for and confirmed, ideally in adolescence. It is a unitary construct with elements of strength and weakness, and the instrument of evaluation in the phenomenal world where expectations govern outcomes. Self-concept is the source of our humanness.

Furthermore, it is important to understand that self-concept is a consequence of action choices made in the interest of staying alive in the metaphorical world of self—survival being experienced there as feeling safe and confident in a world of mind constantly under attack by circumstances and our esteem-starved fellows.

Ultimately, comparison psychology proposes, we are each responsible for our own self-image, and it behooves us to choose our metaphors wisely, in our own best interests.

As a synthetic metaphor, the reader is reminded, self-concept is a factor of metaphor-made metaphor, the memory of reflexive and hylozoic metaphors and their consequences making it possible to derive synthetic ones. Unlike other metaphors—and in the interest of stability—the self-concept metaphor is based on actions and ideas consciously chosen in the interest of self-concept survival.

The synthetic metaphor that is self-concept, imbued as are all forms of metaphor, with survival drive, is concerned with survival of the psychological self, it having undergone the metaphorical shift that transforms "stay alive" into "be cool."

The drive to preserve self-concept, the metaphorical mechanism that makes sense of our phenomenological worlds, is the source of our humanness; those soft and easy, self-deceptive ways some of us choose are responsible for the psychological disarray that affects and infects our lives on this planet.

CHAPTER TWO

Dependency Metaphors and Self-Concept Consequences

(There are consequences to the casual use of metaphor.)

That human society is an organism—just as surely as a hill of termites, a school of sunfish, a hive of bees, a biotic ecosystem, or an outward spiraling solar system—has been noted before.

From the perspective taken here, everything under any sun is a product of the drive to survive structured according to the pragmatic law of survival efficiency.

Put in the context of quantum mechanics (the science of affinities discovered and put to use): a particle finds affinity or it doesn't; marriages, and metaphors, happen or they don't.

The survival motive that drives society also drives our planet and its universe. Our solar system is a metaphorical organism—its muscles and sinews, its pulsing blood and throbbing heart, its bones and marrow—all components of a loosely assembled, fluid and diaphanous, cellular-like structure held together by that law of gravity otherwise known as comparison.

Comparison, in turn, is the mechanism whereby the underlying unity of the universe—the all-encompassing idea from which all motion is generated—may express itself. This "idea" is, of course, the compulsion to survive, to propagate—a compulsion here called survival drive.

It is this underlying impetus, hidden within and buried under coiled eons of reflexive practice, that Freud—unaware of its involvement in all forms of matter—identified as the human unconscious. He didn't use the term "metaphor," but in fact the complexes, the behavioral systems he identified, are all metaphor to their core.

And while we can now say his discovery was a partial one (I personally find it unfortunate that he traced everything to sexual motive rather than survival drive) we must also say that his psychoanalytic answer was the first important step on the path to an understanding of metaphor in the sense developed here.

This underlying impetus to survival, this propulsive thrust to seek out and find all kinds of evolutionary adaptations, drove matter to the point of brain and, centuries later, to self-awareness. It was at this point in time—the advent of self-concept—that the reasoning brain was driven to find reasons for its existence.

Historically, these reasons have been contrived and fatuous, and Sir James Frazer has performed a yeoman-like service in tracing their evolution in his massive masterpiece, ***The Golden Bough: A Study in Magic and Religion*** (New York, 1967).

From the viewpoint of comparison psychology, it is first important to understand why there had to be reasons for our existence.

Comparison requires a base (an operant, see dictionary)—a prime number, in a manner of speaking—that is divisible by no other number than itself or one—an object in space, time, or mind against which to measure itself.

For there to be metaphor, there had to be an object or idea consciousness could act upon—first reflexive and eventually self-willed.

In other words, the brain as survival organism—the comparison factory *non-pareil*—must know how to identify what is marriageable, what is capable of being combined—be it gas or energy or whether a thing be judged as edible or poisonous, tasty or noxious, cathartic or pestiferous.

In fact, the human brain, programmed as it was/is for survival, is biased for cause and effect. For this reason, we are driven to look for origins, to argue that everything must have a beginning. Survival mandates that it be so, else existence is not logical, not safe.

Not only is this bias for cause and effect not carved in stone, nowhere is it mandated that this engrained propensity be allowed to enslave us in frozen absolutes.

As the quantum world now tells us, it is not only possible but necessary to live with probabilities—not everything is cut and dried, pre-made and immutable! As much as we deify it, the brain is still nothing but a survival organ. We are victims of its method, not inheritors of its truth.

We need not be enslaved, in other words, to the need for certainty, the unconscious expression of survival drive codified as staying alive.

The need for a deity, for instance, may be seen as a design-system flaw, engrained in the method by which we compute, and the pragmatic precept (true though it be) that nothing comes from nothing—a product of our black-and-white way of seeing—has led to fundamentalist and potentially devastating consequences.

As proposed here, the world of animate and psychological matter was built through comparison: this subatomic particle found affinity—be it spin, position, or velocity—with that other entity; these leaves are similar, but those berries are poisonous; I can eat this animal, but this animal can eat me; thunder rumbles, the god is near; and always the comparison begins with the desire to merge, to create—in other words, to survive.

(As stated earlier, it is important to recognize that the act of merging has come to epitomize the act of survival. A particle survives in its creation of another entity; a parent survives in the birth of her offspring;

and, to extend the metaphor, in poetry one idea reflects off another, and a poem—if successful—is born, and its author survives. Survival is a rose of many petals.)

Survival is the buzzing business of all creation, a business governed by the pragmatism of staying alive, of reproducing, at any cost.

But this was the old way, I hear you say. We have substituted civilization for the law of the jungle. We now have rules, science, and religion.

And I respond: Too many of us are still motivated by subliminal impulses; society, itself, is an organism with tentacles—intent upon its own survival. Laws are invented and punishments imposed, but just under the veneer of sophistication there pulses a molten lava of primitive survival urge.

As it is with society, so is it with us. Each of us is an organism driven by survival urge, generally unrecognized and uncontrolled.

We say we are sane and suave and have it all together, while all around us children are killing children, people are going insane, mass killers range the plains and classrooms armed with automatic killing machines, and babies die of plague from lack of vaccinations.

Obviously, we cannot forever survive our unexamined self-deceptions. We must find the will to take a long, hard look at our systems of survival—be they physical, social, or psychological. We must dare to challenge those fears we now hide from, to confront and name those metaphorical devices we consciously mislabel in the name of survival.

One such device for survival, and a glaring instance of our willful misuse of metaphor, is one I have termed *dependency metaphors*—avoidance comparisons with roots in our primitive reflexive origins.

Seen from the perspective of comparison psychology, dependency metaphors are survival formulas—vestigial re-castings of primitive survival methods, engrained in protoplasm, adapted to the survival needs of infancy, and then unthinkingly carried forward into adulthood.

Dependency metaphors can always be traced to a survival issue—that ancient metaphor of the gaping mouth, the maw of insatiable appetite, the engrained hunger to be fed.

Of all forms of planetary species, the most dependent is the human infant. As with most embryos, it is dependent, in utero, upon nutrients and protection provided by the mother; however, in the case of the human infant, this dependency is prolonged, because of the human infant's need for protection, into adolescence.

So, it is understandable that the infant clings hungrily to her mother and that on the cobbled road to maturity, one of the issues of adolescence is physical and psychological separation from the parent. It should not surprise, either, that variations on dependency metaphors—once so necessary to the infant's survival—are continued into adulthood.

What is surprising, however, is the extent to which these variations are hidden and the degree to which the problems ensuing from them are obfuscated with jargon and outright self-deception.

I will try, now, to clear away some smoke.

Like other forms in nature, dependency metaphors are capable of mutation—utilizing the beaten paths of synapses to neurons to secure survival—both physical and psychological.

This means that our dependencies on food or our fear of death may (in the way of quantum entanglement and riding the path of popular associations), easily translate into the love of money; our psychological insecurities metamorphose into power grabs and dictatorships; or we flock in droves to the fads of style, religion, and political correctness.

So it is that our love of father may unconsciously take the form of hero worship; patients may fall in love with their therapists; and teachers be transfigured into gurus.

So is it, too, that a perceived threat to psychological survival may translate the ancient survival imperative into a dependency on mother, which can, in turn, be shifted to wife dependence. It might be born again into sexual profligacy and potentially be transformed into serious mental illness.

It complicates the matter even more when, in our recognition of dependency, we respond with anger, displacing our displeasure at self onto the object of our dependency. In so doing, we continue the dependency, which is, this time, hidden under the protective—diversionary—cloak of anger.

Before further discussing the many guises of dependency, I would like to offer a case study (name and biographical details altered) by way of illustration:

Fredrick was born of humble origins in tobacco country and was driven by his father to play football and by his mother to excel academically.

His athletic abilities, despite his large and powerful frame, were limited; but Fredrick was a determined plodder, remaining on the team—at that end of the bench farthest removed from where the coach presided—throughout his high school years despite his average to mediocre performance.

His grades, however, were exemplary, and this was not only because of his talent for that plodding determination displayed in football, or because of his willingness to put his own needs second to the wishes of his parents. Fredrick was born intelligent and was admitted to one of the state universities on academic scholarship.

As will be suggested, however, his success in academics may've turned out to be something other than a positive investment in self-esteem.

In many ways, his willingness to put his wishes second to the wishes of others was the same sort of thing. Even as academics became a place he could retreat to when questions of psychological survival presented themselves, giving in to the wishes of his parents (and later his wife) could purchase an easy, though temporary, security.

But I get ahead of myself.

My knowledge of Fredrick's biography is sketchy and to some extent hypothetical, primarily because he rarely talked about his formative years; but I do recall there being an early marriage, a tour of duty in the military, and an assignment in Germany.

When I met him at the newspaper where we were both employed part time, Fredrick, a senior at the university, was already a husband and a father.

Somehow, despite the challenges of parentage, he had successfully maintained a perfect 4.0 academic average for four years at the university. When I met him, he had completed his course work and was eligible for graduation.

It was in the spring semester of the year I met him that Fredrick began having problems with a graduate-level course, in analytic geometry, as I recall.

Usually, a person who exhibited a strutting display of confidence, he turned suddenly despondent and suffered a dramatic drop in self-esteem—more intense, really, than the situation seemed to warrant. Eventually he withdrew from the course, thereby preserving his average and being graduated with honors on schedule.

There is little in Fredrick's biography, to this point, that can account for the direction his life has taken, though I had opportunity, once, to meet his parents for the span of an afternoon. From that brief visit, it was apparent there were dysfunctional issues in the family dynamic.

I remember sensing a great distance between his parents—a feeling, almost, of their occupying different lodgings in the same residence. His father barely spoke to Fredrick or to me, and I imagined a sense of repressed anger crackling beneath the surface of his presenting persona.

His mother, on the other hand, exuded protectiveness and an almost suffocating sense of solicitude for a son she loved enough to recognize his problems. Her solicitude extended to me, with repeated offerings to replenish my glass of too-sweet, iced tea.

I had the distinct impression that her devotion to Frederick did not extend to his wife, a possibility affirmed in the fact that neither she nor their daughter had gone with us on this visit and by the fact that his mother made no mention of her daughter-in-law, or granddaughter, during the visit.

Though I have no actual knowledge of it—Fredrick discussed his parents only in the briefest of passing references—I am of the opinion that his enlistment in the Air Force, and his marriage to a woman from north of the Mason-Dixon Line, constituted expressions of a desire for emancipation from differing versions of oppressive parental supervision.

It may have contributed, as well, to the absence of financial support from Fredrick's family.

(Unfortunately, to be successful, any act of separation must be taken from a position of strength, the initiator of the action doing so in confident expectation of success.

Should, on the other hand, the act derive from anger growing out of a need to escape dependency—as I suspect was the case with Fredrick—the outcome is likely to fail, in the sense of negative outcomes.)

My understanding of his wife's psychology leads me to suspect Fredrick was driven by her ambition as much as by his own insecurities. After graduation, Fredrick accepted a position in a distant city as manager of a branch bank. Within a few months, however, he had resigned this position for an entry-level position at a local chemical company.

The exact factors responsible for his resignation were not revealed to me, though I seem to recall problems with supervision and conflicts with a senior vice-president.

What is clear, however, is that Fredrick suffered a crisis in confidence reminiscent of that episode with the professor of analytic geometry referred to earlier.

His job as lab tester at the chemical company took advantage of his considerable course work in chemistry and was far less stressful than his position at the bank had been; furthermore, despite sieges of depression

27

returning like clockwork every spring and periods of excessive absence, Fredrick not only held onto his position but excelled, eventually accepting a position on the company sales force where he enjoyed immediate success.

Fredrick went on to become president of his own company.

The last time we met, he was a sponsor of a race car at a major racetrack. With his wife and me as passengers, he drove a souped-up Mustang seventy-five miles an hour down the main streets of the largest city in Georgia!

By this time, his numerous infidelities had begun to exert a strain on his marriage, and the couple eventually divorced.

News from his former wife, with whom I had managed to maintain contact, indicated that he is no longer living in California, that he has been divorced for the fourth time, and is now living with his parents in Florida.

While admittedly there are gaps in this synopsis, it is possible to derive some useful insights into the role dependency metaphors play in the development of that metaphor that is self-concept.

First to be considered is that episode of depression revolving around Fredrick's difficulty with the graduate course in geometry.

It is hard to believe, given his academic credentials, that Fredrick's problems derived from lack of ability.

I trace his difficulty, instead, to the professor who taught the course and who came across to Fredrick as arrogant and unfeeling—reminiscent, perhaps, of personality traits found in his father.

Fredrick's withdrawal from the course, a perfectly logical solution given the fact that he was not officially enrolled in graduate school anyway, did nothing to eliminate the depression, which in fact seemed to intensify.

This leads me to conclude that something in the episode must have tapped into a long-standing reservoir of hidden and not-dealt-with inadequacies, possibly traceable to his strained relationship with his irascible and emotionally distant father.

The very fact of a reservoir of hidden inadequacies confirms the excessive use of dependency metaphors, for in not confronting conflicts and dealing with them, we bury them—hiding them where they collect and fester, each new negativity finding an already-prepared nesting place. In exercising our option not to confront, we run from danger.

In other words, by permitting ourselves to lapse into those vestigial survival formulas of running from a predator, we avoid the hard issues of self-concept self-sufficiency—something I believe Fredrick did—as evidenced by his continuing to play football to please his father, by his withdrawal from the geometry class, and by his resignation from the bank.

The excessive levels of depression associated with both withdrawal episodes—viewed from the perspective of comparison psychology—can be traced to Fredrick's experiencing the cumulative effect of similarly unconfronted conflicts he had experienced before and run from.

That Fredrick was ill-prepared to deal with the unsympathetic vice-presiident—who may've evoked memories of an unapproachable father and an arrogant geometry professor—suggests unresolved issues of masculinity, as might his sponsoring of racing teams, his numerous marital infidelities, and death-defying rides in a souped-up Mustang.

(The issue of masculinity needs not always be a consequence of an over-indulgent mother. When a son lacks opportunity for male modeling because of a distant father, he may come to see himself as deficient in maleness.

As will be said many times in this document, children never blame the parents, only themselves.)

Fredrick's resignation from the banking position, followed by his retreat to a lower-paying, less prestigious position as a laboratory technician, may be seen as resulting from a crisis in self-esteem or as a reversion to dependency.

His success as a salesman does not surprise, for he was good at first appearances; and, speaking from hindsight, when a bipolar personality is on a roll, the only limitations to achievement are the inevitable down times.

His amassing of considerable wealth and his splurging it should not surprise either.

Fredrick's numerous extramarital relationships may also be viewed as an outgrowth of his unwitting employment of dependency metaphors. His mother's solicitude had shown the way and, for a time, his wife followed in her footsteps. Numerous successful sexual conquests (reference the golfer Tiger Woods, for example) can enhance, at least temporarily, a masculine concept of self.

Self-concepts not constructed on a person's commitment to integrity are almost certain to be ephemeral and subject to easy demolition. Ultimately, there is no way to satisfy the gaping mouth of inadequacy, particularly when it exists in the form of an insatiable yearning for wholeness in the face of a threatened and insecure self-concept.

Eventually Fredrick's wife's never-too-strong maternal energies were exhausted, and divorce quickly followed—setting in motion, for Fredrick, an almost ritualistic succession of marriages and divorces.

Several years ago, I was informed, again by his first wife, that Fredrick is now on disability, having been diagnosed as suffering from bipolar disorder.

This illness, as will be pointed out later in this document, is a development perfectly consistent with my sense of the kind of penalties that accrue as a consequence of over-indulgence in dependency metaphors.

It is one of life's great ironies—but in no way a coincidental one—that the patterns of our insecurities have a way of expressing themselves in the actual events of our lives, as represented by Fredrick's reversion to living back home with his parents and his acting his dependencies out in a real and devastating way.

Some years ago, I had a client whose problems, interestingly, had been bundled into that same diagnostic spectrum of bipolar disorder.

The presiding fact of his psychology, as it related to his perception of self, was his abandonment by his father when he was nine years old.

As a consequence of his having beaten his wife, more than once, in fits of anger and delirium, he was legally enjoined to live apart from her and their children—experiencing, again, the double-barreled effects of his childhood abandonment.

These are but two suggestive consequences of the role of dependency metaphors in our lives.

I have witnessed other variations on this motif in addition to those suggested in the biography of Fredrick.

My young friend, Rob, referred to in Chapter 1, once foolishly risked his life diving off a waterfall from a height no one had attempted before, an action greatly applauded by his witnessing peers. Fredrick's previously cited interest in auto racing and speeding on city streets would seem to represent a repressed need for risk taking and a kind of separation-power statement, all possible reactions to feelings of guilt born of dependency.

The fact is, however, that risky actions are never the real issue, any more than is the awed approbation Rob received from his adolescent peers. Driving a souped-up Mustang at excessive speeds down the downtown streets of a major metropolitan city induces, in this writer, intimations of insanity, not awed gasps of admiration.

What I believe is at work in both instances is a near-frantic desire to escape the demeaning perception of dependency and inadequacy, which are initially implied in the fact of human mortality, engrained from early infancy. In Rob's case, these qualities were confirmed by the absence of family and by threats to self-image derived from degrading poverty and eviscerating parental abuse—all experienced metaphorically as confirmation of feelings of massive unworthiness.

Interestingly, actions initiated out of self-concept inadequacy always back-fire, having owed their selection to defensive needs. A positive self-concept requires assertive actions taken in the best interests of a consciously developed concept of self.

Another possible consequence of the unexamined survival drive—in addition to youth's rejection of parental authority and risk-taking activities—may be an unwitting immersion in the herding philosophy of other adolescents, who are themselves undergoing similar rites of passage, largely based on unrecognized survival urges.

From the perspective of comparison psychology, this act of "selling out" for psychological security constitutes the substitution of one dependency for another and is another instance of avoiding responsibility for development of one's own concept of self.

(I hasten to add that the failure to take responsibility for one's actions in the realm of self needs not be produced by conscious decisions, for the image of self will come, whether built by reflexive or conscious choice. Whether or not the consequences of this turn ugly, the consequence that is loss of personal freedom is inevitable.

(This said, it is believed no people who have read and understood the philosophy presented here can ever again be absolved of responsibility for their use of dependency metaphors or for failure to address the conscious construction of self-concept.)

Like so many dependency metaphors, the herding instinct—the finding of security in group acceptance—contains the seeds of its own destruction since only leaders reap ego currency, and even that is transitory riches.

(To my knowledge, neither Rob nor Fredrick was able to avail himself of peer acceptance during adolescence because of personality characteristics that led to alienation from their fellows. Rob, because of self-esteem issues, rejected the opportunity for group adulation of his music.

(It is interesting to note, even so, that both men worked hard at getting acceptance—Rob through his membership in anti-establishment cliques, his death-defying antics, and, early on, his music—and Fredrick, through his racing ambitions, his hungry drive for financial success, and his numerous extra-marital conquests. It is important to note that these actions likely grew from the need to compensate for self-concept inadequacies.)

Whether staying safe under the protective shade of parental love, diving headlong into the ego-immersing ocean of peer acceptance, or exalting in the momentary illusion of sexual prowess, it is all the same.

All are instances of using dependency metaphors and, as such, constitute actions that make no lasting contribution to an honest and self-reliant sense of self.

From the perspective of comparison psychology, these actions represent the elections of dependency metaphors as a way of coping and, as such, constitute instances of failure to take conscious responsibility for one's metaphor of self.

Thus, consequences accrue as a result of a failure to gather unto oneself that feeling of self-concept ownership that is anodyne to the fear of death and its psychological counterpart—feelings of inferiority.

Of course, the creative human animal has found other strategies of avoidance.

A name for one such strategy might be "bogus refractors"—activities undertaken so as to bask in the glow of our neighbors' avowed admiration for our many good works, or—at the other extreme—for the size and value of our homes. These are all bogus investments in bogus self-concepts.

As a consequence, we have our "For-We-Are-Jolly-Good-Fellows" games, illustrated in our block parties or in our publicized support of local good causes. We can also gain public affirmation of our worth by patriotic citizenship, first church membership, and the perceived possession of power and influence.

Now, thanks to social networks, we can present to the world the sanctified, and sanitized, vision of ourselves we wish the world to see.

Some of us find comfort in displaying our wealth, our country club memberships, or our Mayflower heritages.

We drive fancy cars and live in dumps, never realizing that the car represents an unconscious attempt to glow in delusions of grandeur, or to buy imagined respect from people who don't even know us.

A one-time neighbor of mine loved to take his camping trailer to the beach in the summertime because, he said, "The folks down there are real friendly folks." It was a friendliness denied him at home because of how he imagined he was perceived by his neighbors, who were familiar with his human foibles and frailties.

As illustrated in Tennessee Williams's character, Blanche (*A Streetcar Named Desire*), merit found in the friendliness of strangers means nothing.

Sequestered away, safe and sacred, we hoard these fictitious imaginings—dreams of what we imagine, or wish, ourselves to be. We turn them in our hands to catch their luminescence and watch with awe and reverence as they grow and glow and glitter—phosphorescent bubbles with the substance of moonbeams.

The deriving of ego support from anonymous sources, or the perceived admiration of our fellows—pumping ourselves up on the basis of an assumed notion of worth—are counterfeit formulas for achieving self-esteem. These measures are destined to fail because, ultimately, they are "money" (ungrounded metaphors) devoid of purchasing power.

The same force is at work in our brand-name jeans and sneakers, our expensive Italian shoes, and even our labels purloined from high-class stores!

Bogus refractors—phantasmagorical perceptions of personal worth reflected in the eyes of other people—are continuations of the survival strategy of infants who must goo and coo and smile in order to be fed.

As we bask in the glow of reflected glory—victims of unrecognized dependency metaphors—our self-concepts languish or atrophy and do not grow.

Of course, it is possible to see these dependency metaphors as relatively harmless strategies based on innocent one-upmanship, acts that contribute, moreover, to social stability.

And when done consciously, as an investment in a willed construction of self-concept, a number of these things need not be bogus refractors at all—especially if they are practiced anonymously.

This said, dependency metaphors, which are always reflexive, develop a life of their own, and, unrecognized, may well take on properties such as the will to power, the enslavement of others to one's own purposes, and a blind and corrupting need to feel superior to someone else.

These avoidance techniques are not necessarily innocent, as the crusades of the Middle Ages, the Spanish Inquisition, Hitler's "final solution," instances of mass slaying, and acts of rampant racism all demonstrate. Not knowing—and not accepting responsibility for—one's actions (metaphors) is dangerous, not only to self, but to the world.

Each are instances of humans securing self-concept enhancement (national prestige being the same sort of opiate) at the expense or sacrifice of others.

This strategy of feeling good about the self one perceives by the use of—or in the interest of external sources of affirmation--constitute a denial of responsibility for developing one's own self-concept and continues dependency relationships into adulthood.

In addition to dependency metaphors, another "antidote" to our fear of death (transposed psychologically into feelings of inadequacy) may be found in the obsessive use of fantasy or escapism.

As seen here, the obsessive use of fantasy is a metaphorical device people use to escape the labyrinth of ego insufficiency and to thereby avoid having to take ego risks.

It may be a minor thing—a harmless sashay into a sunny dalliance—but it can be more. It can be a place to hide from the world and from challenges to ego sufficiency.

And in recent times, due to giant leaps in computer graphics and programming, video games have been developed where virtual characters capable of performing heroic deeds or acts of great villainy can be embodied with the self-concepts of gamers playing them.

These developments threaten to alter the rules of the game where fantasy is concerned and have occasioned rafts of studies on the psychological effects of games like these on children and adults.

According to Julia Savacool, for instance, in a special written for *USA TODAY* (**Asheville** [NC] **Citizens-Times** 3/30/14/64) well over one hundred studies have documented "…the rise in hostility and aggression in people who regularly play violent video games."

She quotes Brad Bushman, a professor of communication and psychology at Ohio State University as follows:

> We just finished a major review of studies looking at 381 effects of violent video games in over 130,000 people [and] we found that violent video games unmistakably raised levels of aggression and heart rate, and decreased feelings of compassion toward others.

On a more positive note, and one indicating the passivity of reflexive metaphors, Ms. Savacool quotes Professor Patrick Vargas as having found that gamers who played the virtual hero "…acted more generously toward others in a post-game setting"

She concludes her article saying, "These games are here to stay as a central feature of modern childhood."

While doubtlessly a valid assessment, it is still true that, whatever effects on personality these games entail, these consequence are traceable to unconscious effects—anathema to the conscious development of self-concept argued for here.

While Rob may have been using escapism when he immersed himself in classical music, shutting himself off from everything and everybody, (and certainly his obsessiveness with wilderness camping was an instance of literally removing himself from social challenges) he did not have access to the opportunities for escapism that gaming provides.

(Interestingly, when I first met Fredrick, he was, like me, a passionate devotee of classical music. Then, almost between visits, he metamorphosed into a worshiper of blue grass.)

While it is possible that fantasizing may be a useful and highly pleasurable activity (some writers contend it is useful in dealing with stress, and Herbert Marcus sees it as a way of gaining access to freedom, a "split off" uncontaminated by societal tamperings, as gathered from **Eros and Civilization**, Boston, Ma., 1955, p. 14), there is much yet to be learned about the consequences of electronic wizardry on self-concept.

To that end, I would like to stick with what I know from personal experience.

During adolescence, fantasy was for me—as I suspect it was for Rob—a place to hide, a way of avoiding having to deal with the judgments of people, especially my peers. While ensconced in my world of fantasy, I could accomplish all manner of heroic feats.

Though not yet in my teens, I once fashioned a Superman costume, complete with a paper **S** and a flowing cape. I was convinced the costume was all I needed to facilitate my leap from off the front porch into space.

I remember, still, the waves of disillusionment that washed over me as I lay on the ground, my five-year-old dreams of flying gone, my carelessly sewn stitches pulled from out the ruins of cotton fabric spread out around me like shreds of discarded confetti.

Sad to say, I returned from my fantasy world, bruised but unchanged, opportunities for growth and real-world experience having, for the time, passed me by.

While my boyish experiment did not permanently scar me, fantasy, when allowed to dominate, becomes a kind of Xanadu—an addictive venue for escapism, and it can be used as a device to avoid real-world responsibility.

(Certainly, this was the case with Rob; and Fredrick may have found academia a good place to hide from the stresses of real-world demands. And while the long-term effects of computer gaming on self-concept are yet to be determined, this writer rejects the likelihood that they will be positive.)

It may be safely said, then, that no one returns from a world of fantasy (including vampire movies, computer war games, and the Harry Potter series) better equipped to cope with a real world or possessed of a more coherent concept of self.

As an interesting sidelight, and as a useful example of fantasy not being limited to the world of children and adolescents, we need only note the adult interest in, and identification with, a particular sport team and individual athletes.

Identifying with and gloating over the victories of our favorite teams is an instance of a symbolic conversion, allowing us the psychological illusion of having triumphed over impediments standing between us and personal fulfillment. It even legitimatizes, in some cases, gloating and schadenfreude.

It is difficult not to see similar motivations at work in the grandiloquent self-glorifying action and statements of the former president, Donald John Trump and his followers.

There may be no lasting harm in such vicarious identifications, particularly if they are recognized for what they are; however, if we remain blissfully ignorant to our motivations—indulging ourselves in the expression of unexamined survival urges—we are, metaphorically speaking, saving our lives by inflating our egos (albeit it temporary and ultimately self-defeating) through fraudulent means.

We train our soldiers to assert, unquestioningly, their aggressive instincts and wonder why they experience difficulties in pacific adjustments to civilian life!

(In the meantime, the lawns of the world await; every hour, the grass grows higher, honey-do lists accumulate, wives and mothers and bosses fulminate, and lost opportunities for positive, self-enhancing actions— "Enterprises of great pitch and moment…turn awry and lose the name of action.")

The previous allusion to Xanadu being equated to fantasy was not inadvertent. Samuel Taylor Coleridge, the author of the poem in which that mythical retreat was described, was addicted to opium in the form of ladanum (labdanum).

One possible explanation for the growing popularity of mind-altering compounds may be traced to the increased complexity of modern living associated with survival in a world made stressful by capitol invasions, "Dark State" rumors, global-warming controversies, and the Covid-19 pandemic—a number of which, parenthetically, speak directly to self-concept issues promulgated here.

It is possible to interpret these stressors, and the current obsessiveness of extreme conservatives, as the result of unconscious responses to primitive survival motives. Pragmatists, it should be noted, always insist on the primacy of food, shelter, and security.

And these ancient metaphors are easily transformable into simplistic solutions and retrospective retreats to the safer, idealized times of childhood—as is suggested in the circumstance that many right-wing conservatives turn out to be fundamental Christians, pro-life adherents, and likely to oppose social entitlements.

Not to be ignored is our addiction to technological solutions to the problems that beset us. One such solution is pharmacological—the manufacturing of drugs that bespeak instant gratification and immediate relief from every conceivable pain and illness.

Complicating matters even more is the avaricious nature of drug companies, filling the airways with advertisements glorifying their products as panaceas for every difficulty, even psychological ones.

Of course, neuroscientists have long known that the brain possesses natural opiates—pain killers created to rush relief to internal lesions, to injured limbs and organs. There is even evidence of the existence of hormones that reward us for sexual productivity and help our mothers forget the agonies of delivery.

However, too little attention has been paid to pharmacological solutions and to the fact that what works in the physiological world may apply equally well, and unethically, in the metaphorical world of a threatened sense of self.

The fact is, we are chemical beings, and chemicals are utilized every day to insure and assure our survival. Even our immunologic system is endocrinologic!

It may well be that opiate-type compounds are useful to physical survival prospects, but it should not surprise (knowing the way survival metaphors work) that they may speak to our psychological survival as well.

In fact, they may often have the effect of being instant (and artificial) enhancers of self-esteem. People high on drugs feel great about who they are and, as a consequence, fall easy prey to facile solutions—to say nothing of addictions.

(For further discussion of hallucinogenic functions in the human brain, see pages 40-42 below.)

Unfortunately, A.E. Housman states:

Oh, I have been to Ludlow Fair
And left my necktie God knows where,
And carried half-way home, or near,
Pints and quarts of Ludlow beer:

Then the world seemed none so bad,
And I myself a sterling lad;
And down in lovely muck I've lain,
Happy till I woke again.

Then I saw the morning sky:
Heigho, the tale was all a lie;
The world, it was the old world yet,
I was I, my things were wet,

And nothing now remained to do
But begin the game anew. (**ASL** LXII)

One of the great attractions of mind-altering substances is that they provide escape, temporary though it be, from the prison of a pervasive, engulfing sense of depression, helplessness, or feelings of inadequacy.

A number of "participants" I worked with while employed at OIC were substance abusers of the first order.

Many, if not most of them, were poor, high-school dropouts, and black; they were unemployed, and their prospects for economic success were certainly less than positive. Many of them were teenage single parents.

In addition, they resided in an area of the country still afflicted with harsh vestiges of segregation, where the color of one's skin remains a decided factor in employment opportunities and social acceptance.

In short, many of them lived under a cloud of socially enforced poverty, devastating self-doubt, and massive levels of perceived inferiority.

Though no one had ever informed them of it—that they were responsible for their metaphors!—the climate in which they lived was not a propitious one for the development of positive self-concepts.

(It is possible, tragically, to build a concept of self out of the whole cloth of reflexive metaphors—never even knowing about the concept of being responsible for one's metaphors. When the environment conspires to make available metaphors self-demeaning, the consequences are doubly tragic and immoral.

(That the same reflexive outcomes can apply in the case of individuals reared in the lap of luxury makes it no less tragic.)

(This sad and unnecessary state of affairs should not be construed as justification for dropping out of school, for siring [or bearing] children "out of wedlock," or for substance abuse—the major emphasis of this section.

(In fact, the majority of these young people did not use drugs. Those who did, however, knew what it was to feel temporarily good about the selves they perceived—artificially produced though the feelings were.

(There were, among them, a few people who sold illegal substances, drove luxury cars with wads of money in their fancy suits, and who were, in fact, experiencing an effect as unreal as that derived from the products they sold.

(More tragically, they were feeding the pragmatism associated with the drive to physical survival. They were saying by their deeds, and sometimes their actual words, "Access to wealth is denied to me—this is all there is for me—and I am justified in surviving any way I can.")

That the feelings derived from substance abuse (or from selling them) are engineered—rather than earned—versions of self-esteem, that they don't come as a consequence of efforts rewarded, or out of reciprocated love, is beside the point to them. At the depths of pragmatic cynicism, feeling good becomes its own excuse for being.

Of all the means accessible to humans for avoiding responsibility for their metaphors, none is more invidious, in my opinion, than the use of drugs.

This is because not only does the use of illegal substances prostitute health to the appetite of an irresponsible self, or that it provides temporary anodyne to a doubt-wracked self, it literally negates the opportunity for responsible self-development.

Let this then be said:

1. Where there is no positive sense of self there is nothing—just walking husks of survival-driven desperation.
2. The recreational use of drugs is an easy way to icy death.

3. The various forms of physical addictions are pharmacological versions of dependency metaphors.

Similar in many ways to drug-induced escapism are witchcraft ritual and magic. Like many disciples of alter-realities, the practitioners of witchcraft insist upon the validity of their esoteric version of reality.

To the extent that these practitioners see themselves as empowered people, with access to powers that reach beyond the grave, to that extent may their practices be seen as just another ego-survival strategy indebted to and energized by the energies of reflexive survival drive.

Disciples of these practitioners are opting for dependency metaphors, as well, and are choosing another version of the short and easy way.

The fact that their images of self are founded on false pretense doesn't matter until the time comes when the world refuses to cooperate with their illusions.

One young woman I knew conducted seances in her dormitory and professed clairvoyant awareness of my presence anytime I was on campus. Because so many of her devotees were acting out erratically, and having nightmares, I, in my capacity as dean of students, asked her to cease and desist. She left college at the end of that semester.

In another instance, a bright and sophisticated woman of my acquaintance reportedly led a coven of witches on full-moon, midnight nude marches down a dry creek bed in a nearby park.

She had a coven member make a plaster of Paris death mask of me, which she turned into the centerpiece of a black-wreathed sculpture festooned with runic, witch-like hieroglyphics. I was invited to the gala "gathering" where I, and my death mask, turned out to be the centers of attraction.

(The thought crossed my mind that visions of me as warlock may've danced in the head of my hostess.)

In many instances these metaphors of otherworldly powers function as vehicles for intense self-loathing or social alienation or both—though this seemed hardly the case with the woman described above!

Whether it was because of wealth and social standing, or deriving from her perception of paranormal powers, she radiated a sense of confidence and high social aplomb.

When last I saw her—dressed in a brightly flowered, form-concealing gown whose hem caressed the ground she walked upon—she seemed her usual self-satisfied self, undeterred by real-life exigencies, an aura of security possibly facilitated by inherited money.

For reasons unknown to me (she tended to portliness) this woman viewed herself as outside, and perhaps better than, run-of-the-mill society.

It occurred to me that her interest in witchcraft might well have been an unconscious expression of a will to power (survival), born of an unexamined survival drive.

Also, the level of energy certain people pour into devil worship or vampirism may be seen as speaking reams about psychological inadequacy.

An instance in case was a one-time friend of mine, a paraplegic, who was a vampire fanatic. His poems and stories were peopled by these creatures of the night, and he owned an extravagantly expensive black cloak with a crimson velvet lining.

The dreams of freedom and flying were doubtlessly there, but, imbedded as well, was a snarling self-concept lashing out at an injury undeserved.

(This friend, it should be noted was ahead of his time and "into" vampires decades before the current fads of zombie worship, *Vampire Diaries* and *Vampires Everywhere,* swept the country.)

At other times, these escapist maneuvers (to be described below as ungrounded metaphors) seem to constitute a type of reverse English, whereby the self-concept gathers strength from turning unattractiveness into a virtue.

Some years ago, I had a student who was short of stature, mother-dominated, and suffering from extremely low self-esteem. When he was on the streets, he wore a fedora and carried an ornate, eagle-headed cane.

It was as though he were saying, "Take my weirdness and stuff it!"

At the roots of this nose-thumbing, I suspect, lay the deep-seated conviction that outlandishness was his only avenue to recognition and to a sense of importance in a world he perceived as leaving him no alternatives for self-respect.

Seeking identity by employing alter egos is but the latest version of dependency metaphor, another short and easy way.

This "reversal," this turning of self-survival needs against the self is, as stated earlier, the origin of evil in the world. As will be shown subsequently, there are other versions.

The deeper we bury self-concept, the more radical the robes we wear to its funeral!

Anthropological studies indicate that belief in magic is old, with many ancient rituals based on fertility rites—a version of the survival impulse—and on activities ranging from the sacrifice of virgins to initiatory rebirths enacted in caves seen as symbolic uteri.

Metaphor, being what it is, it is not surprising that primitive minds quickly discovered analogies between being born and surviving death.

Since nature was seen as the mother of life, it should not surprise, either, that many tribes sought eternal life via transmigration rituals involving animals and virgin maidens.

Even the movement from shaman to priest to worshiped deity has about it the familiar logic of metaphorical transmigration—always a product of reflexive stimuli.

With the advent of modern science and its insistence upon "verifiable" metaphors, many life-preserving strategies have gone underground, undergoing imaginative transformations and renovated for more modern consumers.

Interest in crystals and "channeling," rituals of animal sacrifice in religions such as Ifa (see **Psychology Today**, September/October 1993, Vol. 26, No.5, 48-50), and the once-popular fascination with the anthropological investigations of Carlos Castaneda may be seen in this light, as may the revival of interest in LSD-induced hallucinogenic revelations.

Many practicing Zen Buddhists appear to center their existence on what I call ungrounded metaphors—views of reality that lack guideposts or limitations and that celebrate meditatively revealed insights that effectively remove them, and their egos, from the "real world."

Their view that abnegation of self opens the path to freedom is a concept greatly at odds with the one being presented here!

Such open-ended metaphors—validated by feelings alone—profit from the very fact of open-endedness and constitute, as do witchcraft and magic, an unwillingness (a reflexive avoidance and a kind of benign hypocrisy) to assume responsibility for their metaphors and, in fact, practice methods literally designed to annihilate self-concept—the perceived sanctuary of egotism run wild.

Even such phenomena as the recent emergence of conservative political movements with their emphases on armaments, flag worship, "right-to-life" issues, the sudden popularity of tele-evangelism and its promised on-earth rewards of wealth and immortality, censorship of textbooks and their publishing houses, the insistence upon an equal status for creation science with evolution, the conservative "seeding" of boards of trustees at theological seminaries, and the sudden upsurge in so-called "tea partiers"—may be seen as responses to a threatened, need-to-be-right-and-safe, primitive survival urge.

So long as people are preoccupied with perceived threats to their survival—be it physical or psychological (and these are very often overt expressions of hidden fears)—they will remain distracted from the real business of life:

Consciously confronting the inadequacies within, rather than jousting with imaginary ghosts in an outer world, and by creating—out of a willed determination to achieve psychological freedom—objects and deeds that survive our dying and further the cause of enlightened living.

World religions, repositories of some of the greatest metaphorical treasures our species has produced, may be seen as evidence of the power of survival drive, even when applied to open-ended metaphors and driven by the survival issues of patronage or assurances of eternal life.

Obviously, survival drive—whether energized in art or expressed in unconscious living—is not concerned with issues of validity or integrity, and the gut feeling of survival accomplished is as chemically satisfying as the actual effect.

This form of reflexive pleasure, needless to say, is not a luxury in which people committed to the conscious construction of self-concept can safely indulge.

(Great religious art, of course, is one of the noblest, and earliest, expressions of the human desire to survive one's dying, and it is regrettable that creators of these masterpieces—geniuses in aptitude, dexterity, and vision—did not recognize the linkage between the drive to survive and self-concept.

(As a consequence, their art, as much of today's artistic creations, is infused by an unrecognized impulse to gainsay the fact of physical dying, a reward promised the obedient by powerful religious institutions who are themselves enabled through tithing to offer generous commissions to promulgators of the faith.)

A similar impulse may be at the roots of Thomas Kinkade's pastoral paintings, attempts to maintain (and get paid for) the illusion of survival by preserving the ideal memories of an idealized past—shades of a shining city built on a hill!

As stated already, great art survives its creator—adding beauty to a world already too consumed with "getting and spending" and inspiring, as well, an empowered sense of self in the artist. It behooves us all that art not be a slave to penury—of the body or of the mind.

As a way of illustrating the subliminal way primitive survival drive expresses itself in other things than art, the following is an extensive excerpt from a paid advertisement "penned" by Helen G. Kelly and published in **The Raleigh** *(NC)* **News and Observer** in March 1989.

(The "I" in the advertisement speaks forGod.):

I am love. My thoughts of you are love-thoughts. With outstretched arms I beckon you. Come to Me. No matter where you are. I love you.

I desire your fellowship. With a joyful heart I create myriads of ways to show you My love. My love has carefully planned the best for you. My will is to overflow your *heart continually with rivers of My love so that the thirsty around you can drink and be refreshed. May I use you for this loving purpose? Everyone needs My love. My love satisfies. It penetrates the deepest crevices of man to cleanse and comfort and make whole. I want you to be whole—to be vibrant with My life—to be a love-vessel for the Potter's use. I see the heart of every man. I see the scars and bruises that only My love can heal. Will you be a channel through whom I can pour the balm of my love? As this love-ointment flows through you to the wounded, you, too, will be blessed. Nothing is wasted. Love never fails. My love reaches the heart. And like a sponge, the heart absorbs the healing rays of My love... Without measure My love is readily available. Just call to Me. Come. As a loving Father, My soul's delight is to lavish my love fragrance upon you.*

Let Me so bathe you in it that the sweet aroma radiating from you will draw others to its Source. Then I can wrap them in My arms and whisper My love in the secret places of their hearts. Nurtured in My love and *in My Word, they, too, can be vessels of My love. In this way My precious love-vessels will multiply all over the earth, and the knowledge of My love will abound more and more in the hearts of men....*

Though the advertisement was written out of sincere religious fervor and at considerable personal expense, a preponderance of primitive survival metaphors becomes readily apparent.

That so many of these metaphors seem implicitly sexual is further evidence of how easily primitive survival drive may be summoned to religious imagery, the prime repository of undeath metaphors.

In support of this argument, I invite the reader's attention to the breathless rhythms of the piece and to the expressions, *out-stretched arms, I desire, use you, loving purpose, needs, penetrates, deepest crevices, love-vessel, love-ointment, multiply,* and *love-fragrance.*

Also, there are such sentences as these: *My love is readily available. Just call to Me. Come. Let Me so bathe you in it* (love-fragrance) *that the sweet aroma radiating from you will draw others to its Source. Then I can wrap them in My arms and whisper My love in the secret places of their hearts.*

And lest the reader think that such survival metaphors are restricted to evangelical churches, one needs only point to popular images of Christ in denominations where He is portrayed as the bridegroom of the church, and where emphasis on rebirth from the womb tomb and the miracles of transubstantiation of wine into blood receive major emphasis.

Additionally, because world religions function as natural reservoirs for primitive survival metaphors—observe, for instance, Christianity's emphases on blood, baptism, transubstantiation (already mentioned), resurrection, and immortality—religions may often become convenient vehicles for man's inhumanity to man.

One instance of this that is particularly troublesome to comparison psychology, is the promise made by world religions of immortality to their adherents, associated with missionary zeal born of the need for consensus.

By committing themselves to certain rules and rituals, followers are promised rewards (as of yet unconfirmed) beyond the grave. And militant Muslims promise adolescent warriors a supply of *virgins* in the hereafter in exchange for their lives and the lives of infidels—an unconscious expression of survival security found in the arms of unanimity.

These rules and rituals—including those motivating suicide bombings—restrict thinking or make it unnecessary; and there are always penalties for those who stray or refuse to profess.

This is a practice not limited to fanatical Muslim rituals. Indeed, similar versions of coercion contribute to the preservation of religious institutions, assuring, as well, the survival of its supernumeraries—hylozoically and psychologically.

The extent to which a religion is dominant in a society—encouraging and enforcing conformity—is the same extent to which it serves the unconscious survival needs of that society and its members.

Furthermore, unexamined metaphors imbedded in the fabric of world religions may encourage dependency; the dependency conditioning of infancy having already been discussed.

For instance, it is easy and perhaps even natural for children to accept as infallible truths the religious metaphors of their parents. After all, they accept their food and shelter!

But problems come when—based on a sense of inner emptiness not satisfied by dependence, or based on the natural urge toward psychological independence—the child-adult comes to believe that he or she has substituted one dependency for another.

The *carte blanche* acceptance of another person's metaphor—be it the metaphor of parent, church, or government—is a form of imprinting tantamount to turning oneself into a photostatic copy of someone else. It is, perhaps, the supreme form of dependency and the ultimate denial of individuality.

Needless to say, it is a fatal blow to the hope for individual freedom, to say nothing of one's sense of integrity.

So it was that clothed in robes of Christian piety, priests tortured thousands during the inquisition, crusaders righteously converted millions of infidels (with or without their consent), and New England protestants burned witches and heretics in the name of a theology perceived as being under attack by Satan—a bugaboo originally invented to frighten children!

In recent times, "white devils" have been taken hostage or killed at the behest of fanatic ayatollahs; blanket murder warrants (fatwas)—accompanied by rewards totaling millions of dollars—have been issued for the writer and merchandisers of a work of fiction that is said to blaspheme Allah;

Arabs destroy each other in Iraq, Lebanon, Libya, Syria, and Egypt; and many thousands die or have died throughout history because of perceived religious heresies, political differences, or dictatorial addictions to power.

So, too, African American children could die in a church choir in Alabama, born-again citizens can burn abortion clinics (and murder doctors) in the name of unborn children, businesses suffer boycotts because their owners are not appropriately religious—or because they are Jews, blacks, or uppity women, and a protestant church be torn apart by questions of "inerrancy."

Lately, national (and international) news has been filled with reports of black men being killed by strangulation, by "driving black," and black women being slain in their beds by hooligans armed with no-knock open-entry warrants. Meanwhile, the free world is rife with controversy regarding the insistence of gays and transvestites on equal rights to marriage, restrooms, and swimming pools.

The response of those opposed, center arguments around the sanctity of laws set by the Constitution, or God--the same God who slaughtered idolators at Sinai and obliterated Sodom and Gomorrah for unapproved (sexual) practices.

It should not surprise that sexual practices that do not contribute to survival of the species is at issue. The survival of survival drive itself depends upon the biblical edict that men and women go forth and multiply. And no one admits to implicit racism.

Straightforwardly stated, marriage is an institution reserved to one man and one woman so that sexual organs can be used to make babies. Any sex act contrary to (or unsupportive thereof) that doesn't support physical survival, is, therefore, verboten.

All of the above examples may be viewed as expressions of unexamined metaphors—versions of survival drive masquerading under the guise of being the will of God or man-made law—ungrounded metaphors if ever there were one! What's worse: the followers of survival drive are self-righteously proud and totally oblivious to their reflexive motivations.

That we will kill at the behest of survival is one of life's great ironies and a testament to our uncanny and mindless ability to subvert survival drive to any function—even contradictory ones (!), all in the name of staying alive.

There are as many variations on the theme of physical survival drive as there are stars in the heavens, and it is not possible to make all of them manifest. It is, therefore, to the end of consolidation that I have formulated the inclusive term "great repository metaphors."

In my use of this term, I seek to consolidate those consensus ideas held near and dear by a people—ideas that may be brief in span or last for generations.

Examples include social pressures to affirm a particular religion; neighbors being pressured to vote a particular way; and the imposition (through intimidation or ostracism) of predominant cultural values.

Repository metaphors are mindsets devised to secure that survival comfort found in consensus. One of the most telling, and earliest, instances of repository metaphors and their motive of survival may be found in the herding instinct of gazelles, bison, the water buffalo, seven-year locusts, and even geese and sheep.

Variations on the drive for consensus may be found in humans, in pre-adolescents, and adolescents; these variations may also be found in the fear of being perceived as different, and in the treatment of non-native and mixed-race children receive. Even today, though much less overt, homosexuals are subject to ridicule, bullying, and social ostracism.

In most respects, repository metaphors are to psychological survival what reflexive metaphors are to physical survival. They are unexamined aversions to difference—instinctive carryovers from that time when strangers from another tribe were greeted suspiciously or with weapons.

It was through the wholesale adoption of these type metaphors (supplemented, perhaps, by fear) that it became possible for millions of educated and cultured German citizens to commit themselves to their "Fuhrer's solution to the Jewish problem."

And it has been argued, recently, that the French Vichy—under German occupation and the pressure to survive execution—was even more severe in acts of reprisal than the Germans themselves in enforcing Hitler's anti-Semitic decrees.

It is the human susceptibility to the power of repository metaphors, and their promise of immediate psychological certainty (an obvious derivative of the survival impulse), that may be found at the roots of most, if not all, consensus movements.

The only protection from repository metaphors is a personal commitment to being responsible for the metaphors that govern our lives. This is the ultimate importance of education and the real purpose behind the writing of this book.

Though she does not use my term, repository metaphors, Francine Klagsbrun in *Mixed Feelings: Hate, Rivalry, and Reconciliation Among Brothers and Sisters* (New York, 1992) has explored in detail those "patterns of family behavior that become imprinted on our minds in childhood [and that] shape many of our adult responses…" (p. 374).

She too is concerned with the way unconscious patterns can influence our life and writes,

> Banishment [of subliminal patterns] begins with awareness, and awareness begins when people *consciously* think about the images and patterns that influence them. (p. 375, my italics.)

Farther down the page she argues:

> …recognizing old sibling patterns and images, we may recognize ourselves replicating those patterns with a lover, a friend, a coworker. By paying attention to the roles we continue to play with brothers and sisters, we can notice ourselves reproducing those roles with a child, a spouse, an employer. Awareness can lead to control over harmful patterns of behavior. (p. 375)

One of the best ways to develop the kind of awareness Ms. Klagsbrun is promoting is through conditioning ourselves to be on alert for the influence of primitive survival drive in our metaphors. Once conscious of these primitive survival impulses, we can willfully reject and replace them with metaphors consciously chosen and acted upon.

In the interest of alerting the reader to the many forms repository metaphors may take, I will try, now, to be specific.

We experience them in fads, slang, and catch phrasings, sayings such as *the gay nineties* and *great society*, in terms such as *yuppie, X and Y-generations,* and *friends with benefits.*

These metaphors capture prevailing sentiments of a time, a group, or a generation, and all too often make the responsibility for conscious thought or critical thinking unnecessary.

(I remember well those highly influential mantras of the late sixties: "If it feels good, do it!" And "You are free to do anything you like, so long as it hurts nobody else.")

We are likely to encounter repository metaphors in partisan politics, in fervid patriotism, in mass-movement protests, and in the kind of mob spirit that fed the French Revolution and led, in the United States, to passage of the Volstead Act. We experience them as well in racial and species prejudices, to say nothing of gay, lesbian, and transvestite bias.

The same energies found in reflexive metaphors may be tapped into for conscious use in positive movements—as in the arts, and in the almost religious fervor associated with animal rights (*save the whales*) and *save the earth* movements, in global warming issues, and in other ecological causes—such as opposition by ecologists to oil pipelines from Canada.

The surge for individual freedom expressed in the so-called "Arab Spring" may also be seen as a case in point—although the primitive force of unexamined survival drive and its need for certainty seems to have surfaced in certain fanatical groups, possible including some such elements in Somalia, Iraq, Libya, Egypt, and Syria.

Repository metaphors can, of course, be consciously altered into synthetic ones, ideations farthest removed from physical survival mandates. For instance, whereas racism groups people into categories and restricts individual freedom, the principles of feminism—definitely a synthetic construction—destroy classifications and liberate both sexes.

The same may be said for recognition of same-sex marriage, sexual preference, and the conscious (anti-reflexive) acceptance of people as people, not as gay or transsexual.

Because they are conscious, synthetic metaphors do not formalize our thinking for us. They do not obscure our insecurities, or inculcate the illusion of "belonging." Mass hysteria, or other versions of repository metaphors—like capitol invasions—do not come within their purview.

Actions taken by Russian president Putin and native-born Russians in Crimea and eastern sections of Ukraine raise anew the possibility of reflexive repository metaphors run rampant. One can only hope for a return to sanity and the rejection of mob spirit.

Generally speaking, repository metaphors are most destructive when they are motivated by unexamined reflexive survival impulses (viz., racial prejudice, religious bigotry, war fever, extreme patriotism, "big lies," "fake news," "dark state," gun control, and anti-mask, vaccine opposition).

From the perspective of comparison psychology, repository metaphors are a real and ever-present danger because, unrecognized for what they are, they cancel out opportunities for the conscious assumption of responsibility for one's metaphors and thereby for one's self-concept.

Insofar as repository metaphors are regressive—controverting the movement of life away from a concern for survival of the individual to that of the conglomerate—they constitute an obstacle to self-concept growth and, ultimately, to the prospect for human freedom.

The possessor of a realized self-concept has nothing to fear from difference and, indeed, welcomes it as an affirmation of self-sufficiency. To the extent that the above issues arouse anger and disapproval in people, they are affirmations of the effect of repository metaphors. Individuals intent on self-actualization will avoid them as they would the plague.

It is not surprising, then, that world religions are likely treasure troves for repository metaphors, a consequence growing naturally (reflexively) out of their promising alternatives to the inevitability that is death—the prime motive at the roots of reflexive metaphor.

Note that even a cursory examination of religious assurances of survival beyond the grave (golden streets, perfect ease, reunion with loved ones) will reveal the ease with which primitive survival drive takes up residence there. Much of the energy that underlies faith in immortality may be traced to the instinctive need to survive.

Humanity's inventiveness in discovering ways to hide from consciousness the fact of its mortality is matched only by its skill in developing defensive strategies to insure survival of the psychological self.

A conscious decision to identify these deceptive practices, and a refusal to be seduced by them, are the first steps on the path to accepting responsibility for the metaphor that is self-concept.

Summary

As has been said, dependency metaphors find their source in the unconscious act of tapping into the motives of primitive physical survival drive, and every device discussed here—whether running to mother; using drugs; resorting to fantasy, witchcraft and magic; unthinkingly using religion or complying with the so-called great repository metaphors—are all traceable to the sought-for survival of either the physical or psychological self.

Dependency metaphors come in many varieties and are limited only by the limits of human creativity. Other versions of them—discussed only briefly, or not at all—include scapegoating, name calling, bullying, overtly using physical violence, and prostituting family relationships to the needs of an unquestioned internal security.

As the disciples of mammon are said to be legion, so are the many strategies accessible for avoiding responsibility for the metaphor that is self-concept; as we become sensitive to the pervasiveness of dependency metaphors, we can learn not to hide behind them. In the name of personal integrity, the veritable foundation of self-concept, it is imperative that we do this.

The cost of not doing so is self-imprisonment, loss of personal freedom, and a telling instance of selling out to the lowest bidder.

The most convincing evidence available to show ourselves that the self-concept is a construct for which we are responsible is the vast number of strategies we have for doing exactly the opposite!

In the next chapter, I propose to show that the negative consequences of running from self-concept responsibilities are not only psychological but physical as well.

CHAPTER THREE

Self-Concept and the Mind-Body Connection

T he previous chapter described some of the dependency strategies humans have contrived to secure psychological survival. In my opinion, it is the unconscious application of physical survival strategies to survival of the psychological self that is responsible for much of the psychological illnesses in the world today.

Responding to insult by resorting to physical violence is an instance of this, as is the fanatical response of members of certain religious sects who view criticism of their faith as attacks on their person and justifiable reason for retaliation.

Anger, an instinctive response to a perceived attack on self, should always be looked upon with suspicion.

Some radical Muslims are so threatened by what they see as heretical Western views that they respond with what their injured egos perceive as commensurate acts of retribution.

> Anger, an instinctive response to a perceived attack on self, should always be looked upon with suspicion.

Anger, always an instinctive response to a perceived attack on self, should always be looked upon with suspicion.

Even in those instances where mental illness is involved, symptoms can almost always be traced to the sense of an injury to the patient's perception of self. One of the recurrent themes of schizophrenia, for instance, being a feeling of persecution.

Most of these responses are, of course, reflexive—born out of an instinctive defense of self—and it behooves us to be alert to the impetus behind our metaphors, learning to take responsibility for them and guarding against the tendency to glide into the easy path of escapist dependencies.

But comparison psychology, grounded on the philosophy of metaphor presented here, may address implications not yet considered for both forms of survival—physical and psychological. In this chapter, I propose to demonstrate that metaphor is at work in physiology, even as it was in the earliest forms of matter.

(If metaphor can be shown to be at work in the fusion of subatomic particles, as I have argued previously, then surely metaphor can "do its thing" in matter as malleable as flesh and mind!)

While it is true that self-concept is a nonphysical construct—built consciously or reflexively by each of us—I believe it possible to show that self-concept has access to a chemistry with tangible consequences in a tangible world. I propose, here, to argue for these connections.

When Vlatko Vedral ("Living in a Quantum World," **Scientific American**, June 2011, p. 430) writes that entangled molecules in the eyes of European robins can alter their chemical reactions, it is certainly not beyond reason to conceive of perceived threats to survival of self as having chemical responses equally influential in humans.

In a process I have named *autonomic mirroring*, self-concept accesses the metaphorical process and has thereby come to be the adjudicator of many, if not most, medical consequences in the modern world.

It is recognized that a world committed to the view that all physical consequences are traceable to physical causes will not take kindly to an argument holding that a purely metaphorical entity can effect significant physiological changes.

Even so, few thoughtful people would deny that changes occur in the physical world every day as a consequence of human enterprises such as medicine, architecture, art, engineering, horticulture, and music—all instances of mental conceptions (metaphors) having been given physical form through the manipulation of physical properties.

Why we should deny the human brain—inventor of everything synthetic that exists on this planet—manipulative powers of its own is but one of many ego mysteries.

One possible answer to this predilection for pragmatic reality may lie in the fact that people feel most secure in a world where everything is explicable, where their modus operandi is grounded in the hylozoically pragmatic: *Get, first, about the business of staying alive, and then trouble your mind with the meaning of things.*

Many studies suggest that the brain is programmed to condition much more than particles, cells, or hormones—the stuff of physical matter. It is, I believe, capable—through the action of metaphor—of enhancing matter, ensuring its survival, and even acquiescing in its own destruction.

I hope to show in this chapter that self-concept produces physical consequences beyond those configured by hand or machine, that the mind-body connection is real and documentable.

For reasons of structure, I will be discussing these processes as they apply to several different categories.

1. Brain Activity and Physical Change

It has been proposed already that a combination of letters bound together to form a word constitutes a metaphor.

It has been argued, as well, that the string of words called *sentence* expresses a unity that is metaphor, that literary constructions as complicated as **Hamlet, Prince of Denmark** constitute a metaphor in their own right, and that metaphor—upon final analysis—is the method and maker of everything we know and perceive, from matter to meaning to psychology.

Even as a poem constitutes a metaphor, transforming a conception (or collections of conceptions) into a physical object, so does an object created from matter constitute a metaphor.

A metaphor, in other words, is more than the idea behind a creation; it is, in every respect that matters, an object in and of itself.

Not only is every object on the planet a consequence of metaphorical function, every metaphorical product is an object capable of being used in the creation of other metaphors.

(As an instance, consider the light beam laser—from the perspective of this study, a metaphor, an idea, made physical.

(Initially created as a device for pointing out features on a screen, its power, which is greatly refined in energy and conductant, is now used for surgical procedures and is believed to have potential for the exploration of space and even time.

(Scientists already use it to alter and energize subatomic particles known only to mathematics. And, most recently, the US Navy has demonstrated its effectiveness in the destruction of drones. Regulations have even been proposed that would punish individuals for pointing lasers at airplanes.

(It is proposed here that any impulse triggering a response in a physical world—be it a chemical reaction, the formulation of raindrops in a thunder cloud, or an *aha!* response to a songbird's mating trill—constitutes an object in time and space and is, therefore, a metaphor, and whether it takes place under a human cranium, beneath the canopy of firmament the Bible calls heaven, or at the anterior end of a protozoan is aside from the point.)

Furthermore, the thought and its consequence are wedded, both being necessary to the other, and they are only separable by decay or death. This is true whether the metaphor manipulates idea or matter.

(As in quantum mechanics, objects—be they neuron, proton, or poem—can be shown to occupy two different places at once, can be both object and idea, so can an object that is metaphor be simultaneously material and idea, and, like quantum particles, be subject to combination and decay. Even decay needs not be fatal, however, often leading to creation of new particle combinations that when consummated always lead to survival enhancement.)

A thought, seen from the perspective of comparison psychology, is an electrochemical response to external or internal stimuli. It is experienced as feeling and interpreted by comparison in the neocortex. In terms of this argument, a metaphor is subject to definition as reflexive, hylozoic, or synthetic.

When, for instance, Professor Seth Lloyd writes about elementary particles colliding and performing a "logical operation"—p. 6, **Programming the Universe** [Alfred A. Knopf, 2006]—he is talking about metaphor, though he doesn't use the term. The "logical operation" is the completion of the comparison and the *aha!* affirmation of survival.

This first metaphor was almost certainly physical—born, possibly, of the merging of virtual and electronic particles—and was formed of energy, gas, or cosmic dust in a material world, the consequence of elementary particles discovering affinities and melding--thereby making a metaphor.

Because these composite creations (merged particles) were capable of seeking out and finding other affinities—a fundamental property of the impulse to merge imprinted in the laws of the universe as survival drive—they were and are subject to the laws (processes) of survival, one of which we now know, thanks to Darwin, as evolution. Evolution is a powerful, survival-of-the-fittest (among other things) metaphor.

Centuries, or even eons later, it is proposed that metaphor, employing the metaphorical process, discovered metaphor, and that suddenly the original metaphor—survival drive, once limited to the use of material particles only—gained access to the use of symbolic constituents, an evolutionary development making possible the substitution into slots once limited to virtual and actual particles, the immaterial particles of idea. At that moment, a new and more versatile version of metaphor was born, and survival has never been the same.

Although discussed earlier, these constructions merit further clarification: those earliest forms of metaphor occurred before the evolution of the human brain, and, as a consequence, their level of consciousness was primitive.

Even so, these metaphors persist today in the construction of matter and in the unthinking, or programmed, expression of survival drive, represented, for instance, in the impulses toward violence, procreation, and bigotry.

That second hypothesized form of metaphors, the hylozoic, is a product of an evolved level of consciousness and is primarily involved with the engineering of objects and machines that promote physical survival. Because they are concerned with survival practicalities, they may be also seen as providing a basis for the metaphor of pragmatism.

Though hylozoic metaphors are more highly evolved than their predecessors, they occupy that middle ground between the motive to survive physically and the drive to survive psychologically. This said, they must be seen as an important step on the path to the metaphor of self-concept.

This is because hylozoic metaphors—such as success with killing game or shooting arrows—led inevitably to comparisons. One hunter was more accurate, faster afoot, and more successful with women than others. Success in these areas led to the concepts of the successful provider, the alpha male, the leader, and the chieftain.

From this point, it was only a matter of time until physical prowess led to vanity and jealousy; rivalry for position and status made their appearance; and ego—the earliest form of synthetic metaphor—came to be. Like all metaphors, the hylozoic metaphor found its point of origin in the original manifestation of the drive for physical survival.

The synthetic metaphor, the third level of metaphor—destined for elevation to the third power of consciousness in the evolved metaphor of self-concept—was, like all metaphors, the product of comparison. The saga of its progression from subatomic particle to biota, from invertebrate to vertebrate, from mammal to monkey, from chimpanzee to the reasoning human brain is a compelling one.

Survival drive, according to the hypothesis argued for here, has done itself proud. The pilgrimage continues, however, and I would now like to turn to the process that embodies the metaphorical method.

Careful study of the metaphorical process will reveal the involvement of the three forms of metaphor in the mind-body arena, where mental properties can and do have physical effects.

The idea, for instance, that reflexive metaphors may effect changes in human cells is not new or nearly as controversial as one might think.

In fact, many students of the brain have commented, in an almost matter-of-fact way, on this mind-boggling (pun intended!) phenomenon.

Eric Kandel and Daniel Alkon (see Joseph Alper, **Science,** July/August, 1986, 44-86) established years ago that neurons in the brains of sea snails undergo lasting changes as a result of learning trials.

This discovery indicates that experience activates chemical changes that alter brain structure, a point driven home by William Greenough's discovery ("Memory," **Newsweek,** September 29, 1986, Begley, Springen, et. al., 50) that rats exposed to toys in their cages grew 20 percent more synapses than rats in nearly empty cages.

Lynne McTaggart has argued persuasively (**The Bond,** Free Press, 2011) for the influence of environment on genes and other bodily functions. Human culture has been shown to have the same kind of influence on structural configurations.

An article by Joe Durden-Smith, "Male and Female—Why?" (**Quest**, October, 1980, 94) points to differences in the cortexes of men and women, with women having thicker cortexes in the left hemisphere and men's being thicker in the right. He quotes Doreen Kimura of Canada as having said that these differences occur because:

> The men have been hunters, loners, requiring pro-nounced visual skills and goal-direction. The women have lived together in groups with children and the old (94).

Durden-Smith goes on to say that it seems "evolutionarily adaptive that women should have acquired different abilities—social, accultura-tive, nurturant ones—that men, by and large, don't have."

In short, culturally experienced values have organic consequences, consequences that facilitate survival based on different requirements.

Gary Lynch has identified ("PT Conversation [with Gary Lynch]: A Magical Memory Tour," *Psychology Today*, April, 1984, 29-39) a sug-gested process by which some of these physical changes take place.

Interviewed by Janet L. Hopson, Lynch argues that the effect of the enzyme calpain actually alters the shape of brain cells. According to Lynch (34):

> This enzyme sits there totally quiescent. But if you drive a cell to fire repeatedly, calcium enters the cell. When this happens, we hypothesize, the incoming calcium turns on the enzyme, which then chews up a mesh-work of proteins that serve to anchor little receptors—little catcher's mitts [note the metaphor!] in the membrane of the target bump.

These changes, Lynch says (32), also occur in the cerebral cortex. The emphasis here is on the word *repeatedly*. Perserverating elicits calpain which in turn elicits calcium, which in turn alters matter.

The prehensile grasp of our simian ancestors was undoubtedly a consequence of their need to elude predators faster afoot than they were. Dr. Ramachandran, a neurologist of some repute who will be quoted often in this work, goes so far as to argue that this prehensile proclivity contributed to the making of tools and even language.

Again, we see that changes are incurred without the aid of conscious thought (self-concept being a modern invention) affirming that there are, indeed, physical and social consequences to reflexive metaphors.

(This writer is aware of the controversy surrounding Lynch's pronouncement about calpain and of his rivalry with Eric Kandel [George Johnson, *In the Palaces of Memory: How We_Build the World Inside Our Heads*, New York, 1991, p. 23], but to this argument it matters little since both theories support the concept of reflexive constructs effectuating physiological changes.)

As reflexive thought processes trigger cellular changes in the brain, so have epileptic seizures (abnormal thought processes engineered by lesions in the brain?) been shown to result in lasting brain and body changes.

That an electrochemical response (a reflexive metaphor) can stimulate the creation of new synapses is certainly confirmation of the argument that brain processes affect body.

Dr. James O. McNamara of Duke University and the Veterans Administration Medical Center in Durham, NC, has identified a process he calls "kindling." Known for his study of the causes of epilepsy, Dr. McNamara is said to be:

> ...tracking the pathways of a "kindling" process, first identified in 1969, that apparently turns temporary stimulation into permanent changes in the brains of rats.
>
> The kindling process [in epilepsy] researchers believe, starts with a repeated mild electrical stimu-

lation of one small part of the brain …Researchers suspect nerve cells stop firing—and a seizure ends—when they are exhausted….The most startling aspect of the process, however, is that once an area of the brain is kindled, it undergoes a permanent change that leaves it susceptible to bursting spontaneously into electrical activity with no or little apparent stimulus. (*The News and Observer*, n.p., n.d.)

The point of the quote is, of course, the reference to permanent changes etched into the brain as the result of "kindling"—a clearly reflexive activity suggesting that thoughts (electrical impulses) have physical consequences in epilepsy and, it is assumed, in other brain functions, particularly repetitive ones. It also suggests a process of memory with significant implications for brain functions in general.

For instance, the late Dr. Paul D. MacLean, father of research in the limbic regions of the brain, suggested the possibility that:

…patterns of emotional behavior leading to excessive visceral expression are repeated so often in childhood as to become permanently engrained in the visceral [limbic] brain, with the result that they are perpetuated in later life. ("Psychosomatic Disease and the 'Visceral Brain, *Psychosomatic Medicine* **XI**, No.6, 349, November–December, 1949, Paul B. Hoeber, Inc., Medical Book Department of Harper & Brothers cl950 by American Psychosomatic Society, Inc.)

The idea that permanent pathways develop in the brain as a consequence of repeated "excessive visceral expressions," even as they do from the invoking of calpain and the kindling process in epilepsy, illustrates a physical consequence of brain activity and also suggests an intriguing movement away from the reflexive toward the synthetic.

Lest the reader perceive the good Doctor MacLean as too outdated or psychoanalytic to be relevant here, it is important to point out that one of our modern neurologists, V. S. Ramachadran (*The Tell-Tale Brain*, New York, London, 2011) refers to "repeated volleys of signals activating pathways," p. 278).

"Excessive visceral expressions," it is implied, derive from emotional perturbations. If proven correct, the implications for self-concept theory are obvious. An individual who returns again and again to feelings of inadequacy might well engineer a path, physical and psychological, to pervasive and lasting feelings of unworthiness in the realm of self-concept.

Perceived slights traceable to self-concept inadequacy—and I get ahead of myself here—could conceivably take on an intensity (through repetition) unwarranted by the seriousness of the incident evoking them, thereby leaving "tracks" in neuronal structures that facilitate their use in the event of sustained feelings of inferiority, in much the fashion as that accomplished in the brain by calpain and kindling, also referred to by Ramachandran (*op. cit.*, p. 151).

Survival impulse, under the auspices of comparison, requires that like qualities be stored together, with one similar incident evoking all others. In an event such as this, however, injuries to the metaphor that is self-concept would obviously be synthetic rather than reflexive, since by definition self-concept is a synthetic metaphor. (That the system may work in reverse is an argument saved for later.)

Bernie S. Siegel, MD, supports the argument of engrained, or reflexive, mental consequences in his curiously flawed book, **Love, Medicine and Miracles: Lessons Learned About Self-Healing From a Surgeon's Experience With Exceptional Patients**, New York, 1986, p. 3:

> Other doctors' scientific research and my own day-to-day clinical experience have convinced me that

the state of the mind changes the state of the body
by working through the central nervous system, the
endocrine system, and the immune system.

In addition to outlining a process whereby physical changes are effectuated, the quotation also raises the important issue of mind-body connections. The argument here is that self-concept induces chemical reactions, as the endocrine and immune systems effect physical changes.

(My characterization, above, of Dr. Siegel's work as "curiously flawed" should not be passed over without comment: the statement grows out of my impression of Dr. Siegel's grandiloquent style and his tendency to leap to conclusions equally as grandiloquent.

(His effusions about love and spiritual guidance strike me as unscientific, and his apparent belief in his god-like powers, along with his willingness to call himself a healer, evoked in me the following journal comment upon my first reading:

> The work is mystical, marked by the egomania of a
> short man who insists on being more. I think he's
> guilty of taking a series of coincidences and combin-
> ing them to form the basis for a philosophy that is
> speculative and evangelical. He seems to think he's
> discovered a new religion.
>
> His ravings about love strike me as sheer gibber-
> ish, and his notions of actually communicating with
> the dead are outlandish.

(This proviso, it should be noted, applies to Dr. Siegel's personality and writing style, not his scientific acumen. This having been said, I will continue to cite Dr. Siegel when his insights support my thesis.)

Evidence suggests that life experiences and reflexive thought processes induce changes in the actual physical structure of the brain. While these processes are reflexive in nature, it is important to note that they are incurred as a result of external stimuli.

If the external world impinges upon internal reality, as these citations indicate, it should not surprise that the opposite occurs as well—that mind, as the mind's experiences, has power over the matter that is brain and body.

The processes of reflexive metaphor have made and continue to make brain adaptation and modification possible, and it is important to note that the involvement of mind state leads inevitably to mind-body effect and, eventually, to synthetic self-concept—an entity, it will be argued, capable of enforcing physical consequences in the interest of its own survival.

2. Mind State and Physical Change

Even as reflexive responses to a physical world may affect brain structure, so may a pervasive mental state have a lasting impact on brain function. It will be argued here that a persistent mind state, informed by self-image, can influence and condition physical reactions inside the brain.

Gregg Levoy cites experiments conducted by Dr. William Frey, director of the Dry Eye and Tears Research Center in Minnesota (*Psychology Today*, July/ August, 1985, 10), which suggest that a factor of cognition is involved in chemical reactions.

Frey is quoted as saying that when the fifth facial ophthalmic nerve is severed irritant tears are affected while emotional tears are not. "Conversely," he writes:

> ...interruptions in the neural pathway between the lacrimal gland and certain areas of the limbic system of the brain—those associated with memory, behavior and emotional responses—seem to inhibit emotional tears, but not irritant tears.

He continues:

> Margaret Crepeau found that, among 137 men and
> women, healthy people are more likely to cry and
> have a positive attitude toward tears than are those
> with ulcers and colitis, two conditions thought [back
> then] to be stress related.

One conclusion to be drawn is that different mind states occasion different chemical consequences—evidence, certainly, that one's state of mind may dictate physical responses.

Equally interesting, from the perspective of this argument, is Crepeau's discovery that individuals with positive mind states are, to her way of thinking, less likely to suffer from ulcers and colitis—illnesses still associated by many with emotional stress.

Mind state is, for obvious reasons, a condition of self-concept. People who openly express their emotions—people who are not under stress for reasons of obsession with the survival of their physical or psychological selves—are likely to be endowed with sufficient ego strength to dare the risk of vulnerability. They are also less likely, evidence shows, to suffer physical illnessses.

An additional argument supportive of the effect of mind state on physiology occurs in Dr. Richard Bergland's *The Fabric of Mind* (Viking Press, 1986), page 148.

Discussing anorexia nervosa—a psychological disorder that, it is argued later, derives from a negative image of self—he writes:

> The mysterious disease, anorexia nervosa, stemming
> from a feeling of continuous satiation, has been
> linked both to bombesin and vasopressin.

(Bombesin is related by Bergland to depression in Table 14.3, p. 142, and vasopressin to pain, Table 14.6, p. 145. "Continuous satiation, it should be noted, is the literal translation of the term *anorexia nervosa*. In point of fact, anorectics are many times nauseated by the very thought of food."

The presence of bombesin and vasopressin suggests, too, that an attack on the organism—be it by invading microbes or by a pervasive state of mind—is interpreted by the brain as metaphorically equivalent—a point supported by Frey's discovery of the presence of stress chemicals in tears.

It is on page eight of the work by Frey already cited that he discusses the fact that the lacrimal gland removes manganese—a mineral suspected of causing mood alterations—as well as three chemicals known to be released into the body during stress: leucotomy-enkephalin, an endorphin thought to modulate pain sensation; adrenocorticotropic hormone (ACTH), which is considered the body's most reliable indicator of stress; and prolactin, a milk-regulating and calm-inducing hormone in mammals.

This flushing action of chemicals (and remember we are here discussing emotional tears—a physical consequence of an emotional state) adds force to the argument being presented here in several interesting ways:

1. It is obvious that these chemicals are present for a reason, and getting rid of them, once they have been utilized, obviously serves some therapeutic (survival) purpose.

2. The presence of manganese in tears, for instance, may be viewed either as cause or consequence of depression. Whichever the case, excessive amounts doubtlessly do not serve the end of homeostasis.

3. Presence of these chemicals—despite Barry Marshall's discovery of the involvement of bacteria in colitis and ulcers—suggests that a state of anxiety is responsible for these chemicals

being present. For that matter, who can say with certainty that stress does not enhance vulnerability to viral invasions?

4. A positive self-image (as expressed in willingness to vent emotions honestly and without fear) contributes to the maintenance of system homeostasis and the absence of stress illnesses.

The presence of ACTH or manganese in emotional tears is not surprising, but the existence (and flushing) of prolactin is at least bemusing.

What is prolactin, the hormone most closely associated with milk, that survival agent of first and early order—doing in the system at a time of survival stress?

(Ramachandran, interestingly, characterizes prolactin as an "affiliation hormone" that, in company with oxytocin, promote[s] social bonding. [*op. cit.*, p. 147.])

Furthermore, the discovery (cited in **The News and Observer** [8-11-88, 12A] and reported in **Nature***)* of the existence of a hypothalamic hormone-prolactin release inhibiting factor—suggests the likelihood that retaining prolactin may calm at least one function of the primitive drive to survive—it is said to dampen fertility in both men and women—indicating that the drive to survive psychologically may supersede the more primitive drive to survive physically.

This possibility is supported by the article's stated assumption that protracted states of stress contribute to this excess of prolactin, thereby accounting for the need for the inhibiting factor.

It would appear, then, that the presence and subsequent flushing of prolactin indicate that prolactin serves a soothing function; the absence of these chemicals in the brains of autistic individuals, who are universally recognized as lacking the qualities of empathy and compassion, further suggests the role of prolactin as a calming chemical helpful to mothering.

Supporting this possibility is Siegel's assertion (*op. cit.*, p. 29) that prolactin and cortisol participate in activation of the immune system, confirming my suggestion that the brain does not recognize differences between physical and psychological pain.

It would seem, as stated earlier, that it is in response to a perceived assault on psychological survival that the brain mindlessly pumps survival juices into the system. There being no physiological need for this infusion, the effect is likely to be an overstated one and therefore contra-indicated outcome.

Prolactin, along with other chemicals, is presumably present in the interest of maintaining or restoring equilibrium to a system under stress. However, in the absence of a meaningful therapeutic intervention (assuming that the stress-causing condition continues), attempts to relieve stress are likely to be an endless battle, one potentially harmful to the combatant.

The intriguing effect of excess prolactin on fertility will be discussed later in this document, but the presence of endorphins in emotional tears suggests, again, that the brain responds to self-concept stress by secreting pain killers, as it does to physical pain and injuries.

For instance—in support of this argument—high levels of nerve growth factor (NGF) have been found in the saliva of fighting male mice (*Omni*, March, 1988, "Tapping the Healers Within," Carol Kahn, 104), indicating a role in both fighting and (possibly) healing. Assuming the same kind of response in humans undergoing stress, maintaining the kind of even temperament made possible by a strong sense of self would help in obviating NGF and other potentially harmful chemicals.

An additional supportive case of mind-state influence over matter was found in an article in the *Reader's Digest* (July, 1993, 115-117, and excerpted from "Peppers: A Story of Hot Pursuits by Amal Naj," New York, N.Y., 1992).

Writing of the ingredient capsaicin, found in pepper and identified as responsible for its burning sensation, Naj writes:

> When capsaicin comes in contact with the nerve
> endings in the tongue and mouth, pain messengers

75

called neurotransmitters carry the worst possible message—"Fire! Fire!" to the brain. Alarmed, the brain puts the body into high gear: the heart beats faster, the mouth salivates, the nose sniffles, the gastrointestinal track works harder, the head and face break out in a torrential sweat.

Paul Rozin, a psychologist at the University of Pennsylvania, says (p. 117) that:

> …as the body tries to protect itself from the chemical, the brain, perceiving that the body has been injured, releases endorphins—natural painkillers. Since the pepper doesn't really do any harm, taking a bite is like giving oneself a mild dose of an opiate.

In this instance, the brain is tricked into believing that harm is being done to the organism and responds with painkillers and, undoubtedly, other restorative hormones. This supports the contention that the brain responds in similar fashion to emotional distress. The consequences need not be like that of an opiate.

There are other mind-body connections as well.

Norman Cousins points to a relationship between mind state and physical events resulting in pain. He writes as follows (***The Healing Heart,*** op. cit., p.188):

> One of the nation's leading experts on migraine, Dr. H.G. Wolff, has written that migraine generally starts with constriction of arteries inside the brain, followed by extreme dilation of arteries in the scalp.
>
> …Dr. [Elmer] Green enlarges this view with the finding that emotional and psychological stress

has an adverse spillover effect on the body's various
organs, the brain not excluded.

To the extent that *emotional and psychological stress* (my italics) result
from negative thought processes, and these processes result in dilation
of arteries in the brain, it is apparent that synthetic metaphors can have
consequences, even as reflexive ones do. For instance, I have noted in
numerous individuals the admittedly circumstantial pairing of emotional
instability and migraine headaches.

An additional indicator of the power of mind over matter merits
emphasis here. I refer to the healing properties of the placebo effect discussed in great detail by Cousins in his work, **Anatomy of an Illness
as Perceived by the Patient: Reflection on Healing and Regeneration**
(New York, London, c1979).

(The placebo effect is persuasive evidence for the existence of mind-body,
or metaphorical, force. A physical—reflexive—consequence is achieved by a
nonphysical, or synthetic, expectation—welling having been made actual.

(The metaphorical equation—this equals that—is thus confirmed,
and belief in a magical pill has freed us to tap into the primal patterns of
reflexive, comparison-based healing. It is a compelling instance of metaphor at work!

(Naturopathy, which emphasizes treating illness with natural elements identified with human traits—including, in olden times, the use
of particular herbs and roots, such as the mandrake root—is further evidence of the role of metaphor—even in folk medicine!

(As discussed below, autonomic mirroring is the proposed mechanism at work for effecting these kinds of changes.)

Cousins writes (p. 56) that the placebo "translates the will to live
into a physical reality." (Note the supportive metaphor!)

The fact that a placebo will have no physiological
effect if the patient knows it is a placebo only con-

firms something about the capacity of the human body to transform hope into tangible and essential biological change.

The transformation of "hope" into "biochemical change," aside from being a linguistic metaphor, suggests an instance of mind state (metaphor) affecting substance, as is the elevation of hand's temperature by autogenic suggestion (pp. 190-191, *The Healing Heart*).

Anees A. Sheikh further supports the concept of mind over bio-chemical matter in an article entitled "Pictures of Health," (*Omni*, February, 1989, 105-112), writing that imagination has power to cause actual physical changes in the lips and cheeks of humans from the act of mentally recreating a lemon slice.

He also cites a study by Edmund Jacobson in which visualizing the act of lifting an object causes the arm to register increased electrical activity. (See, also, V.S. Ramachanran's, discussion of mirror neurons—*op. cit*, pp. 117-135.)

(This "electrical activity" referenced not only demonstrates the way a metaphor has physical consequences but also speaks to the hypothesis that the brain may not distinguish between the survival needs of the body and the survival needs of self-concept.)

Of even greater interest to the argument that the mind has power over its own matter is reference to the admittedly controversial results said to have been achieved by O. Carl Simonton, a radiation oncologist in Dallas:

> By combining relaxation with personalized images, he has helped terminal cancer patients reduce the size of their tumors and sometimes experience complete remission of the disease. (105)

Sheikh cites other instances of mind controlling physical response. In one instance, he reports that the human retina responded to an imagined color rather than an actual one. (105)

These instances suggest that a conscious employment of metaphors, particularly positive ones, may adduce to enhancement of physical survival—that mind does indeed have influence over matter.

From the perspective of this argument, self-concept is to mind what brain is to body.

Finally, of great interest to this study are the interesting results of the Encode Study, a federally funded project involving 4,440 scientists from thirty-two laboratories around the world (See *The New York Times*, 9/15/12).

This study found the human genome to be packed with more than four million gene switches (previously characterized as "junk") that have been shown to have critical roles in how cells, organs, and other tissues behave.

Of especial importance to this study are the facts that many complex diseases appear to be caused by changes in these switches and, more to the point, that minor changes in environment can so alter gene switches as to induce autoimmune diseases, such as autism or rheumatoid arthritis.

Certainly, the presiding influence of self-concept should be at least as influential in eliciting and responding to genetic change as environmental factors, which have the disadvantage of being "outside" rather than "inside" the organic system.

Most of the kind of changes discussed here clearly take place under the auspices of reflexive metaphor—self-concept issues not being an issue with sea snails!—but changes effected in matter to enhance survival possibilities—whether of mind or body—do demonstrate that mental and environmental processes have real physical consequences.

3. The Stress Effect

Stress is a mind-state effect and is focused on separately because of its importance to the argument being argued for here.

Stress may be, in fact, the best evidence available for the thesis that mind state has physical consequences. I am very indebted, here, to the previously cited work of Dr. Selye.

Even so, my emphasis is not on biological but psychological stress—stress being defined here as a state of mental tension resulting from the transmutation of physical survival stress into stress caused by threats to psychological survival. Aside from being a consequence of the fear of death or of physical harm, stress is also a consequence of insecurities experienced in the realm of self-concept.

This is not to deny that stress has physical properties and consequences.

The brain, as has been often stated, brings the same chemistry to affronts to self-concept as it does to injuries (or the threats thereof) to the physical self.

The adrenalin surge in the interest of physical survival is well known, but it has only been in recent years that scientists have come to suspect that the very same surge accompanies exposure to psychological stress—what will be defined here as a physiological response to a perceived attack upon a nonphysical self.

It is believed that stress is not simply the sum of chemicals found in the blood stream but is actually a mental state with physical consequences. It is perceived in the mind as feelings of dis-ease and feelings (like all metaphors) are real, with consequences of their own.

Feelings take place in the body; they are electrochemical happenings; and they have significant endocrinologic consequences. Feelings of self-doubt are perceived (to use a couple of metaphors!) as a raised pistol pointed at self-concept and, unrecognized and unattended to, are as insidious as a tiger's claw.

While it is recognized that this definition of stress differs from that condition proposed by Dr. Selye, it is important to again point out that biologic stress, in so far as it involves the invasion of foreign objects—be they microbes or javelins—is not the subject of this investigation.

(Recent evidence that stress may be a trigger for activation of the acquired-immune-deficiency-syndrome [AIDS] virus is, however, of considerable interest, since societal attitudes toward the victims of this illness place them under additional self-concept strain.)

The primary emphasis of this exploration is on the effect of mind-generated "stressors" on physiological functions. It should be noted that Dr. Selye does not deny the existence of these kinds of stressors. Additionally, to the extent that mental strategies such as mind blank— the conscious decision to displace or ignore a threat to self concept—or rationalization may be characterrized as "adaptive reactions," Dr. Selye's definition of stress does not contradict the thesis argued for here.

In fact, on page 64 of *The Stress of Life* (New York, N.Y., 1956; revised, 1975) Dr. Selye stipulates that "stress is the common denominator of all adaptive reactions in the body."

(Since "adaptive reactions" may include efforts to protect the psychological self from "pain," they are most certainly accompanied by stress.)

On page 84 of the cited work, Dr. Seyle writes about "indirect pathogens," saying that our response to allergens (pollen, cat dander, etc.) is not directly caused by the external agents to which we have been exposed but:

> ...by our [body's] excessive adaptive mechanisms. It is such indirect pathogens that are the main causes of the so-called "stress diseases" or "diseases of adaption," such as high blood pressure, heart attacks, peptic ulcers, migraine headaches, pains in the neck, certain types of asthma, toxicomanias, alcoholism, excessive obesity or lean*ness due to abnormal diet-patt*erns.

These and many other diseases are not the direct results of any pathogens but of our defective *bodily or mental reactions* [italicized to emphasize mind-body connections] to the stressors encountered in daily life.

Our "adaptive mechanisms," which all carry a component of psychology, react inappropriately as a consequence of misfires in the brain or endocrinologic systems. Evidence will be shown that "excessive adaptations" in the realm of psychological survival have major impact in brain and endocrinologic areas as well.

It is the contention here that stress reactions accompanying a perceived threat to the psychological self may be accurately characterized as indirect pathogens.

It is further proposed that even Dr. Seyle's celebrated discovery—the general adaptation syndrome (GAS)—relates to my definition of stress.

Certainly, the perceived psychological affront may be viewed as "the stage of resistance"; and the onset of an established mental illness in whatever form as "the stage of exhaustion." (*op. cit.*, p. 104).

Finally, it is important to emphasize that Dr. Selye regards mind state as a significant factor in stress reactions, as indicated by his formulation of the term "eustress," his antonym for distress. He writes on page 74 of the work previously cited:

However, the fact that eustress causes less damage than distress graphically demonstrates that it is "how you take it" that determines, ultimately, whether one can adapt successfully to change.

It goes without saying that "how you take it" is a quality of self-concept in play at the time the response determination is being made.

It will be proposed here, then, that while stress serves a useful and even vital purpose in physical survival (an antelope in a life-or-death race with a leopard needs all the quick energy it can get!), stress summoned for protection of the psychological self may have serious physical consequences as well.

The concept that psychological stress engenders harmful chemical byproducts has already been discussed with reference to the once highly held view of the causes for ulcers and colitis and the "bemusing" role of prolactin; but Jo Durden-Smith, in the article from *Quest,* cited earlier points to another, admittedly controversial, kind of stress consequence.

Quoting Roger Gorski, she writes that Gunther Dorner in East Berlin

> ...believes that humans do have a sex center and that
> it is feminized in homosexuals because their mothers,
> *under stress* [my italics], produced at certain critical
> times during pregnancy a hormone [could it be pro-
> lactin?] that suppresses the action of the testicles (96).

It is conceivable that, in pregnancy, a perceived threat to the physical self could have the consequence of less emphasis being placed on biological survival—perhaps leading to a reduction in the size of reproductive organs for the fetus. It does not necessarily follow, though, that smaller testicles lead to homosexuality.

However, Gorski's research—acceptable or not from today's perspective—does suggest the fact of significant physical change occurring as a consequence of intense stress.

An interesting sidelight on this discussion is suggested in the results of a study by L. Roizin, reported by Sylvanio Arieti, MD, in *Interpretation of Schizophrenia* (New York, 1955, p. 401.)

> It is appropriate at this point to mention an ingenious
> work of [L.] Roizin, which deserves great attention...
> Roizin worked with roosters which were experimen-

tally blinded and fed artificially. In comparison with control cases, he found very marked atrophy of the testicles of the blind roosters, although the general weight was not considerably diminished.

Dr. Arieti does not suggest reasons for this phenomenon (though he does cite evidence, p. 401, for signs of "involution in the ovaries of schizophrenic women"), but it is conceivable to me that blindness might have effects similar to those experienced by bomb-shattered women.

No one of us who has observed Chanticleer strutting through his wire-protected, chicken-yard kingdom, surrounded by Pertelote and her less-favored sisters, can doubt that roosters possess a degree of braggadocio "associatable" with self-concept.

At this point in the kingdom of "chickenhood," the agency of survival drive—doubtlessly fueled by testosterone—is at its peak of confidence; inside his guarded fence, empowered by his greater bulk, he is, for a preciously limited period, the lord of all he surveys.

What happens, though, if this proud denizen of survival plenitude is blinded? It is difficult to conceive of a greater stress producer than the sudden onset of the inability to see.

Add to this the factor of having been denied, through genetic disinheritance, possession of an acute sense of smell—that earliest and most potent sense—which might have provided, in the face of blindness, some degree of survival adaptability.

Now he is denied use of his second most powerful sense, his strong auditory inheritance. This is so by reason of it having been rendered irrelevant; for, given the absence of smell, he cannot identify what he cannot see. (See *The Encyclopedia Britannica*, III, 684A, 1968).

Furthermore, his sexual drive is apparently governed by the external factor of light (*op. cit.*, *Britannica* 684B). Certainly, it is true the rooster suffers a reproductive disadvantage, unable either to respond to the visual flirtations and flutterings of Pertelote or "to own his prerogatives" on the field of battle.

We should not overlook the significance of Roisin's roosters having been artificially fed. The instincts of hunting and providing—so important in courtship—are certain to undergo atrophy as well.

Assuming blindness, Chanticleer's aggressively assured preeminence at the feeding tray would no longer be assured; in fact he might not even be hungry. Additionally, one suspects, his reverberating reveille—a once-puissant warning to potential interlopers—would be heard less and less in the land.

His food and protection assured (with him no longer required to fight for physical or sexual survival), it would not be surprising to see Chanticleer's self-esteem wither as his sex organs did, as it should not be surprising if both losses were swiftly translated into stress-produced self-concept survival doubt.

(I am reminded of Dr. MacLean's discussion ["The Triune Brain in Conflict," **Psychotherapy and Psychosomatics**, Switzerland: 28, 211] of two male rainbow lizards "humiliated in defeat."

(He writes, "They lost their majestic colors, lapsed into a kind of depression, and died two weeks later."

(It would appear here that we have a documented instance of survival doubt and its negative consequence in the realm of self.)

Though Arieti and Roisin do not consider the possibility, it is at least conceivable that the withering of sex organs could be attributed to the factor of self-concept stress, rather than solely to blindness; a similar kind of stress might have accounted for the results in the Dorner study.

Some additional support for Dorner's view may be suggested from results of a study conducted by Dr. Simon LeVay of the Salk Institute of Biological Studies in La Jolla, California (Natalie Angier, New York Times News Service, *The News and Observer*, 15A, 9-1-91).

Dr. LeVay found, in a study of autopsied brain samples from nineteen homosexual and sixteen presumed heterosexual males, that "the hypothalamic nucleus in the homosexual men was, on average, as tiny as it was in the women."

Again, it is posited, that psychosocial stress may well have played a role in these effects since that portion of the hypothalamus is thought to be responsible in autonomic mirroring for those diseases Dr. MacLean characterizes under his term "organ language"—see page 105 below.

(Attention is drawn, by the way, to the repeated hypothalamic references in this document—references, it is believed, with significant ramifications for the mind-body argument.)

It is proposed, then, that the bombing and strafing suffered by German mothers in the Second World War, in like fashion to Roizin's unfortunate roosters and Arieti's schizophrenic women, may have contributed to a stress-induced loss in self-esteem, to say nothing of other stress-induced consequences to the embryos they carried.

It is also likely that the brain's mindless dispatching of T-cells to the defense of a besieged sense of self would contribute in unknown ways to the chemical assault upon the embryo.

While these experimental results should not be interpreted as a cause for homosexuality, it is nonetheless ironic that such stress would have the effect of limiting reproduction in the affected individuals, that physical survival drive (reproduction) is "trumped," in a manner of speaking, by the drive to survive psychologically.

This kind of stress, magnified a thousand times in the case of schizophrenic women, might well place a premium on psychological survival to the extent of de-emphasizing the survival importance of ovulation.

Certainly, each of these instances suggest the possibility of psychological stress having very real physical consequences.

It may well turn out that psychological stress is history's single greatest threat to survival of Homo sapiens, particularly when viewed as a consequence of psychological conflict being intensified by the emergence of the modern self-concept.

To return to less-speculative terrain: Dr. Brian Stabler, associate professor of psychiatry with the School of Medicine at The University of North Carolina at Chapel Hill, has documented the role of stress in the health of children.

He is quoted in *The Raleigh* (NC) *News and Observer* (3-22-87) as saying, "Researchers found that stress caused the level [of blood sugar] in Type A children to rise significantly."

Type A children, according to Dr. Stabler, are impatient, aggressive, or competitive, children, who are, in the language of metaphor, anxious in defense of self.

Type B children, on the other hand, are passive, quiet, and relaxed, and they show significantly lower blood sugar levels, Dr. Stabler said (see Dr. Redford Williams's investigations cited below, pp. 88-90).

While this writer professes no medical expertise, the following hypothesis is presented as an example of the way the brain might respond to stress and the kind of physical consequences that could accrue as a consequence of self-concept stress:

When the self-concept is under duress, let us suppose the brain responds the same way it does when physical survival is threatened—by mandating the secretion of massive amounts of dextrose, a source of quick getaway energy.

Unfortunately for self-concept, the massive expenditure of energy required in the flight-or-fight response to physical threat is not mandated in the case of a psychological threat, where little or no muscular response is required. This means that insulin must go to work to control excessive sugar. Since the threatened self-concept is perceived as being continually under siege by inadequacy feelings, there would be a constant need for insulin.

Eventually, the body's cells and tissues would lose their ability to respond to insulin; this, in turn, would require the pancreas to make progressively more, resulting in what Dr. Ronald Kahn of the Joslin Clinic in Boston calls type II diabetes. (*The Raleigh* [NC] *News and Observer*, May 29, 1988, A-20.)

Should this hypothesis have merit, it would provide a direct example of how synthetic mind state effectuates identifiable physical changes in a living organism.

Redford Williams, MD, an internist at Duke Medical Center, has more scientifically outlined a similar process of mind state and physiological consequences in an article from his book excerpted in ***Psychology Today*** (January/February, 1989, 36-42, ***The Trusting Heart: Great News About Type A Behavior***, c1989, Times Books.)

According to Williams, heart attacks result from the formation of blockages in blood vessels. He believes that "the process starts with some injury to the inner lining of the artery." He continues:

> Large and frequent increases in the body chemicals
> involved in the stress response, as have been found in
> Type A people, are likely contributors to such injury.

In other words, physical damage actually occurs from stress consequences.

He goes on to implicate norepinephrine, epinephrine, and cortisol (p. 36) as being "stress hormones" involved when the sympathetic branch of the autonomic nervous system recognizes the need for a fight or flight response. "Type A people appear to react as if they are always running from a grizzly," he writes. Such stress, continued and repeated, would almost certainly have physical consequence.

In his introduction (xiii), Dr. Williams traces to anger the origin of the problem Type A people have.

He writes:

> Hostility and anger not only account for the increased
> risk of developing coronary heart disease among Type
> A persons but may also increase the risk of suffering
> other life-threatening illness as well.

The process, according to Dr. Williams, involves excessive stress responses experienced "frequently over a long span of time." (p. 86) He continues, "This is particularly the case in Type A men during 'vigilance tasks' (p. 89) when testosterone levels showed larger increases that Type Bs."

Dr. Williams goes on to argue (p. 103) that Type Bs are better able to control emergency-branch responses in that portion of the hypothalamus called the sympathetic branch (he calls it the calming branch) that is located in the posterior part of the hypothalamus. He writes:

> Just as the larger emergency-branch responses of Type
> As can stimulate processes of arterial injury leading to
> arteriosclerosis and heart attacks, the stronger calm-
> ing-branch responses of Type Bs could serve to pro-
> tect them by turning off the harmful actions of the
> emergency branch on their heart and blood vessels
> before damage is done.

As has been stated already, those individuals (Types B) content with their estimate of personal worth have less reason to instigate "processes of arterial injury" than do those people (Types A), having always to mount constant wars against perceived attacks on their self-concepts— another instance where self-concept has a direct effect on the prospects for longevity.

On page 107, he continues:

> Meanwhile, it's becoming increasingly clear that when
> stressed, particularly in ways that activate their mis-
> trust of others and thus generate anger, more hostile
> individuals show enhanced activation of emergency
> (sympathetic) branch and hormonal responses that
> make up the fight-or-flight response. If experienced

89

more frequently and more intensively, day in and day out, such responses could very definitely contribute to increaseed disease risk.

The evidence Dr. Williams cites involving the fight-or-flight response is, of course, supportive of the argument that mind state involvement leads to physiological consequences.

The reference to mistrust of others generating anger is particularly supportive of self-concept involvement, since people in the self-protective mode perceive themselves as being constantly under attack. Anger is always a defensive response.

As impressive as Doctor Williams's research efforts are, and as compelling as they are in support of the thesis argued for here, he and I part company when he leaves science behind and embraces religious philosophy.

The fact is a trusting heart (confidence in one's ability to cope) is a product of a healthy self-concept. While commitment to a particular religious path may have this effect—with certain unhealthy side effects for self-concept integrity—the issue at stake here is not religion.

The issue is that behaving responsibly—doing those things and thinking those thoughts necessary to an honest perception of self—contributes to an empowered self-concept and to all the benefits that accrue therefrom.

Dr. Seyle (bless him!) reports in his maddeningly undocumented way that:

> Psychologists estimate that less than 20 percent of the population has an "inner locus of control," the kind of self-possession in which people are guided by their own standards... (*op. cit.*, p. 167).

The "inner locus of control" Dr. Seyle refers to is, of course, an in-charge self-concept, a synthetic "self-possession."

It is believed that the results of Dr. Williams's investigation of vigilance behaviors confirms it: a person constantly on edge in angry defense of an insecure self-concept will possess higher levels of testosterone (*op. cit.*, p. 91) and suffer its inevitable consequences in the form of illnesses—illnesses (as will be suggested later) that mirror the internal mind state.

Less scientific than Dr. Williams's study, but more explicitly to the point of the argument addressed here, is an article by Stuart M. Berger, MD, in ***Parade Magazine***, entitled "Take Control of Your Health" (May 3, 1987, 10). Berger writes:

> A person's mental state can contribute to disease. Research has linked prolonged stress, for example, with a wide range of illnesses, including high blood pressure, heart disease, arthritis, ulcers, migraines, kidney and digestive disorders, complications of pregnancy and allergies.

That there is a connection between stress and physical illness now seems generally accepted, and more evidence will be cited below. Still, the exact process by which this is accomplished remains hypothetical, despite the remarkable work of Dr. Selye and his colleagues.

One important clue to process, and one closely related to the self-concept's role in illness, is provided by Carol Kahn in "Tapping the Healers Within" (*op. cit.*, 101).

In this article, Ms. Kahn points to a direct connection between the self-concept and the immune system. She writes:

> Studies by Levi-Montalcini have shown that NGF (nerve growth factor) is also necessary for normal development of the hypothalamus, a brain structure that regulates a number of hormones. It also appears that T cells, the immune system's frontline defense

against infectious diseases have receptors for NGF. *This could help explain the mind-body connection that has long been observed between emotional well-being and health.* (My italics)

In the interview portion of the article, Ms. Kahn asks about the previously referenced presence of NGF in the salivary glands of fighting male mice and whether this means that the immune system is subject to the effects of emotion. Ms. Levi-Montalcini responds:

> Oh, it has always been known that psychological conditions affect the welfare of people through the immune system, but it was never proved structurally that there was any relationship. Now we believe NGF is somewhat of a linking messenger. (104)

This "structural relationship" provides what may well be the most persuasive evidence found so far for the connection between stress (and by extension self-concept) and the immune system. (See also Dr. Siegel's comments, p.93 below.)

Attention is specifically directed to the role of NGF in development of the hypothalamus.

Richard M. Restak, MD, addresses the same relationship between emotional state and a weakened immune system (***The Brain***, Bantam Books, New York, c1984, pp. 168-169) when he recounts the famous experiment of Steven F. Maier, professor of psychology at the University of Colorado.

Professor Maier exposed a group of rats to a series of unavoidable electrical shocks with the result that they developed a weakened immune system.

Restak writes:

Overall, Maier's findings provide some measure of support for the commonly held belief that a person's "state of mind" can weaken his or her ability to resist infection and, it now appears, make the person more likely to come down with cancer as well.

It might be said, to paraphrase Dr. Seleye that the immune system has reached the "stage of exhaustion" from mandated failure.

Self-concept inadequacies, when they assume the status of mandated failure in the mind of the patient, are believed to have similar effects on the human immune system.

If Dr. Restak's endorsement of mindstate influence on the immune system is somewhat equivocal, this cannot be said of Norman Cousins' commitment to the concept in ***Anatomy of an Illness***.

Cousins believes that his own famous illness was brought on by stress and "adrenal exhaustion" (pp. 32-34), and on page 53, he discusses the physical ills he believes accompany stress:

> The fact that stress doesn't come from germs or viruses doesn't make its effects any the less serious. Apart from severe illness, it can lead to alcoholism, drug addiction, suicide, family breakdown, joblessness. In extreme form, stress can cause symptoms of conversion hysteria—a malaise described by Jean Charcot, Freud's teacher. The patient's worry and fears are converted into genuine physical symptoms that can be terribly painful or even crippling.

The conversion of the metaphorical states of "worry and fears" into painful and crippling illnesses is an instance of metaphor-making consequences and is, very likely, an illustration of autonomic mirroring to be discussed below.

The fact that stress has consequences for physical well-being is well established and widely believed. Stress, then, provides a clear example of the way mind state can affect physical well-being.

That stress has physical consequences, relating even to longevity, is indicated in studies conducted by Elizabeth H. Blackburn (see *Scientific American* 10, 11, 84-87).

Dr. Blackburn, a Nobel Prize winner, has established that psychological stress shortens telomeres—stretches of DNA at the end of chromosomes—in white blood cells and, furthermore, stresses that longer telomeres are linked with exercise and stress reduction. This supports comparison psychology's emphasis on the importance of exercise.

She is quoted (p.86) as saying:

> The more traumas, the shorter the telomeres. Our study showed a striking correlation between the number of years of chronic stress experienced by caregiver mothers of a chronically ill child and the degree of telomere shortness.

She goes on to link cancer with short telomeres as well as cancer cell involvement with the immune system—a system proven to be negatively influenced by stress.

Though Blackburn does not suggest it, I recall a study in which short telomeres were related to conservative mindsets—a possibility supportive of the precept in comparison psychology that holds a continuous state of defensiveness (a factor of stress) leads to shortened life spans.

In a related study (Liz Szabo, *USA Today*, 4, 24, 12), lead author Idan Shalev is quoted (in *Molecular Psychiatry*) as saying violence leaves longterm scars on children's bodies, not just on the skin but by altering their DNA, causing changes equivalent to seven to ten years of premature aging.

Interestingly, Shalev finds that the best way to strengthen telemores is through better nutrition, exercise, and stress reduction—activities specifically recommended in comparison psychology for enhancement of self-concept.

The connection between stress, shorter telomeres, and psychology deserves greater attention, as should the likelihood of a direct linkage between psychological stress and an embattled self-concept. It goes without saying: a confident, consolidated sense of self is less subject to stress and stress consequences.

We fight for survival of our nonphysical selves even as we fight to preserve our physical bodies. Failure in either realm has the same consequence—in one, death; in the other, bodily dysfunction or mental illness or both. (Loss of sanity is the metaphorical equivalent of death.)

4. Depression and Other Mind State Effects

There are, of course, mind state effects in addition to that of stress, and it is likely that the tangle of mind state will remain a thicket rife with known and unknown, yet-to-be-invented imbroglios.

One of the most deadly of these mind-state effects is that mind-crushing sickness endemic, almost, to these modern times. I refer to depression.

Richard Bergland, in his work *Fabric of the Mind*, already cited, has written brilliantly about depression and its connection to hormonal functions—what he refers to as "wetness of the brain."

He believes the role of hormones to be one of the most underrated facts in the universe, while the brain's electrical functions he regards as being greatly overrated.

Even though Dr. Bergland does not address the argument being presented here, his work provides important insights into the causes of depression. On page 170, he discusses that massive feeling problem as follows:

> Depression, more than any other human behavioral disorder, has clear-cut endocrine abnormalities. As many as one-half of the patients with unipolar depression have changes in the brain/pituitary/adrenal axis that are so dramatic that they can be measured in the blood.

If depression is, as this writer contends, "a state of exhaustion" deriving from stress caused by repetitive and prolonged attacks on self-concept by a presiding sense of inadequacy, it follows that a negative self-image may well be an agent for the kind of chemical changes Dr. Bergland documents.

Certainly, depression is a mind state with profound implications for physical and mental well-being.

While the high levels of cortisol Dr. Bergland finds in depressed patients may or may not alleviate the pain of injured feelings, it is safe to assume that so potent a hormone is not lying around doing nothing.

(Cortisol is an adrenal hormone, and adrenaline is correlated with pain in Table 14.6.)

Dr. Bergland further suggests that:

> ...many behavioral diseases may result from a mistuned blood-brain barrier that allows the brain to receive too few or too many hormones. Depression, for example, may result from capillaries that are too tight and do not allow the "hormones of happiness" into the brain. (p. 153)

Depression is a mind state that, like migraines, may impact blood vessels on the surface of the brain. A friend of mine who suffers greatly from periodic depression accompanied by anxiety swears she can feel her brain literally tighten up as depression sets in.

The "mistuned blood-brain barrier" referred to above is viewed here as a physical consequence of prolonged maladaptive mental actions.

Certainly, with its drawbridge raised, its crenelated battlements drawn tightly in upon itself, the brain provides us with an apt metaphor of the besieged and protected self—impervious to onslaughts from the enemy outside but isolated also from the chances for good from within.

Still with reference to the blood-brain barrier, Dr. Bergland says (p.171) that electroconvulsive therapy (ECT) opens the blood-brain barrier (and it will be recalled that ECT is one of the most effective treatments for prolonged and severe depression). On page 170, he writes as follows:

> Cortisol, the hormone formed by the adrenal gland after it receives a command from the brain and pituitary, is typically elevated in the blood of these [depressed] patients. While cortisol levels go up in the morning and down in the afternoon in normal people, in many who have a unipolar depression, such fluctuations are lost. If an attempt is made to shut down cortisol secretion by the administration of a synthetic hormone called decadron, it will be evident that the brain and pituitary are working overtime to stimulate cortisol secretion; decadron doesn't shut down production in a normal way.

Again, the presence of elevated levels of cortisol in depressed individuals supports the hypothesis presented earlier that the brain ministers to psychological pain the same way it addresses physical pain—additional evidence for the way metaphor works, based on discovered affinities.

The fact that levels of cortisol don't go down in the afternoon (as happens in normal populations) supports the idea that in mental illness the defending of a besieged self-concept is a never-ending task.

This presence of elevated levels of cortisol also supports the mind-body connection and the way states of mind can have physical consequences. The fact that decadron fails to stop the accumulation of cortisol is indicative of the levels of pervasive and interminable psychological pain the victim of unipolar depression experiences.

The threatened self-concept, much like the physical body—and it is important to note that self-concept mirrors the human body and is a metaphor of it—elicits treatment for a continually recurring pain. It is an instance of the classic double-bind, the depressed individual being trapped forever on a chemical roller coaster.

In addition to the mind state effects of stress and depression, there is also the fact of that intriguing mental manipulator called the placebo.

Reference has been made already to Norman Cousins's interest in this effect, but what he says about it has relevance to this argument as well—certainly with respect to mind-state effects. He writes:

> Medical problems relieved by placebos include severe postoperative pain, seasickness, headaches, coughs, and anxiety. Also affected by placebos are rheumatoid and degenerative arthritis, blood-cell count, respiratory rates, vasomotor function, peptic ulcers, hay fever, hypertension, and spontaneous remission of warts (*op. cit.*, ***Anatomy of an Illness***, p. 58).

It is obvious that something in the mind (belief in the efficacy of medicine, in this case) is activating important factors of healing. (The stronger the self-concept, the stronger the human will.)

It is no coincidence that Dr. MacLean, urged on by his psychoanalytical bent, (See p. 101 below) refers to some of these very diseases as psychosomatic. These illnesses, he believes, originate in the hypothalamic region of the visceral brain—the seat, it will be argued, of autonomic mirroring, discussed below.

Cousins also reports (in the work cited) test results by Dr. Stewart Wolf in which placebos are shown to have changed body chemistry and reduced the amount of fat and protein in the blood (p. 58); on page 59, he cites improvements in depression and arthritis as a result of placebos.

The effectiveness of placebos is directly related to the patient's belief in the efficacy of the medicine, and this writer sees faith as a derivative of will—will and self-concept being connected through the conscious evocation of survival drive.

Speaking of the effects self-confidence and the power of will (two additional qualities of mind state) have on human illness, Cousins writes of his doctor's willingness to cooperate with his self-therapy practices:

> He fully engaged my subjective energies. He may not have been able to define or diagnose the process through which self confidence (wild hunches securely believed) was somehow picked up by the body's immunelogic mechanisms and translated into anti-morbid effects, but he was acting...in the best tradition of medicine...(p. 48)

His perception of his physician's confidence in him was, he believes, a factor in his healing—the doctor's belief in him serving as the basis for his own enhanced confidence. The references to self-confidence and "hunches believed in" speak, in this writer's opinion, to a strong sense of worth centered on a stable concept of self—a persuasive instance of self-help in healing.

It is proposed that the body's immunologic processes, once freed from the stress of self-doubt through the agency of a stable sense of self, are left free to do their work.

Cousins speaks directly to the function of will in *The Healing Heart* (*op. cit.*, p. 198):

> The will to live is not just a frame of mind but a specific biochemical force. [I call this force survival drive!] For all we know, the will to live may be one of the connecting links between the belief system and the healing system.

This will to live, while inherent in all forms of animal and plant life, is an expression of survival drive. Freed from stress and unbelief, it is almost certainly strengthened by a positive sense of self. The stronger our self-concept, the more pleasure we seek, the more chances we take, the more successes we enjoy, and the longer and healthier we are likely to live.

Thus, a link between enthusiasm for life and longevity may be hypothesized. If this is correct, one might argue that, by assuming responsibility for self-concept, an element where human control is possible, could well be added to the equation of human longevity. It is an experiment (and possibility) open to us all.

The power of human will, documented in cases of patients who refuse to die, can be shown to vary from individual to individual, within families, and even between identical twins.

It is not unreasonable to propose that should such a thing as a self-concept meter exist, it would affirm the difference a positive (responsibly constructed) self-image makes even here.

To summarize: Depression is despair at the chances for survival (physical or psychological). It is the fate of MacLean's rainbow lizards, of Roizin's castrated roosters, and of Ariete's schizophrenic women. Along with loss of will, it is a consequence of self-concept gone awry or rendered impotent.

For the placebo effect to work, the patient must believe; for homeostasis to exist in the world of mind, the self-concept must be whole.

5. Autonomic Mirroring

Autonomic mirroring (to borrow a term from Dr. Maclean) is the "effector mechanism" that makes possible the changes described in each of these chapter headings. It is the engine (self-concept is the engineer) whereby things perceived in the mind work out their consequences. In essence, it is an application of the process of metaphor to the physical body.

Autonomic functions are generally presumed to be automatic and unconscious—witness Norman Cousins' definition of the autonomic system (*op. cit.*, p. 186) as "the system that governs the various functions that occur for the most part without our conscious knowledge or control."

But the fact that autonomic functions are subject to supervision by the neo-cortex (observe the effects of biofeedback and Transcendental Meditation, for instance) raises legitimate questions as to just how unconscious and unintentional these functions really are.

At the heart of the theory of autonomic mirroring is the conviction that metaphor is at the root of everything on the planet, and that includes the adoption of illnesses that imitate the individual's state of mind.

There are, of course, important reasons why certain autonomic procedures should be kept below the radar screen of consciousness as much as possible; one of the most important of these lies in the historical fact of survival made difficult by human existence in a jungle environment rife with predators.

In these venues, where a state of constant alertness is necessary for physical survival, the more matters that can be handled "behind the screen," the more energy is available for escape. With alarm bells going off every second, the organism would be distracted from its prime directive of survival—a manic attention to everything being attention to nothing.

However, in addition to physical survival there is that other form of survival, the psychological. It appears that the presiding entity of self may have taken unto itself survival issues the world has yet to recognize.

Individuals with insecure self-concepts are (to use a metaphor) like out-numbered soldiers who must navigate a mine field, here, maneuver through a swamp of quicksand, there, and infiltrate jungles a-swarm with evil foes. They must wend their way through potential catastrophe, expecting at any moment the shriek of sirens, the whining of strafing war planes, or the boom of exploding improvised explosive devices (IEDs).

The insecure self, like the threatened infantryman, will seek refuge wherever it can find it, through any means at its disposal.

Among the means available to it, in addition to drugs and alcohol, are the fore-mentioned use of dependency and repository metaphors, the strategies of scapegoating, and the use of self-generated stressors—compulsive fixations that distract the severely threatened individual from his primary source of pain.

In addition to these devices, there is yet another way the threatened individual may deal with a sense of impending catastrophe or a pervasive conviction of unworthiness, and that is through the unconscious use of autonomic mirroring. I suggest that this survival strategy is made possible through the agency of metaphor and its use of hypothalamic functions.

In a manner of speaking, autonomic mirroring is an instance of one form of survival (the psychological) being purchased at the expense of another—an incapacitating autoimmune illness.

From this perspective, the psychological self gains relief (temporary though it may be) by transferring baggage from the express train of mental stress to the slow-moving freight loaded down with physiological cargo.

More subtle than scapegoating (though it may actually be another form of the same), autonomic mirroring is a way of applying the psychological equivalent of the mind-blank option to physiological functions.

Briefly stated, the term "autonomic mirroring" describes a metaphorical practice whereby a distressed state of mind gets embodied in a specific, metaphorically similar, physical illness affecting some aspect of body function.

As Dr. Siegel implies (see p. 105 below], it seems likely that the mental state fastens upon that one autonomic function that comes closest to mirroring (duplicating) the psychological problems it is experiencing.

(The concept of autonomic mirroring owes something to Charcot's "conversion hysteria" and to certain psychoanalytic speculations by Dr. Maclean; however, the emphasis here is on that process of metaphor in which the mind says, "This psychic state finds its counterpart in this similar physical manifestation.")

It works this way: the self-concept, responding to a pervasive threat to the sense of self, and threatened by the prospect of worthlessness, taps into the primal patterns of comparison that underlie everything, organic and inorganic, on the planet.

This process, which utilizes the precise method of metaphor, transforms one thing—say an issue of emotional stress—into something else, diverting an issue of psychological discomfort to one that is physical, nobody's fault, and to which no sense of guilt or inferiority is attached.

In other words, an autonomically generated entity is created, one that corresponds in shape and symptom to those self-generated psychological stressors discussed earlier. It can be an extremely painful (potentially life-destroying) substitution.

For instance, over twenty years ago, I lived next door to a young woman, fresh out of high school, who was sent against her wishes to an out-of-state university.

Highly inhibited and aberrationally timid, this young woman had been reared in an environment lacking in that kind of sophistication the university took for granted or encouraged in its students. Once at the school, she was stricken by homesickness (or by perceived rejection) so severe that she withdrew within the month, returning home in a state approximating nervous exhaustion.

Once home, she married almost immediately, moved into a trailer on her parents' property, and got quickly pregnant—only to discover the man she'd married so hastily had a history of excessive drinking and was a diagnosed alcoholic.

In a matter of years, she was divorced and had moved home with her parents. To my knowledge, she never dated again, and, the last time I saw her, her hands and feet had folded into themselves, looking almost fin-like, and she could only get around in a wheel chair—into which she had to be lifted.

She had been diagnosed with a particularly crippling form of rheumatoid arthritis, an autoimmune illness resistant to every form of medication then available.

I propose that this is a compelling instance of self-concept inadequacy having taken on the form of her view of her inner self as being unlikable to the point of deformity—a mind state that crippled her as surely as would have a physical attack with a club ax.

While it is not yet possible for this kind of transformation to be documented in a laboratory, it strikes this writer, who knows the woman well, as a convincing instance of autonomic mirroring. If true, it represents a terrifying instance of self-image turning the physical body into a monstrous reproduction of itself.

It is also evidence for the underlying conviction upon which comparison psychology is based: metaphor is at the root of all creation—even a Caliban of the mind.

As said, the concept of autonomic mirroring owes something to Dr. Maclean and to comments made in a work already cited ("Psychosomatic Disease..." *op. cit.*, 350.) Here, Dr. Maclean discusses "a kind of organ language."

After referring to the inability of patients with psychosomatic illness to verbalize their emotional feelings—an inability intensified by the fact of its denial—he writes as follows:

> In other words, emotional feelings instead of find-
> ing expression and discharge in the symbolic use of
> words and appropriate behavior, might be conceived
> as being translated into a kind of *"organ language."*

He goes on to say, speaking of psychoneurotics, that their greater facility with language "affords a reduction of traffic on the autonomic circuits and thereby helps to ward off the development of lesions."

The implication seems to be that utilization of the neocortex (the site of reading, writing, and reasoning) provides a substitute mechanism for the usual autonomic passageways, one that is less physical (less prone to lesions) and therefore less harmful.

(The young woman described above as suffering from rheumatic arthritis was significantly lacking in verbal skills.)

It is relevant, as well, that Dr. Maclean's use of "symbolic" words and "appropriate behavior" specifically address metaphorical functions. In my opinion, a greater facility with language, language being metaphor, suggests an ability to express one's emotions, rather than repress them.

This does not mean that these individuals might not develop psychological issues—after all, human trauma comes in all shapes and sizes, some more threatening than others—but these issue would be less likely, if Dr. MacLean is right, to be autonomic and of the autoimmune variety.

(The assumption that a greater facility with language somehow reduces traffic on autonomic circuits may suggest a basis for the evolution of synthetic metaphor and point to the creation of a new version of survival—the psychological.)

There are lesions and there are lesions.

Dr. MacLean's hypothesis suggests one way metaphor might function on the physical level, but more importantly, it demonstrates how a physical consequence may be shifted to a metaphorical one.

(The distinction Dr. MacLean draws between psychosomatics and psychoneurotics, and the different ways they handle their emotions, is a very useful one; for it illuminates two paths humans may elect in protection of the self-concept in addition to those dependency strategies discussed in Chapter 2. A consolidated sense of self, constructed by the conscious use of synthetic metaphor, might well eliminate the need for subconscious escapisms.)

While his point may be to illustrate the mind's knowledge of the body's illness, Dr. Siegel (*op. cit.*, p. 32) describes a consequence that reads much like autonomic awareness—a mirroring by the mind of hidden inner processes.

He quotes a Jungian therapist who had recently undergone emergency surgery to remove several feet of dead intestine as follows:

> I'm glad you're my surgeon. I've been undergoing
> teaching analysis. I couldn't handle all the shit that
> was coming up, or digest the crap in my life.

The connection between metaphor and organ language is obvious, as there is obviously some form of mirroring going on. If the therapist had indeed translated his emotional unhappiness (and the teaching analysis was obviously threatening his self-concept) into a condition requiring surgery, this would constitute an exact instance of autonomic mirroring.

After undergoing a mastectomy, a woman is reported to have told Dr. Siegel that she needed to get something off her chest (*op. cit.*), and on page 66, he writes, "The body responds to the mind's messages, whether conscious or unconscious." He goes on to cite a series of mind statements: "He's a pain in the neck/ass. Get off my back. This problem is eating me up alive. You're breaking my heart."

What Freud might term "naming from the unconscious" may actually be a metaphoric kind of knowing made possible by autonomic functions of (to use Dr. MacLean's term) "the visceral brain."

The following Siegel quotation (*op. cit.*, p. 67) suggests a means whereby autonomic mirroring might be effectuated:

> Nerve fibers enter the hypothalamus from nearly all other regions of the brain, so that intellectual and emotional processes occurring elsewhere in the brain affect the body. For example, about five years ago, child-development researchers discovered "psychosocial dwarfism," a disturbingly common syndrome in which an unhealthy emotional atmosphere at home stunts a child's physical growth. When a child is caught in a crossfire of hostility and feels rejected by his or her parents, thereby growing up with little self-esteem, the brain's emotional center, or limbic system, acts upon the nearby hypothalamus to shut off the pituitary gland's production of growth hormone.

One regrets that the good doctor doesn't find it necessary to document his sources—and the process as described seems more than a trifle strained. However, should the "psychosocial dwarfism" he cited be authentic, it would be a perfect instance of autonomic mirroring. The physical body would have been made to conform to a negative self-image.

Marilyn Ferguson (*The Brain Revolution*, N.Y., N.Y., 1973, p. 149) reports that "the brain creates its own images of the body parts." On the same page, she compares phantom-limb pain to

> ...a mirror image epileptic pattern in the opposite hemisphere. Even when the original damaged area is

surgically removed, the mirror focus may continue to
cause seizures for many months.

(Efforts to secure permission to cite the above passages came to
naught. Ms. Ferguson's publisher in New York stated that the company
no longer represented her, and efforts to contact her new publisher were
unsuccessful.)

That the brain creates mirror images of body parts is a concept of
great value to this argument, for it describes a process whereby an image
(a metaphor) may have direct impact upon the autonomic system—the
site of the immune system and other bodily functions that assure the
survival of the organism.

And Dr. Ramachandran (*op. cit.,* p. 25) provides support for this
perspective when he writes, "I discovered there was an entire *map* [my
italics] of the missing (amputated) hand on his face." And on page 256,
he refers to body image as "a unified…, real-time representation of your
physical self."

Needless to say, body image is a metaphor of an existing physical
entity—the body—and one with important ramifications for physical
and mental well-being. The fact of the existence of a "real-time representation of your physical self…" suggests the existence of a metaphorical
sense of self.

If body image is rendered inaccurate from amputation—by it continuing to mirror the absent limb with all its persistent complications—
who is to say that the same mechanism might not be in play when
self-concept is defective? Certainly, the metaphorical process is involved
in both permutations.

More important to the concept of autonomic mirroring, though, is
the possibility that even as body parts are mirrored in the brain so may
the image of self be engrained metaphorically in the fabric of the brain.

This "intaglio," it is proposed, has the capacity to reform parts of
the body in its own image—a more palatable version of homunculus and

the ultimate extension of autonomic mirroring. It is the Platonic concept of "Idea" with an ironic twist.

Returning to the autonomic system:

Norman Cousins's description of it was presented in abbreviated form above; however, he lists there additional functions—including the reproduction and circulation of blood cells, the manufacture of hormones and their energy, the delivery system along which this power moves to different parts of the body, including the heart, the breakdown by the body's chemicals of different foods into materials of maintenance and growth, and the storage of information by brain cells.

As can be seen from this listing, the autonomic system is occupied with important physical survival functions.

And it should be noted that, while Mr. Cousins does not include the functioning of the immune system, he could have. It is one of Mr. Cousins's major theses that, with training, it is possible to utilize autonomic functions in the maintenance of a healthy body.

This training's effectiveness appears to be itself a consequence of autonomic mirroring put to conscious use in the form of a sought-for positive outcome. It also suggests the direct involvement of self-concept, since a responsibly constructed self-concept is necessary to the healthy functioning of both body and mind, as held by comparison psychology.

In the article cited previously, Dr. MacLean wrote at length (and with splendid scientific acumen—much of it in the highly arcane language of the trained neurosurgeon) about the limbic system and the processes through which it contributes to psychosomatic illnesses—mind-created illnesses not owed to germs or viruses.

The illnesses he discusses are linked directly with the autonomic nervous system.

On page 338, he refers to the hypothalamus as being "the head ganglion of the autonomic nervous system" and as being the "effector mechanism of emotional expression."

(This description of the hypothalamus as the "effector mechanism of emotional expression" drives home, it is believed, the importance of the hypothalamus to the concept of autonomic mirroring.

The hypothalamus is seen as more than just the "effector of emotional expression," however; I see it as the actual organ of transmutation—the means through which physical functions are made metaphoric.

Therefore, it is no coincidence that this brain organ has been referred to repeatedly in this document. It is the gateway to autonomic mirroring.)

Let us return now to Dr. MacLean. He goes on to link the hypothalamus and other connecting brain organs with the feeling process—a primary function of the limbic system and the likely rails on which psychosomatic illness rides—by quoting Dr. James W. Papez as believing that the hypothalamus, the anterior thalamic nuclei, the gyrus cinguli, the hippocampus, and their connections "elaborate the functions of central emotion, as well as participate in emotional expression." (339)

Discussing the cingulate gyrus as an important autonomic center, he refers to "the bearing of emotion on asthma" and says, "It should be noted that the anterior part of the cingular gyrus can exert a powerful vagal effect on respiration." (343)

He also points to the fact that stimulation of this area can cause a considerable rise in blood pressure; he goes on to suggest a link between the renin enzyme system and persistent hypertension.

On pages 349 and 350, he states that hypertensive patients suffer "chronic unexpressed rage"; that patients with peptic ulcer suffer "unconscious dependent needs"—an eventuality I wish were indeed the case, since I view dependency as the most direct path to emotional insecurity; that the asthmatic patient suffers from her/his inability "to fulfill" a need for "emancipation"; or that asthmatic breathing is a form of "wailing" that occurs when the patient attempts to break the parental tie—instances, in this case, of far-reaching psychoanalytic metaphors, too extreme even for me!

It should be pointed out, though, whether or not one believes these motives underlie these illnesses (and to this reader they reek too much of psychoanalytic theorizing), they are diseases clearly related to specific autonomic functions and could be easily used for the kind of avoidance purposes suggested in my theory of autonomic mirroring.

(From this admittedly extended and highly subjective perspective—one that at least Dr. MacLean would approve of!—hypertension might be seen as related to arterial pressure [a metaphor, perhaps, of a stress-filled mind]; and asthma might become a complication of breathing [a product, perhaps, of a sense of ego suffocation—the latter possibility supported in my experience by the case of a highly insecure friend of one of my daughters who suffered asthma attacks whenever she was away from home].

This said, it is important to alert the reader to the fact that metaphors—because of their very formula—always require the *aha!* response of affirmation; and, as a cautionary reminder, the reader is again informed: No metaphor is right or wrong, just efficient or not.)

Dr. MacLean also refers to a "psychiatric and psychoanalytic" study of patients with rheumatoid arthritis conducted by A. O. Ludwig and says the studied patients "are unable to express their very strong emotions, but instead react to emotional crises with *intense autonomic activity*." (350) [My italics]

The "intense autonomic activity" observed by Dr. Ludwig describes (I believe) the ongoing process by which autonomic mirroring is accomplished.

Under the pressures of self-concept inadequacy, his patients "choose" not to express and confront their feelings and, instead, (through employment of the human capacity for displacement) divert their tensions elsewhere.

I contend it is no coincidence that some patients are victims of rheumatoid arthritis (reference page 79 above). Speaking metaphorically, they have bound themselves with ropes of their own unconscious production.

(Along the same speculative lines, I, personally, have been diagnosed with osteoarthritis—a fact that could conceivably lead to speculations that I suffer from an autonomic disease of the motor system—a metaphor, perhaps, of my difficulty in extricating myself from life difficulties or from emotional strictures.)

Writing again about the process whereby mind state "might" contribute to psychosomatic disease, Dr. MacLean writes (350):

> It might be imagined that the "rage" of the hypertensive patient, arising out of unsatisfied "oral" demands, has a similar mechanism to the rage-producing hunger in the animal.
>
> In both instances the visceral brain might be postulated as participating in the release of the hypothalamus to sympathetic discharge. But in the hypertensive the conscious need for restraint would exert through the neocortex an inhibition of the somatic expression of rage for which the autonomic responses are brought into play, and so interfere with the physiologic safety valve of muscular activity. On the other hand, the "emotional hunger" of the patient with peptic ulcer might be considered as chronically activating that part of the visceral brain which is linked to the hypothalamic nuclei governing gastric functioning with the result that the stomach is being constantly prepared for food. Similarly one might speculate about possible mechanisms for asthma, ulcerative colitis, and other diseases where the emotions are thought to contribute to the development of lesions.

This is powerful, albeit very early, support for the concept of autonomic mirroring. The "emotional hunger" Dr. MacLean refers to, and that he suggests might result in a peptic ulcer is a metaphor of a troubled mind state.

(The reference to "the physiologic safety valve of muscular activity" is seen as supportive of the importance assigned to actions in the actualization of self-concept.)

Should an ulcer occur under the circumstances Dr. MacLean proposes (and Marshall's discoveries implicating bacteria, not stress, cannot be ignored), it has been well documented here that stress is deeply involved in immune system functions, and it might very well make one more susceptible to various kinds of infection—including bacteriological ones.

Even though MacLean's argument reeks of psychoanalytical thinking, such a phenomenon would be an instance of just what is being discussed—a physical representation of an aching emptiness—an emotional state translated into an organic representation.

Earlier in the same article, Dr. MacLean argues that while the hippocampal formation (which consists of the amygdala and the hippocampus, both with direct access to the hypothalamus), does not compare in efficiency with the neocortex (348) it nonetheless possesses "the capacity to participate in a nonverbal type of symbolism."

He writes:

> This would have significant implications as far as symbolism affects the emotional life of the individual. One might imagine, for example, that though the visceral brain (the limbic area) could never aspire to conceive of the colour [sic] red in terms of a three-letter word or as a specific wave length of light, it could associate the colour [sic] symbolically with such diverse things as blood, fainting, fighting, flowers, etc. Therefore, if the visceral brain were the

113

> kind of brain that could tie up symbolically a number of unrelated phenomena [metaphor in action!], and at the same time lack the analyzing ability of the word brain to make a nice discrimination of their differences, it is possible to conceive how it might become foolishly involved in a variety of ridiculous correlations leading to phobias, obsessive-compulsive behavior, etc. (348)

The non-verbal symbolism (evidence for the existence of other forms of metaphor) hypothesized here—a concept easily seen as supportive of what Dr. Arieti calls paleologic thinking—see *Creativity: The Magic Synthesis*, (New York, 1976, p. 67)—with its corollary of neurotic illnesses resulting therefrom, constitutes another instance of autonomic mirroring—the organ affectted, here, being the brain.

This older and "less intelligent" reptilian brain would obviously have more intimate relations with the autonomic system than does the cerebral cortex, thus providing (if supported by further research) a more likely location for the kind of metaphorical transmutations hypothesized to be taking place in autonomic mirroring.

It is also important, with respect to the concept of autonomic mirroring, to stress the connection between the hippocampus and the posterior part of the hypothalamus, a connection pointed out in Dr. MacLean's diagram on page 346 (*op. cit.*, Fig. 4).

He stipulates that these connections express those "predominantly sympathetic" responses of "fight, flight, wakefulness, etc."

These connections, it should be noted, are tied to internal responses to an outer world and are similar in this respect to those survival forces thought to be behind changes detailed above in "Mind State and Physical Change."

These sympathetic responses (be alert, attack, run fast, stay alive) demonstrate the very process of metaphor being argued for here; and flight responses correspond, of course, to mind-blank in the world of psychological survival.

The kind of "thinking" done in the posterior area of the hypothalamus occurs in that realm of primitive reason called by Dr. MacLean "the visceral brain." It is also the likely realm of autonomic mirroring and a possible junction for psychoneurotic, psychosomatic, autoimmune illnesses, and other forms of physical malfunctioning.

The anterior end of the hypothalamus, on the other hand, connects with the amygdala, and, according to Dr. MacLean, these connections are "predominantly parasympathetic" and address the functions of "feeding, digestion, elimination, sleep, etc."

These functions deal with sustaining the physical organism rather than fending off external threats; however, I hasten to add that the issue is still one of survival.

The sympathetic branch of the hypothalamus may be said, then, to concern itself primarily with external threats to survival, while the parasympathetic branch is concerned with inside, "housekeeping" matters.

I don't propose to lean too heavily on these metaphorical distinctions, but it is tempting to hypothesize that autonomic mirroring takes place in both branches of the hypothalamus and its associated organs.

From this perspective, the sympathetic branch—that system responsible for the impulses of fight or flight from invasive threats to survival—be they physical or psychological—would stimulate the use of weapons from the adrenalic arsenal such as overt hostility, emotional outbursts, or outright physical violence.

Overuse of these "attack-or-defend weapons"—according to this hypothesis—would result in illnesses cataloged under what has been called anxiety-related diseases.

On the other hand, transmuting psychological obsessions to a concern for physical survival would activate the parasympathetic branch, shunting illnesses in the direction of those organs responsible for bodily upkeep.

Individuals who settled on, or unconsciously selected, these avenues for an obsessive expression of psychological unhappiness would, in terms of this argument, be utilizing and deflecting their insecurities through the device of autonomic mirroring.

Some support for this contention *may* be found in the previous MacLean citation (p.125) relating to the difficulty arthritic patients experience in expressing themselves verbally. (This was in contrast to a notable facility with language on the part of psychoneurotics.)

Dr. MacLean asserts that this is the general case with patients afflicted with psychosomatic illness and writes as follows:

> It should be remarked that one of the striking obser-
> vations regarding the patient with psychosomatic ill-
> ness is his apparent intellectual inability to verbalize
> his emotional feelings. (350)

Dr. MacLean goes on to suggest that there is little direct exchange between the visceral brain and the word brain in the psychosomatic patient and that emotions are fed for immediate expression to the autonomic centers—resulting, as already mentioned, in a kind of "organ language."

(It would not be surprising, by the way, should it turn out that psychoneurotics do enjoy higher language skills than their psychosomatic counterparts. After all, psychoneurotics are ensuring their survival by use of the most powerful weapon in the sympathetic nervous system's arsenal—verbal symbolism!)

The fact that there is "little direct exchange" between visceral and word brains (the cerebral cortex) suggests, again, that patients may unconsciously employ autonomic mirroring as a side-tracking mechanism, making it unnecessary for them to confront self-concept issues.

Physical illnesses, after all, are not generally seen as the patient's "fault" and are more easily borne than are feelings of psychological inadequacy, looked down on in society as signs of weakness.

I am reminded of an article I failed to save by the late Everett Allen, one in which he described his inadvertent observation of a hospital patient deliberately causing herself to vomit, thus validating to an observing world that she was genuinely sick.

That this unfortunate woman would knowingly resort to so demeaning a strategy may well mean that her need for human sympathy was greater than her need for self-respect, her need for illness greater than her fear of shame, of being seen as guilty of faking.

It even may have been that she had so lost touch with the world's view of reality that she only felt secure in her prefabricated world of illness.

Psychosomatic illnesses may well originate from these or similar motives, but whatever their origins, it is believed that these illnesses, accompanied by their very real suffering, are metaphorical transmutations of deep-rooted feelings of psychological worthlessness.

The possibility was suggested earlier that the two branches of the autonomic system might be thought of as facilitating two forms of expression—the sympathetic for the so-called stress diseases and the parasympathetic for organic ones.

This suggestion implies the existence of some system of traffic controller that, in a manner of speaking, shunts one metaphorical bus to the right and another to the left.

This proposal assumes the existence of just such an arbitrator—in the form of self-concept. It is the most important, and most ignored, entity in our lives.

An argument for the importance of self-concept in autonomic mirroring finds further support in an article in *The News and Observer* (Raleigh, NC, March 6, 1988, 22A). The reporter, Daniel Goleman, writing for the *New York Times* News Services, contends that:

> New studies are drawing a portrait of one of the most mystifying personality types: those people who maintain a stiff upper lip under all circumstances.

Personality is, of course, an expression of self-concept. Repressers protect their threatened selves by use of the device referred to above as mind blank—a conscious decision to avoid taking responsibility for self-concept.

Mr. Goleman says repressers are not just successful at masking emotions. Often, he says, they are not even aware of their own inner stress. (Of course, they are not aware of their stress; they have done something else with it!) "As a result," he continues, studies are showing these "represser" personality types are more prone than others to some diseases. "These individuals have a higher risk for asthma, high blood pressure, and overall ill health," he writes.

(Asthma, the reader will remember, is associated with the parasympathetic branch of the autonomic nervous system. High blood pressure would appear to be stress related and associated with the sympathetic branch. Both are sometimes seen as autoimmune illnesses or precursors thereof.)

More generally, Goleman stipulates, the represser's style has been associated with a reduced resistance to infectious diseases—a possibility supportive of the telomores hypothesis presented above.

Researchers at the Yale School of Medicine, Goleman writes, found that in 312 patients treated at an out-patient clinic there, the repressers tended to have lower levels of certain disease-fighting cells of the immune system, and higher levels of cells that multiply at the time of allergic reactions.

Repressers of the stiff-upper-lip type not only reduce the effectiveness of their immune systems (this has been shown to be one of the effects of stress), they also divert energies from important psychological responsibilities.

In short, they circumvent their opportunity for a responsible construction of self-concept and may literally truncate longevity possibilities.

In the context of this argument, by not taking responsibility for self-concept—that is, by not confronting and resolving their frustrations and feeling good about having done so—they are exposing themselves to higher risks of mental and physical illnesses.

The direction these illnesses take (the branch of the autonomic center chosen) is based, this writer believes, on the quality of self-perception.

Under terms of this hypothesis, angry repressers would likely end up with diseases of the sympathetic type—diseases that mirror their anger. Introverted repressers, on the other hand, would fall victim to the so-called organ diseases of the parasympathetic branch.

Those people who do not repress, and who are not trapped in a world of hidden obsessions, do not linger overlong in either branch of the central nervous system and, from the perspective of this argument, are spared the agony of self-inflicted illness.

Whatever course taken, the individual is responsible for construction of self-concept and the choices he makes. Needless to say—from the perspective of comparison psychology—the decision to avoid this responsibility is fraught with negative consequences. As we choose (or fail to choose) our thoughts and actions, so do we choose our consequences.

Autonomic mirroring may have provided the mechanism, but self-concept is the driver of the bus.

This chapter has sought to show that brain can, in the interest of physical and emotional survival, respond reflexively (think metaphor) to external stimuli and literally modify physical organs.

It has been suggested that this organ of comparison (the brain) adapts to internal emotional stimuli (such as psychological stress and depression), also in the interest of survival, psychological or physical.

From these points, it was argued that brain matter is influenced by the non-material stuff of idea, here called metaphor.

Autonomic mirroring—the metaphorical process whereby the non-physical is made physical, the physical is made nonphysical—is presented (in alliance with a positively constructed self-concept) as a possible clue to the mind-body connection.

Metaphors—actions or ideas—that deal with self-concept are (or ought to be) conscious and therefore synthetic.

That the employment of conscious metaphors is a possibility is suggested in another article by Julia Savacool, published in **USA Today** (5/4/14/3U). In the article, entitled "Stress-Busting Resilience Can Be Learned," she argues that "mental fortitude training and resilient self-development [should] become a mandatory part of children's education."

Earlier on she quotes Mustafa Sarkar and David Fletcher (in the journal **Sports, Exercise and Performance Psychology**) as saying, "It's up to people to do what they can to maximize their potential [for resilience] within their constraints."

As contended throughout this work, resilience is an inevitable consequence of a responsibly constructed self-concept.

According to Sarkar and Fletcher, "a proactive and positive personality; a sense of flexibility and adaptability; feeling in control; having balance and perspective" are all self-controlled variables supportive of psychological survival, necessary components of "cognitive reframing"—a phrase that supports the presumption that responsible development of self-concept is indeed possible.

Summary

As has been stated, the mechanism of change is comparison, and all comparison is metaphor. It matters little whether things change as a result of evolution, lifestyle acculturations, or as a consequence of chemical reactions taking place in the brain.

Change is a consequence of metaphor—a thought held in the mind of nature or of humankind.

As stated repeatedly, the force in the universe that generates comparison is survival drive, expressed either physically or psychologically; and in this chapter I have sought to demonstrate that the desire to survive psychologyically (in the realm of self-concept) has physiological and psychological consequences of great moment.

Autonomic mirroring was presented as the mechanism that drives the mechanism. Through its offices, the process of metaphor, omnipresent in the universe, has been metamorphosed into mind.

Metaphor is truly at the root of everything.

Autonomic mirroring, then, has access to the gears and chassis of survival; it leaps the gap between the finite and the mental; and it makes possible a transition from the strictly mental to the physical—a reversal of the usual path of metaphor, and one prefigured in the importance of physical actions to self-concept.

Ultimately, of course, autonomic mirroring is the conveyer of consequences growing out of self-concept inadequacies, self-concept being the arbiter of physical and psychological homeostasis. Even as autonomic mirroring may be seen as a version of bridge between mind and body, it is a bridge leading, always, to Bunyan's Slough of Despond.

The practices one employs in walking the bridge of life determines self-concept quality, and the argument here is that one consequence of ignoring responsibility for construction of self-concept invokes the reaction that is autonomic mirroring—a reversion to the survival tactics of reflexive metaphor, one with dire and potentially life-threatening consequences.

Assuming responsibility for conscious development of self-concept is the prime responsibility of those individuals determined to make their lives stand for something. The mind-body connection is real, thanks to self-concept's bridging the distances between.

CHAPTER FOUR

Disorders of the Hungry Heart

I will always remember her sitting across from me at the Pizza Inn. On her left sat her two daughters. We had been in place for about an hour, and the girls were getting restless. In fact, they were climbing under the booth, spilling tea and sugar, crumpling up soggy napkins, and generally making a terrible mess.

What stands out in my mind, though, was the pervasive mood of darkness that engulfed her. She ate with a monomaniacal intensity, keeping her eyes down and ingesting slabs of pizza without pause. Again, and again, she returned to the buffet. She was alone in her own place, and as she ate, her dark face seemed to get darker.

The feeling was an irrational one, but it seemed to me she was cloaked in shadow, and that a baleful immanence, an energy I can only characterize as evil, filled the booth.

This was a young woman whose home I have visited, who has told me secrets she had never divulged to anyone, whose acts of sweetness and generosity were known and celebrated through her community. Still, had a wrinkled crone sat across the table from me, chanting a litany of incantations, the impression of being in the presence of something demonic could not have been more real.

What I was experiencing, I now know, was a sense of self-loathing so intense as to be immeasurable in human terms. When she finally stopped eating, it was as though she had raised herself from a deep well. It was this young woman (whom I shall call Mary) who set me on the path this chapter explores—eating disorders and autonomic mirroring.

While my objective in the previous chapter was to establish that metaphor underlies everything, that existence is a product of survival drive's imprinting itself in the form of idea on the plastic face of matter, and that these changes take place through the operation of a metaphorical process called autonomic mirroring—itself under self-concept direction—in this chapter I hope to demonstrate the terrifying power of metaphor when, in the interest of psychological survival, it is focused on self-image.

I propose to accomplish this through examination of those devastating illnesses, anorexia, bulimia, and compulsive eating. It was to that end that I began this chapter with the episode at Pizza Inn where I described Mary in the midst of one of her periodic food binges.

Mary is a victim of the combined illnesses anorexia and bulimia—called by some researchers bulimarexia (see *Fasting Girls: The Emergence of Anorexia Nervosa as a Modern Disease,* Joan Jacobs Brumberg, Harvard University Press, 1968, p. 12). Mary has been binging, purging, and dieting since she was fourteen.

To people who have experienced firsthand the trauma of a full-blown eating disorder, the scene depicted at the restaurant—even my dramatic rendition of it—will not appear extreme.

In fact, people familiar with the terrible toll these illnesses inflict upon families will agree that Mary's problems cannot be explained away as an expression of a naive desire to reduce her body to fit the dimensions of a new summer bikini.

Nor is it possible to see her as a pubescent teenager responding to the mandates of peer pressure and the fashion magazines.

There is something serious at work here, something dark, menacing, and capable of killing. In fact, hundreds have died in this century and thousands more are in jeopardy.

(According to the American Anorexia and Bulimia Association, these illnessses strike one million Americans every year, and 150 thousand die annually. See Brumberg, *op. cit.*, pp. 19-20.)

First, a brief biography of Mary:

At the time of our relationship, Mary was a twenty-five-year-old black female with two daughters by different fathers. She was born in Brooklyn, New York, the first of three children, and was subjected to periodic episodes of outrageously cruel physical punishment by her mother—acts of abuse she assumed were her lot as a result of being the oldest. Her mother knew, Mary told me, that she would never "tell"—a horrifying prostitution of a child's unquestioning love!

Mary's mother was an alcoholic and a drug addict, and the beatings were always vicious. Eventually, for reasons Mary still does not understand, but likely an act born of love, her mother resorted to outright abandonment of her—once on a train, and again on a city bus.

The abandonment, of course, made the newspapers and, for the remainder of her childhood, Mary lived in a variety of foster homes—in one of which she was subjected to her first instance of sexual abuse, by the son of her foster parents.

When she reported the abuse, the foster mother, supported by her son's denial, refused to believe her and insisted instead that Mary be placed in another home.

It was during this second placement that she met the father of her first child. She was in the seventh grade, and he came up and started talking to her during recess. He was a "cool" dresser, she said, and very nice. He talked in a friendly and caring way, asked about her family and schoolwork, and never said or suggested anything that could be taken in a negative way.

He even introduced her to his mother. Eventually, when he suggested sex, she said she wanted it as much as he did.

Some months later, after they'd had sex in his apartment, he said he wanted her to meet a few of his friends. There were six of them, and each of them raped her.

After delivering a daughter born of the gang rape, Mary moved to North Carolina to live with her grandmother. There she met the father of her second child—again, a "cool" dresser—who is currently in prison for dealing drugs.

He, too, was "good-looking and built," sporting a gold front tooth—all elements she looked for in her husband to be. Some months later, when he was arrested, she moved to a nearby city to live with an aunt. It was then that I met her and became her counselor.

Mary was strongly religious and belonged to an all-black, charismatic Baptist church that encourages 10-percent tithing and periodic periods of fasting.

When I met her, she had not dated in more than two years (though she is attractive and could have her pick of any number of suitors) and expressed no interest in doing so.

With those at her church having no knowledge of her eating disorder, she refused me permission to discuss her illness with anyone, her doctor and minister included. After a number of months (though she still called occasionally), she cut off communication with me as well.

There are a great many contraindications in Mary's condition. In the first place, she is black, and statistically, few blacks fall victim to eating disorders (see Brumberg, *op. cit.*, p. 28)

> Ninety to 95 percent of anorectics are young and
> female, and they are disproportionately white and
> from middle-class and upper income families.

Not only is Mary African American, she is a mature female and on welfare. Also, many specialists have purported to find mother-daughter problems (in Mary's case, an understatement!) at the root of the problem. Brumberg writes:

> When a parent is implicated in anorexia nervosa, it is almost always the mother. Kim Chernin, a psychoanalytically inspired feminist writer, argues that eating disorders are rooted in the problems of mother-daughter separation and identity (*op. cit.,* p. 29).

Susie Orbach, author of the important psychoanalytic work: ***Hunger Strike: The Anorectic's Struggle as a Metaphor or Our Age*** (W. Norton & Company, New York, 1986) also traces anorexia to problems daughters have relating to mothers. She writes (*op. cit.,* p. 43):

> The mother-daughter relationship is inevitably an ambivalent one, for the mother who herself lives a circumscribed life in patriarchy, has the unenviable task of directing her daughter to take up the very same position she has occupied.

Writing of mothers with their "un-emerged" selves, she proposes: "The cause, then of the hunger striker is the preservation of this "*un-emerged* self." (*op. cit.,* p. 109)

To return to Mary: there is an additional incongruity in Mary's story found in the fact of her being separated from her mother before puberty and living apart from her most of her life. (Her mother died when Mary was eighteen.)

The point is that Mary's relationship with her mother is not typical of those presenting problems of anorectics living with their mothers.

This incongruity, however, does not mean that her relationship with her mother is not relevant to her psychology.

Even though Mary's background may be atypical, she is obviously bulimic/anorexic, and her divergence from the typical only makes her case more interesting.

Eating disorders, in the opinion of this writer, go back a long way—all the way to self-concept origins. This is because, viewed in the context of comparison psychology, it was not possible, prior to the advent of self-concept, to project internal unhappiness on external causes.

The use of food as symbolic language (see Brumberg, *op. cit.*, p. 46) is, as argued previously, an instance of synthetic metaphor. It is a transmutation, in other words, that could not have taken place without existence of the entity that is self-concept.

It is even possible to argue that the awareness of self (the first synthetic metaphor) is an act of envisioning the non-physical and as such may be seen as the founding paradigm for the concept of soul.

The initial (and still primary) use of food is for survival of the physical self—a usage that, in itself, makes the alternative prospect possible—the fact of death, the survival antithesis.

The awareness of this fact of antithesis is itself a synthetic act and evidence of the existence of a sense of self. Thus, the making of food symbolic in Christianity turns its metaphorical counterpart physical and corruptible—the very opposite of that sought-for, crystalline perfection with all its implications for eternal life.

It should not surprise, then, that the earliest recorded uses of food as symbolic language occur in religious practices. Food and physical survival are directly related, and the symbolic use of food in religion speaks to this connection in psychology.

All religions derive—it will be argued here—from the survival impulse applied, metaphorically, to the desire to survive mortality.

(Animal and human sacrifices were originally religious, food-related practices; it is metaphorically logical that food—the stuff of physical survival—become the vehicle of transmutation, first through animal and human sacrifice and eventually the Eucharist.)

The transmutation so typical in religions continues too in eating disorders applied to psychological survival.

Dr. Brumberg traces the earliest uses of food as symbolic language to the High Middle Ages and to Catherine of Siena—though she characterizes Catherine's behavior under the term anorexia mirabilis and not *anorexia nervoso!,* a fixation she sees as modern. She writes *(op. cit, p. 45)*

> Some pious women did deny themselves ordinary
> food in order to become receptacles for the food that
> was god, but power and service to others, through
> "holy eating," was the ultimate goal.

One may wonder how Dr. Brumberg is able to tap into the minds of the ancients and read their innermost motives, but the point can be made, in any event, that the use of food as symbolic language (though it be out of the motives of "power and service to others") is still a synthetic act and an act directed to self-concept preservation.

Aside from the purely physiological side-effect of starvation-based euphoria (which can be "read" as divinely inspired), fasting also has the added benefit for self-concept enhancement—from within and without.

Those early Christian fasters felt good about their piety, as did the outer-world-observing believers, and this external admiration contributed further to positive (ungrounded) self-image and, perhaps, to even more intense fasting.

Mortification of the flesh (flesh being symbolically equated to food) enhances the sense of self at the expense of the physical self—something certain aspects of religion and eating disorders have in common.

Food, then, whether put to symbolic use or used to satisfy appetite, has always been about survival of the tribe or tribal members.

Catherine Siena's self-starving may have been based on the most pious of motives, but they were still about survival—in a heavenly hereafter. From the perspective of comparison psychology, her actions were really less about religion than survival of the psychological self.

In fact, it can be argued that it is the metaphorical state of self that is addressed by all forms of religious practice. All religions teach purification of the soul through perfection of the self through worship, and, at the risk of cynicism, the point should not be lost that fasting served the survival interests of established religions, particularly when it provided evidence that survival on the food of the spirit was possible.

(Of course, it was in the best interest of church survival that self-concept abnegation be done in the interests of soul, not self.)

The fact that self-starving serves the interest of psychological survival is also suggested by the number of women and young girls who, during Victorian times, offered themselves up as "miraculous maids"— see Brumberg's discussion of Jane Balon (*op. cit.*, p. 59) and Ann Moore (*op. cit.*, p. 59).

(Ms. Balon was said to have neither eaten nor drunk for almost three years, and Ms. Moore brought considerable fame and fortune to the town of Tulbury—until she was caught in the dastardly act of eating and forced to confess.)

Needless to say, a person who can survive off air and prayer is obviously a personage of great importance to a world anxious for proof of divinity, the certainty of eternal life, and the "rightness" of Christianity.

(The issue of deception by self-starvers, which has been known to go to bizarre extremes, will be held for later discussion.)

It is believed, then, that the survival of self-concept is the driving force behind self-starving. This need for psychological survival (which can be experienced as intensely as the drive to survive physically) can become extreme when opportunities for self-individualization are limited, and one version of this is demonstrated by the response of certain women to the Victorian ideals of women as spiritual and delicate beings.

Dr. Brumberg says that during those times, constipation came to be "incorporated into the ideal of Victorian femininity."

> Some women "boasted that the calls of Nature upon them averaged but one or two demands a week!" (*op. cit.*, p. 178)

Dr. Brumberg's distinction between anorexia nervosa and anorexia mirabilis referred to above is an interesting one, and one cannot help chuckling at the way she describes the difference in these two forms of expression. She writes (*op. cit.*, p. 46):

> Although Catherine of Siena and Karen Carpenter [a popular singer who died of anorexia] do have some-thing in common—the use of food as a symbolic lan-guage—it is as inappropriate to call the former an anorectic as it is to call the latter a saint.

The distinction (which comes close to making a moral judgment?) is not necessary if one sees the symbolic use of food as a statement about psychological survival. Food is being used in either case to say something, and the something being said is about the worth of the person involved.

The act of self-starving, then, is a statement about self, going far back in human history. And the perception of self-concept involvement in eating disorders is one aspect of the subject on which the literature seems to be in complete agreement.

Katherine Byrne *(A Parent's Guide to Anorexia and Bulimia: Understanding and Helping Self-Starvers and Binge/Purgers* (New York, N.Y., 1987, p. xv) says that the literature "almost incontrovertibly supports" the effectiveness of psychotherapy in the treatment of eating disorders—a statement I take to mean that most therapists see anorexia and bulimia as psychological illnesses—and let us not forget, self-concept is a metaphor!

She goes so far as to say that people with eating disorders "must have professional help."

(I will have more to say later about the possibility of physiological causes, but at this point it is only necessary to assert that the presence of psychological dysfunctions of whatever sort are viewed in comparison psychology as evidence of self-concept problems.)

And Dr. Brumberg (*op. cit.*, p. 28) points to direct involvement of identity in eating disorders.

> Because of the anorectic's paralyzing sense of ineffec-tiveness and anxiety about her identity, she opts, furi-ously, for control of her body. (Hilde Bruch argued that the anorectic makes her body a stand-in for the life that she cannot control. She experiences a distur-bance of "delusional proportions" with respect to her body image.)

The reference to the anorectic's "paralyzing sense of ineffective-ness" and the phrase "anxiety about identity" support the argument that self-concept is a factor in anorexia.

The "disturbance" that Bruch takes note of is an oft-noted con-sequence of an eating disorder that this writer sees as an instance of a negative self-image actually over-powering optical verity.

The unrealistic self-image of the anorectic is a facsimile of self-con-cept. The body she sees corresponds to her perception of her worth as a person, not the physical body that comports it.

(Attesting to the ability of the mind to overpower reality is an instance of an amputee perceiving water as running up his phantom limb in defiance of the law of gravity. [Dr. Ramachandran, *op. cit.*, p. 25]).

Katherine Byrne also supports the fact of self-concept involvement (*op. cit.*, p. 97):

> Most self-starvers think of themselves as fat or on the verge of being fat, even when their bones show through the skin.

On page eight, she writes, "Low self-esteem is the one universally shared characteristic of starvers and binge eaters."

Nowhere have I found a more telling commentary on the destructiveness of negative self-concept (particularly with reference to eating disorders), than the statement by Jane R. Hirschmann and Carol H. Munter in **Overcoming Overeating** (N.Y, 1988, p. 41):

> Powerless people do two things: they try to please those on whom they are dependent, and they attempt to be as much like those in power as possible. Sadly, the more they idealize people in power, the more they hate themselves.

(In some interesting ways, I found the Hirschmann-Munter book to be more about philosophy than psychology.)

The point of the quotation is that people who see themselves as weak respond by seeking psychological survival through emulation of those around them they perceive as having power. The more they try, the more they fail, and eventually they come to see their failure as further evidence of personal inadequacy.

The fact is that power is as selfishly guarded as money and life, and these people are not likely to get more of either.

Susie Orbach, it should be noted, also sees anorexia as a type of response to self-concept suppression:

> Whenever a woman's spirit has been threatened, she
> has taken the control of her body as an avenue of
> self-expression (*op. cit.*, p. 19)

Ultimately, of course, governance of how one feels about oneself is the point at which power begins, and it goes without saying that women, even ones with the status of Catherine of Siena, have been (and continue to be) held largely powerless.

It should not surprise, then, that women have availed themselves of opportunities in the metaphorical world. The fact that the powerless come to hate themselves means, literally, that they cannot win for losing—a double bind that is true for schizophrenics and anorectics as well.

Historically, women have been driven to please their God, their priest, their husbands, and their society. In the process, they have been left little room to develop and perfect their one inalienable inheritance, the ownership of self. (Hopefully, thanks to the women's movement, this circumstance is capable of being changed.)

That the vast majority of individuals succumbing to the eating disorders continues today to be females (Gloria Steinem sets the number at over 90 percent [*Revolution from Within: A Book of Self-Esteem*, c. 1992 by author, p. 221]), speaks to a continuing absence of power and control over their lives.

It is not coincidental that anorexia is a metaphorical form of self-crucifixion.

(That some women are now demanding the right to political and personal possession of their own selves is, in this writer's opinion, the basis for the "backlash" Susan Faludi confronts in her book of that title.)

The fact of political pressure dedicated to the conforming of women to the needs of a male-dominated survival system should not, however, be taken as support for the idea that people are not in charge of their metaphors.

As a straight line is said to be the shortest way to a distant point, so may a pervasive aura of oppression nudge a person in the direction suggested by social gravity. This does not mean that women cannot stand erect and refuse to budge. Many women have done so, to the lasting credit of the species, and a telling commentary, besides, on the power of taking responsibility for one's metaphors of self.

(I am personally committed to the ideals of feminism on the self-serving grounds that freedom denied to one may also be denied to me, and political impediments to self-actualization are unconscionable.

(Ultimately, however, the freedom of women and all oppressed populations will only be accomplished through self-enfranchisement in the form of liberated self-concepts. This act of self-freeing has to be a conscious, personal choice, otherwise it cannot be.)

Reference was made earlier to the instances of deception practiced by victims of eating disorders, and the reader is reminded of the case of Ms. Moore (see page 129 above), who was observed in the act of surreptitious eating.

Byrne (*op. cit.*, p. 34) proposes that binge eaters "tend to deny that they are binge eating and purging, long after the evidence is compelling, and others confront them with it."

Dr. Brumberg reports that:

> …anorectics have resorted to all of the following kinds of deceptions: drinking enormous amounts of water before being weighed; using terrycloth towels as napkins to absorb food and food supplements; recalibrating scales, and inserting weights in the rectum and vagina. (*op. cit.*, p. 16)

These deceptions may be perceived as deriving from differing motives, but it is my conviction that each of them derives from a conscious extrapolation of survival drive. Ms. Moore, for instance, is driven to appear exceptional, saintly, and remarkable—all expressions of desired elements in quest for self-concept survival.

The bulimic denies her purging, even when her secret is known, out of a desire not to appear abnormal (or evil), even though in her heart of hearts she "knows" that she is. The anorectic resorts to her subterfuges out of a morbid desire to preserve her illness at any costs, it having become so integral a part of her conception of self that, ironically and perversely, she cannot conceive of herself as existing without it.

The fact that some of these actions violate acceptable standards of decorum is but further evidence of the levels of self-disgust these victims may harbor inside and the lengths to which they will go to receive even artificial (known to be false) evidence of worth.

Byrne, for instance, relates a dramatic instance of what she calls "signaling": A woman's bulimic daughter "vomited in the family bathroom and did not clean up at all." (*op. cit.*, p. 44)

In my opinion, the girl's vomit, in addition to expressing anger for her condition, and a cry for help, is also a metaphor of her perception of her inner self, and it's a very important signal indeed! On some level, the vomit is her, perhaps even a metaphorical suicide.

The extent to which my client Mary's deceptive practices were learned are largely unknown to me because of her excessive protectiveness; however, she did counsel with me on a regular basis for almost an entire year without once mentioning her eating problems.

Despite my urgings that she do so, she refused to inform her gynecologist of her anorexia prior to visiting him to complain about intense stomach cramps.

Though she informed me of her eating disorder and regularly attended twice-weekly counseling sessions, it was months later I learned that she had been binging and purging on a regular basis and lying about it.

That day in my office, when she finally admitted to her deception, I was taken aback by the utter lack in affect of either guilt or remorse. It was evidence, I later came to understand, of the internal horror she so assiduously hid within.

Furthermore, when the very fact of survival of self is at stake, lying is an issue of secondary concern.

The surprising extent to which mothers are implicated by their daughters in eating disorders was mentioned earlier with the accompanying proviso of controversy.

The fact is, however, it is an accusation that keeps coming up. Dr. Brumberg writes, for instance, that an:

> ...early clinical report did state clearly that the anorexic girl would never speak to her mother except in tones of the greatest violence." (*op. cit.*, pp. 143-144)

Byrne addresses the issue of mother blame as follows:

> Like their sister starver, binge eaters will often say, "Mom is the villain." This has been the overwhelming conclusion whenever eating disorders in children are examined.
>
> According to two well-known therapists, Marlene Boxkind-White and William C. White, Jr., researchers and clinicians and even feminist writers, are likely to hold women responsible, [and] all deplore the controlling mother who is seen as perfectionist, domineering, and over-involved with her children.

Both therapists call this entrenched view "myopic, destructive, and unjust." (*op. cit.*, pp 39-40)

I do not seek to resolve the controversy, but an interesting sidelight is provided when the matter is looked at from the perspective of comparison psychology.

Each of us is free to choose his metaphors, and as Dr. Freud is said to have said, "Sometimes a cigar is just a cigar."

What Keith Haraty writes about dreams and dream symbols ("Language of the Night," **Omni**, Vol 15, No. 11, 1963, 50) is also true of our metaphors. However, having made the point that dream symbols can mean different things to different people, he writes:

> Yet despite these individual differences, many common symbols appear in our dreams, just as many familiar threads run through our shared daily cultural experiences.

The same freedom of metaphor is available to persons with eating disorders, but the fact is that all of us have mothers, and mothers are among our earliest and most powerful survival metaphors.

It is to our mothers that we turn for food, for comfort, and for solution to our problems of survival—physical and psychological.

It should not surprise, then—given the human penchant for dependency metaphors such as scapegoating—to say nothing of the fact that mothers present to daughters their first emblem of femininity—that anorectics blame their mothers. Their mothers, after all, provide them with their first matrix of femininity, and it is a common human frailty that we blame our pain on those we are closest to.

Even though our first mother experience involved food, and mothers provide their daughters with their most important model of femininity, this does not mean that mothers are responsible for anorexia in their daughters, though any parent is capable of a shove in that direction.

(Mothers, after all, are responsible for instructing daughters as to the role of women in society, and very often they *do* seek to impose their notions of how to avoid ending up being like them. Furthermore, mothers have been known to try to relive their lives through their daughters.)

Mothers may, and in fact often do, serve as a point of focus for their children's psychological unhappiness, but children are perfectly capable of inventing their own villains, and there are a great many metaphorical survival objects available, in addition to mothers.

As cannot be emphasized too often, self-concept is (or ought to be) made up of consciously chosen ideas and actions, and the reflexive path is all too often the closest-at-hand option.

Still, in that ideal world envisioned in comparison psychology, all mothers would be alerted to the importance of self-actualization in their children, avoiding as the plague any tendency to see them as extensions of themselves.

Another survival metaphor of great potency is sexuality. After all, it made possible our entry onto this stage of life (apologies to Prince Hamlet), and it offers hope for survival beyond the scope of our own biographical skits.

It should not surprise, therefore, that the issue of sex—albeit from the perspectives of denial and negativity—comes up again and again in the literature about eating disorders.

Part of the reason for this may be traced to sternly entrenched puritanical attitudes toward the act of intercourse—the exact opposite of saintliness being concupiscence.

The young are taught one thing at home and church and something else in the media. Small wonder that ambiguities predominate in eating disorders!

But these ambiguities are not the whole story or even the main issue. Hirschmann and Mooter introduce an important aspect of the problem in the very fact of biologic destiny (*op. cit.*, pp. 41-42):

> Our young anorectic girls embody the most tragic
> outgrowth of this belief [that it is not possible to be
> too rich or too thin.

> They represent the ultimate effort to be thin. As Susie Orbach demonstrates in **Hunger Strike**, the girls end up literally destroying themselves as they attempt to take charge by eradicating fat—their symbol [metaphor!] of need, desire, and femininity.

Those very qualities that make them desirable to men (and reflexively supportive of their egos, in addition to the survival of the species) become their enemies. Caught in a double bind not entirely of their making (but for which, ultimately, they are responsible), some of them respond by crucifying themselves.

Have they not been taught, "He who would save his life must lose it?" It is, of course, apparent that women need not be captives of their biology—any more than men need be. Still, since primitive survival drive thrives best off the hidden and subliminal—and sexual desire in among the most hidden—it behooves us all to work at being aware.

(At the risk of yet another parenthetical aside, I cannot resist the irony of a quote included in a note to Susan Sontag's **Illness as Metaphor** [Anchor Books, copyright by the author, 1989, p. 16.]

> It is a description, provided by John Middleton Murray, publisher of the **Journal of Katherine Mansfield**, written as she lay dying on her deathbed of tuberculosis.

Characterizing the language used by Murray as typical of that applied to tuberculosis—a wasting disease—Ms. Sontag says,

> The words evoke similarities, if not to anorexia nervosa, to anorexia mirabilis. I have never seen, nor shall I ever see, anyone so beautiful as she was on that day; it was as though the exquisite perfection which was

always hers had taken possession of her completely. To use her own words, the last grain of 'sediment,' the last "traces of earthly degradation," were departed forever. But she had *lost her life to save it. [my italics]*

Ms. Mansfield had apparently persuaded herself that the cure for her illness lay in the application of willpower—an ironic expression of psychological survival drive. To that end she refused to continue medical treatments and fell victim to her own drive to survive—a perversity very like that driving suicide bombers in Iraq, Afghanistan, and now Syria and Egypt.)

Anorectics also deny themselves food (the medicine of physical survival) in the interest of self-concept survival, and they, in a sad perversion of religious teachings, are driven to saving their lives by losing them.

To return to the issue at hand: it would be a mistake to think we are discussing mere adiposity. Fatness becomes a symbol of that which arouses desire, of forbidden urges, of the dark side of maturity, of maternity, of measuring up.

It is even implicated in the fact of menses—that bloody announcement of bodily fecundity. Byrne quotes from a presentation on Hilde Bruch Day in April of 1986 (*op. cit.*, p. 13) as follows:

> Menstruation has been shown to be directly related to a minimal body weight, below which menses are suppressed. In a remarkable study of self-starving and non-starving school girls, A.H. Crisphas found that the starver's "ideal" body image is precisely that weight above which menstruation begins.

Bryne goes on to suggest that this connection is unknown to the "starver" and therefore "is not a conscious motivation."

I am not convinced, however, that the connection is truly unconscious. Some girls of my acquaintance have been terrified at the prospect of having "their periods," and this terror is perfectly capable of delaying or stopping altogether the menstrual process.

Since adiposity is related to femininity (and fertility), it is conceivable that there could be a forced connection between anorexia and menses.

In other words, anorexia not only keeps one girlish, it has the added advantage of preventing menses—the undeniable evidence of womanhood, fertility, and all its potentially stressful consequences.

In any event, it is not necessary to know the process, only to harbor the fear. The body and the subliminal force that is survival drive knows what it needs (or wants) to know.

Given the need, the body will find a way; and one of the possible ways suggested here is autonomic mirroring. Certainly, whether willed or unwilled, the forcing of the body to conform to an inner vision is an application of the metaphorical method and is one of the many ways of self-victimization.

Fertility is a survival metaphor of great moment and one with significant implications for self-concept.

Dr. Brumberg writes:

> In puberty…girls experience an increase in adiposity,
> particularly in the breasts and hips. This increased fat
> is a necessity for the menstrual cycle. (*op. cit.*, p. 27)

It is obvious that important changes are going on in a girl's body, changes hard to ignore and changes with lasting significance for how she sees herself.

Sometimes these changes are unwelcome and terrifying, and the opportunity for metaphorical transmutation is seized upon. The issue may be recast in any number of ways—in an obsession with fatness or, in some cases, as an actual blocking of the menstrual process.

Anorexia is a known means to these ends. Dr. Brumberg writes (*op. cit.*, p. 26) that "because of the cessation of the menses [in anorexia], infertility is hypothesized."

Kolodny (*op. cit.*, p. 57) addresses the bulimic directly. "If you're female, bulimia can cause menstrual irregularity and may affect your future ability to conceive and bear children."

This form of conditioned infertility (through the agency of autonomic mirroring) could, like the willed blockage of menses referred to above, be a form of denial based on the fear of growing up, or even a way of punishing oneself for forbidden impulses.

From this perspective, anorexia becomes more than a translation of fat into bad; it becomes an expression of self-hatred so intense as to be murderous.

In addition to these obvious physical changes, young women today—possibly more than ever before—are compelled to confront the issue of what role sexuality will play in their lives.

How this issue is dealt with comes to have enormous implications for self-concept. It is at this point that some of them may hit upon the use of food as a self-generated distractor—a straw man constructed for the purpose of avoidance.

Even as we can transform food and fasting into evidence of our saintliness, or use it as the sorcerer's apprentice, seducing us to fatness, so can we assign sexual meanings to food. From this perspective, food becomes "something magical and forbidden that must be kept off limits or swallowed whole." (Hirschmann and Munter, *op. cit.*, p. 161)

In a manner of speaking, food becomes a metaphor for sexuality—food being necessary to survival of the individual as it is to survival of the species.

> You reach out for food which you have invested
> with magical powers, then yell at yourself for having
> eaten. You thereby circumvent the original source of

your anxiety and relabel it "fat." (Hirschmann and Munter, *op. cit.*, p. 161.)

Nothing can "invest with magical powers" like the forbidden "lusts of the flesh." And while this use of food may temporarily "lay the ghost" of anxiety, the usage is replete with sexual overtones.

And, of course, the fatter we become the less desirable we see ourselves as. Now we can hate ourselves for being fat and infertile, and another layer of armor, another self-generated distractor, stands between us and an honest confrontation of self.

Hirschmann and Munter confirm the fact of individuality in the choice of metaphor, but they also mention the lust word directly:

> Equating our thoughts with deeds, we inhibit the bad ones. Some compulsive eaters fear the forbidden emotion of anger. Others fear *lust* [my italics], and still others fear jealousy. The list is as endless as the variety of emotions one can feel. What's apparent is that, as adults, we continue to fear what we consider to be unacceptable thoughts, feelings, and wishes, and we compulsive eaters attempt to erase these thoughts with food before we even know that we have them. (*op. cit.*, p. 184)

It is not, when seen from the context of comparison psychology, surprising that victims of eating disorders "metaphorize" thoughts of lust into thoughts of eating or of abjuring food.

Both lust and food are survival-related, and the last is not viewed as nearly as heinous as the first.

That we translate the feelings of anger and jealousy into metaphors involving food is often a reaction deriving from negative comparisons of our sexuality with that of someone else's—an action taken in defense of our psychological selves.

It is easy to see why food (signatured as a survival agent of the first order) quickly takes on the quality of the forbidden thing. It appeals to the senses, it is taken inside, and it has "growth potential."

This is particularly true when the eating of food is made to take on "orgiastic overtones" (Brumberg. p. 18). Because sexuality is endowed with so much energy (by survival drive and subliminal social attitudes— very often the same thing!), it is an ideal vehicle for self-hatred.

The involvement of sexuality in self-concept perception is also suggested in the way many compulsive eaters and starvers respond to compliments on having lost (or gained) weight.

Hirschmann and Munter quote Rima (*op. cit.*, pp. 223-224) as saying:

> What I am aware of when people compliment me is that I feel confused. I feel that I am supposed to thank them for the compliment, but I don't want to. What kind of compliment is it anyway? They're really saying that I looked terrible before.

Byrne (*op. cit.*, p. 116) has encountered the same reaction:

> The starver who has been no more than a collection of bones and who gains five or ten pounds and begins to look a little human may encounter an acquaintance she has not seen for some time, and be greeted with "You look so much better!" The starver translates this as, "You've gained weight," which in turn translates into, "you're fat."

The defensiveness expressed by Rima's and Byrne's starvers suggests that it is not implicit criticism that these women are responding to.

144

It seems more likely that both women are forced by the comments to confront their own sexual insecurities. Since one purpose of the illness is to obscure that very issue, it is not surprising that they are "confused" and even hostile.

The role played by sexuality in both anorectics and bulimics is addressed by Bernard Mackler, PhD, in "Afterword: A Therapist's View," an essay coming at the end of Byrne's work already cited. He writes he has:

> ...seen people with anorexia who are more mature than patients with bulimia. Usually, however, I believe bulimics are more "mature," because they more often work, relate to others, and have an active—although empty—sex life. Anorexia forecloses relationships with others. Responsible and sometimes even excessive work may occur among anorectics, but sex is out.
> (p. 137)

The issue of maturity is not, of course, the reason for the citation. The fact that sex is abjured by the anorectic and is without genuine feeling and emotion on the part of the bulimic indicates that attitudes toward sexuality are implicated in both illnesses.

The fact that "sex is out" for anorectics and engaged in without pleasure by bulimics suggests the absence of sex drive in both illnesses is a consequence, perhaps, of placing so much emphasis on surviving psychologically that physical survival drive as expressed in sexual desire has been over-ridden.

There seems to be no question that the drive to survive psychologically has assumed the dominant position in their lives—explaining, perhaps, their disinterest in sex and why the fear of dying is no deterrent.

Hirschmann and Munter point to a specific way sexuality is employed by compulsive eaters. They caution them about denial, saying,

"Imagining that when you become thin you will become very sexually active isn't a reason for you to remain fat." (*op. cit.*, p. 229).

Fat and even the absence of it are both painted with the red flag of denial.

My client Mary credited her abstinence from sex to her religious conversion, but she also lamented the circumstance of both her daughters being by different fathers.

She was emphatic, too, about the fact that her mother was both promiscuous and fat, things she swore would never be true of her. In actuality, anorexia has displaced her passion in all facets of her life, except when she binged. It was during those times that sex, associated with overpowering guilt and disgust, became the overriding issue in her life.

As important as it is to self-concept, sexuality is only one of many survival metaphors, including mother and food, embedded in the structure of these hungers of the heart called eating disorders.

Although it lacks the magic and the mystery of such dynamic metaphors as mother, food, and sexuality, one oft-noted personality characteristic of anorectics is their insistence upon control—a symptom and, it is believed, evidence of a besieged self-concept.

Byrne supports the importance of control in the anorectic's psychology.

She says that internal and external forces act upon the anorectic in such a way as to undermine confidence. "The result is a need for total control." (*op. cit.*, p. 134).

Earlier on, she asserted that "people with eating disorders are maddeningly resistant to change, especially if they cannot predict or control the consequences." (*op. cit.*, p. 97)

In a poignant portrait of the plight of the starver—a term she prefers to anorectic—she described the awful presence that the illness assumes in the starver's identity.

She hates the tyranny exercised over her by her fear of fat. And she hates the tyranny it makes her exercise over others…. Nevertheless, she is terrified of being cured, because the illness has become the central fact of her life, her identity, her reason for being, her evil thing. The illness has become "who she is…" If it is taken away from her what will be left? What will she be? What will make her special when she isn't the thinnest girl in town? (*op. cit.*, pp. 120-121)

This is the story of a person cut off from her moorings of inner worth—a consolidated sense of self. The illness has become her identity, and preserving it is equivalent to saving her psychological life. Small wonder they bring such energy to bear! Anorectics are saving their lives by losing them.

The issue is not so much one of being the "thinnest girl in town" as it is replacing a savage sense of inadequacy with a fierce and willed determination to be in control of something. It is a stratagem that backfires in spades!

Nancy J. Kolodny also affirms, in **When Food's a Foe: How to Confront and Conquer Eating Disorders** (Boston, 1987, p. 36), that anorectics deny their hunger and learn to suppress it, "sometimes even reveling in it as proof of their strength and self-control."

Dr. Brumberg (*op. cit.*, p. 29) contends that anorectics are usually "stubborn, rigid, and strongly defensive about their behavior." She concludes:

The anorectic is, then, a "good girl" who alternates between compliance and rebellion. In the beginning, at least, her refusal to eat is a form of over-control that is subtly hostile and rebellious in its nature.

I believe the hostility and rebellion derive from the forementioned psychological investment in the disease and, as well, from the unfulfilled need to succeed at something—a powerful self-concept issue—and express the human penchant for blaming others as anodyne for a constant barrage of self-blame. (Anger, the reader is reminded, is always defensive.)

The issue of compliance, while a valid one, may sometimes receive greater emphasis than is actually merited. It is often because of the anorectic's perceived inability to conform that she/he makes compliance an issue.

It is this anger at self that fuels the anger and rebellion expressed toward intimate others and that fosters the obsessive need for control of everything, themselves and the world.

Dr. Brumberg also provides support for the self-starver's need for control gained through the exercise of power. She quotes Farquharson and Hyland (**Anorexia Nervosa**, p. 1090) as saying, "Associated with a sense of inferiority, they [anorectics] have a strong desire for prominence and dominance." (*op. cit.*, p. 220.)

People who perceive themselves as weak may seek external evidence that they are not irretrievably lost. If they can manipulate others, they know they matter. The need for power, like anger, is always an admission of weakness, born of defensiveness.

Whether Catherine of Siena and the many who followed her used food as evidence of their piety, and in reverence for the Eucharist, or food became a device for garnering self-worth or power or prominence, any of these motivations would be supportive of the argument of self-concept survival being involved in anorexia.

The perfection these women sought is not vastly different from that sought by my client, Mary, as was not the mortification of the body they suffered for the love of Christ. Like them, Mary also seeks to measure up to an image in her mind—an image based both on the survival metaphors of the body beautiful and life everlasting.

(That image, despite her faith, is in no way an ideal one. Her faith may provide momentary surcease from her unremitting sense of badness, but, ironically, she is not genuinely close to any members of her church and cannot bring herself to confess her "sinful" eating disorders or to do what is necessary to get rid of them.

("This is true even though she knows that anorexia can kill and even though her daughters are aware of her illness and get upset when she binges and forces herself to purge.)

("What an interesting variation this is on Mary's keeping her mother's abuse a secret! She is keeping her illness alive the same way she kept hidden her mother's cruelty, and her mother's beating her was the very source of Mary's overriding sense of unworthiness.)

Tragically, the absence of real emotion in her religion is descriptive of the starved landscape that is her phenomenal life. Anorexia devours everything but itself.)

Where the need for control is so obsessive (and control should be seen as a potent survival metaphor) it is obvious that the self-concept is under assault.

Interestingly, it is the fear of losing control that necessitates control. As their self-concepts flounder in the waters of desperation, the one life pre-server available to anorectics is the act of control—of themselves and others.

Perhaps the best support I have found for the involvement of self-concept in eating disorders was in **Overcoming Overeating**, the work already referred to by Hirschmann and Munter.

The book does not refer directly to eating disorders—in fact the words *anorexia* or *bulimia* do not appear in the index—and they do not refer to self-concept as a presiding entity of control to the extent I have. Even so, it is obvious that they regard compulsive eating as a self-concept problem.

Compulsive eating is, of course, an eating disorder, even as anorexia and bulimia are. Food is used in either case as symbolic language, as a metaphor embodying internal dissatisfaction with self-concept.

(This writer finds it revealing that when his schizophrenic friend calls, inevitably the first order of business is a cataloging of what he has eaten that day. Schizophrenia is a self-concept disease and his recitation is supportive of the role of food and what it represents in the survival of the threatened sense of self.)

The writers cited above begin by identifying two types of hunger, mouth hunger and stomach hunger. Stomach hunger is viewed as the necessary act of feeding the physical organism, while mouth hunger is psychological—an unconscious tapping into the natal experiences of "feeding and calming."

From the viewpoint of comparison psychology, the first form of hunger (metaphors all!) corresponds to physical survival, the second to survival of the psychological self, also in need of "feeding and calming."

The work ***Overcoming Overeating*** seeks to help compulsive eaters experience eating from the impulse of natural hunger, and to this end the work places repeated emphasis upon not feeling guilty, not dieting (through the application of willpower), recognizing the "fight-back" response, and learning to "feed oneself on demand." (p. 126) "Eating," the authors write, "is not a transgression. It is your basic right." With reference to the "fight-back response," they argue, "When people are told to stop doing something they need to do, they don't simply stop. They fight back."

In other words, people who are told not to eat do so anyway, as an act of rebellion, yes, but also as a way of preserving self-concept. It is from application of the enormous power of the physical survival drive that they derive their spectacular determination not to "stop."

Hirschmann and Munter go on to define their purpose for writing their book as follows:

> It is the thesis of this book that you do not have to
> spend the rest of your life trying to control your desire
> to eat. However, the cure for compulsive eating does

require as a first step that you scrutinize your fight-back response to diets. In other words, you must take your reaching for food when you're not hungry…as evidence that you have a deeper need which must be addressed. (p. 13)

The "deeper need" is, in my opinion, self-contempt born of some yet-to-be-identified inadequacy in the realm of self-concept. It is survival of self that is at issue.

On page 187, the authors write, "For compulsive eaters food is the centerpiece of a ritual to ward off danger." It is, of course, the danger of dying physically or—transmuted metaphorically—the danger of hating self that the ritual of compulsive eating addresses, the same being true for anorectics and bulimics.

(Their "fight-back response" was not the most persuasive aspect of their argument—at least from this writer's point of view.

(The resistance to dieting [and indeed the refusal to eat at all] is a psychological survival impulse. Whichever form of expression is selected, it constitutes a statement about survival of self-concept.

(I would agree that it's important to examine one's "fight-back response," simply because such an examination may divulge a guilt response or provide a clue to specific areas of weakness needing reme-diation in the structure that is self-concept. Then it—they—becomes identified and amenable to correction.

(But to say that we fight back at the attempts of society to conform us is to utterly understate the nature of the conflict. What is at issue is survival of the self, accompanied and intensified by the engrained fear of physical death.)

Janet Polivy and C. Peter Harman, both with the University of Toronto and authors of the Foreword to *Overcoming Overeating*, propose that:

> Basically, they [Hirschmann and Munter] focus on returning eating to its natural place in one's life, as something to be enjoyed rather than feared, and on improving one's self-concept so that one's problems are dealt with directly rather than compounded by mismanagement through compulsive overeating. (pp. x-xi)

They go on to contend that, essentially, restrictive dieting "drives a wedge between a person and his or her body, a struggle ensues, and generally the situation deteriorates." (p. ix)

The "wedge" is a consequence of the dieter's perception that if her/his body were perfect, life would be perfect. When the body does not become perfect (and *ipso facto*, life isn't either), the problem becomes the dieter's fault: "No wonder my life is such a mess. I can't stop stuffing my face!"

The battle then begins: Grim determination versus cowardly surrender. As Hirschmann and Munter put it:

> Each time you eat compulsively, you move from your unlabeled discomfort, to food then scold yourself for having eaten and being too fat [punctuation is that of the authors]. This process of eating compulsively gets you off the track of what's really troubling you. And to make matters worse, you become convinced that the trouble is your eating and your weight. (p. 14)

Once the dieter is convinced that the problem is one of character, it is a matter of simple metaphorical transference to food and fatness as embodiment of all one's problems. It is important to note that every form of eating disorder seeks to "get you off the track of what's really troubling you."

Polivy and Harmon say that one consequence of compulsive dieting is that the dieter "mangles" the natural connection "between eating and normal hunger signals." (p. ix) This same disjunction occurs with bulimics and anorectics:

> If anything, it becomes more firmly established and
> means that the normal homeostatic survival process
> has not been disrupted; it's been "mangled."

The process, as I see it (whether dieting, starving, or binging), is one of interposing one's will between the body and one's concept of self—an instance of placing physical survival at risk in the interest of psychological survival and, as such, utilizing the very method of autonomic mirroring.

Once the machinery of autonomic mirroring is in place, and the natural connection overridden or replaced, the result is reflexive starvation—or gluttony.

The succeeding consequence in anorexia and bulimia is that the body and self-concept are forced to feed off themselves; the overeater fattens the body at the expense of self. In either case, ultimately, the outer self is made to conform to the image of an inner negative perception.

That such a process is at work is pointed to by a statement by Polivy and Harman (*op. cit.*, p. ix) when discussing the mangling of the natural hunger signals. They write: "These signals are what the diet is designed to overcome."

If, in fact, the purpose of eating disorders is to "mangle" these natural processes (suggesting a more drastic design than simply losing or controlling weight), the dieter's (also the anorectic's and bulimic's) real intent, speaking metaphorically, is implementation of the process of autonomic mirroring—a "surgical" intervention designed to lop off the "offending member."

In shutting down the natural machinery, the compulsive dieter/ anorectic/ bulimic may actually be saying through clenched teeth, "Shut down the infernal machinery that keeps me alive and suffering."

Believing as I do in the power of self-concept to alter physical structure, I think the existence of such a process might explain the level of acidic intensity Mary brought to her dieting and purging.

In counseling with her about the double bind she had created for herself, I would often ask in frustration, "Why must you continue to crucify yourself?" Inevitably my answer was the same grim smile, simultaneously affirming and negating.

The fact is, Mary hung on to her eating disease with the same degree of intensity she conveyed when discussing the vicious beatings her mother administered: "She knew I would never tell." The overriding issue for Mary was survival of the psychological self. The machinery of this survival was inflicted upon her the same way her mother's beatings were. While not her fault, it was her burden to bear—her only way of coping with inherent unlovability.

If this kind of maniacal self-injury is characteristic of severe eating disorders (as I think it is) this could be seen as an instance of autonomic mirroring mangling the body to save the self.

Lest the reader think I have crossed the line into fantasy, I would now like to introduce Dr. Brumberg's speculations about the possibility (in her view and mine a dubious one) of eating disorders having a physical origin.

Her arguments, interestingly, have the effect of supporting the existence of the process of autonomic mirroring. She writes:

> Most recently, research conducted at the National Institutes of Health reports that depressed patients and those with anorexia nervosa both oversecrete CRH, a corticotropin-releasing hormone produced in the hypothalamus that travels first to the pituitary

and then to the adrenals to make cortisol. Normally,
excess cortisol production occurs in response to fear
and as a sign of stress. (*op. cit.*, pp. 25-26)

Reference to the presence of cortisol in stressed and depressed
patients was, the reader may recall, made earlier (reference respec-
tively, Redford Williams, and Richard Bergland, pp. 90 and 95 above).
Reference to the role of the hypothalamus is also noted.

These "stress chemicals" are present because the body ministers to
a threatened self-concept the same way it treats a physical threat—more
evidence, it is believed, of self-concept involvement in the so-called eating disorders.

The hypothalamus reference is also illuminating to the argument
presented here, it having been implicated in autonomic mirroring and
identified as the mind-body mechanism (p. 136).

The presence of these factors in anorexia supports the proposition
that the mind-body phenomenon is involved in anorexia.

To the extent that autonomic mirroring is involved, it could certainly be argued that the person afflicted with an eating disorder is
employing tools other than willpower and that a restructuring of body
(note the pituitary reference!) to conform with self-image is taking place.

Of the hypothalamic connection, Dr. Brumberg has written as
follows:

Although there is as yet no definitive answer to the
puzzle of anorexia nervosa, the thrust of biomedical
investigations leads to this conclusion: if anorexia
nervosa is associated with an organic abnormality,
the hypothalamus is the most plausible site for the
origin of the dysfunction.

That the hypothalamus is the brain organ in which the effect of anorexia is located suggests to me not disease but process. It will be recalled that the hypothalamus was characterized above as "the effector mechanism of autonomic mirroring."

She goes on to cite three reasons why the hypothalamus might be involved in anorexia:

> At least three possibilities exist. It may be that starvation damages the hypothalamus, that psychic stress somehow interferes with hypothalamic function, or that the manifestation of anorexia nervosa including the psychological aberrations, are relatively independent expressions of a primary hypothalamic defect of unknown etiology.

The fact that the hypothalamus is "the most plausible site for the origin" of anorexia supports (of course) the theory of autonomic mirroring. Eating disorders are almost certainly psychological diseases—else why would psychotherapy be successful?

Anorexia results in identifiable physiological illnesses; and the medical evidence suggests that whatever is going on it is effectuated in the hypothalamus.

In addition to Dr. Brumberg's three possibilities, I would like to suggest a fourth—that the hypothalamus is involved not as an expression of a "defect of unknown etiology," but as a consequence of autonomic mirroring, the process whereby a mental state is given physical form.

Victims of severe forms of eating disorders are consciously—through the exerting of will power, transforming their physical bodies to correspond to their negative images of self—a function of metaphor and an expression of autonomic mirroring.

Evidence that mind state may in fact have anatomic consequences in eating disorders is suggested in an article published in **Omni Magazine** in November 1993.

Douglas Stein, author of the cited article entitled "Compulsive Eating, Ritual, and Addiction," p.14, discusses the involvement of the nucleus accumbens (NAC) in compulsive eating patterns.

According to Stein, University of Wisconsin associate professor Anne Kelley and her student Vaishali Bakshi have successfully conditioned eating responses in this area of the brain.

Their studies, he says, indicate that eating cues are filtered through forebrain areas and down into the limbic regions of the brain, where they are charged with emotion.

It seems likely that, though Stein does not suggest it, this is the point of hypothalamic involvement.

More to the point of the argument here, however, is Stein's statement that "almost any association connoting the rewarding value of food can tap into the wide-spread opioid circuits and trigger a compulsive eating 'program.'"

He goes on to argue that:

> Chronic drug use can alter neuronal architecture
> long after the drug is gone. These long-term changes
> may underlie behavior, bodily responses, and mental
> states related to foods, too, and their associations....
> Possibly, the "software" makes us crave our drug and
> by "running the system," it perpetuates abnormalities
> in the "hardware."

(Interestingly, recent studies have confirmed this brain effect in the brains of consumers of nicotine.)

I see what Stein describes here as the actual process involved in autonomic mirroring. The metaphorical "shape" that capsules our psychological inadequacies is translated into a metaphorically similar disease entity.

In the case of victims of eating disorders, the "software" that is mind state (read "self-concept") runs the "hardware," thereby perpetuating "abnormalities" in the neuronal architecture of the brain.

Finally, Dr. Brumberg offers support (inadvertent though it be) for the concept of autonomic mirroring being involved in eating disorders when she states (p. 26) that:

> Physicians are justified in their close attention to the anorectic's body, because the disease is typically accompanied by characteristic physiological abnor- malities. Anorexic patients experience hypothermia, edema, hypotension, bradycardia (slow heart beat), and lanugo (excessive body hair).

The existence of these physiological conditions obviously does not support the idea that eating disorders are caused by viruses or organ malfunction. Interesting, too, is the fact that many of the "physiological abnormalities" cited are also implicated in autoimmune illnesses.

From the perspective of comparison psychology, the fact of identifi- able physical illnesses confirms the power of mind over body. Metaphorical constructs are numerically unlimited; the means of expressing them are not.

In this writer's opinion, it is not coincidental that at least two of these symptoms (edema and lanugo) contribute to negative transforma- tion of the physical self; and the reference to the pituitary reminds one of Dr. Siegel's proposal (*op. cit.*, p. 137, ff.) that:

> ...when a child...is caught in a crossfire of hostil- ity...the limbic systems...act upon the hypothala-

mus to shut off the pituitary gland's production of growth hormone.

It is believed that all these symptoms are indicators that the "surgical intervention" of autonomic mirroring referred to above is in process.

Eating disorders, then, are a method of embodying one's problems in the interest of protecting self-concept. More precisely, they are a way of managing a degree of self-detestation so intense that the utilization of a mechanism of avoidance is mandated if life is to be bearable.

The implementer of mind-directed physical change—the means whereby the mental becomes physical—is an instance of autonomic mirroring at work. Like all stratagems of avoidance that cross the line into deviance, eating disorders have dire, long-lasting, and even fatal consequences.

I have attempted to demonstrate at various times in these pages that my client Mary's symptomology contains those general elements said to be descriptive of eating disorders.

I would like now to return to that aspect of Mary's biography that contributes most significantly to an understanding of her illness, and of the way I believe eating disorders operate in general.

The aspect under consideration is that of her relationship with her mother. The point was made earlier that her relationship was not typical in that she was separated from her mother at an early age and never lived with her again.

(In point of fact, Mary's mother persuaded protective services to "give her back" once. However, after a brief period of custody, she abandoned Mary again, this time on a bus. Also, even though Mary's mother died when Mary was eighteen, she had managed an arms-length relationship with her mother during those years.)

Mary's relationship with her mother, estranged as it was, is nonetheless important to her image of self. As has been stated, she saw her mother as having been fat, substance-addicted, and promiscuous—characteristics she was determined to avoid.

At the same time, she was quick to say that she loved her mother, whom she viewed as sick and therefore not responsible for her behavior.

On any number of occasions, I told Mary it was all right to be angry at her mother, that there was no excuse for her mother's having treated her as she did. Mary always responded in the same way:

> You're trying to make me hate my mother, and I'm
> not going to do that. She didn't want to hurt me. She
> was just sick.

My insistence that my goal was not to make her hate her mother, that I only wanted her to express her feelings, was always rejected, and she held firmly to the belief that her mother loved her and knew that Mary returned that love.

As long as Mary is able to hold onto these convictions—that her mother was not responsible and loved her after all—she can avoid facing that very thing her illness was contrived to hide.

This is because admitting her anger and blaming her mother would have the effect of requiring her to face the greater evil—the fact of that quality of badness in her that made her mother reject her in the first place.

In a manner of speaking, by making excuses for her mother, Mary is making excuses for herself.

Mary once called to tell me that Oprah Winfrey had announced on her show that it was not necessary to be angry at one's abuser. Oprah, she said, was not angry at her abuser (because she had encouraged him by asking questions about sex) and had forgiven him.

In the interest of not permitting her the luxury of strengthening her defenses, I responded that if Oprah would express her anger, quit blaming herself, and then really forgive her abuser, she would likely be more successful in keeping her weight under control.

This, of course, was not the reason Mary called; she had called to gloat.

I then broached the subject of her health, and she responded that she had not purged in "about a month." She went on to add, however, that her weight was now at 126—four pounds below her original optimum goal. When I pointed that out, she ended the conversation.

Twice before, I have made reference to Mary's statement that her mother knew she would never tell the world about the beatings she had received at her hands. It is a statement I return to again, for there is something both beautiful and tragic in the statement.

Mary was twenty-five when she said it to me, but when she said it, I caught glimpse of the five-year-old child smiling through sun-brought tears, the child I once saw in a wrinkled black-and-white snapshot.

What is it about that simple statement that evokes powerful feelings in me, even today?

There is courage in it, evidence of an undaunted will, a hint of family protectiveness, and a glimpse of undeterred loyalty to the mother who victimized her.

It is somehow something more, though: it is a statement of love made against a background of stark poverty and violent abuse, of a grim-faced girl smiling bravely into the face of a world gone mad with cruelty.

It is a portrait reminiscent of Thomas Hardy's "Darkling Thrush," in which the thrush sings his song to a universe "shrunken hard and dry...."

Mostly what I hear in that simple sentence is: "I will deserve her love no matter what she does." Behind the shield of her illness, she says it still —to her mother and to an unfriendly world.

It is the cry of a besieged self-concept trying to stand for something.

Mary's problem, then, is not that she hates her mother, and she does not—as many adolescents do—blame her unhappiness on a handy symbol. She has gone beyond the point of childish scapegoating and has instead diverted her feelings of rejection and personal repulsiveness into a full-fledged deviance capable of killing her.

Let me try to be more specific. Hirschmann and Munter describe the normal processes (*op. cit.*, p. 16):

> We are all born knowing how to eat. We get hungry, we cry, and we are fed. Through endless sequences of getting hungry and being fed, we make contact with the world and learn that it meets our needs reliably. Early in life, feeding and calming are inextricably linked. Hungry infants panic, and when the world responds to their panic with food, they calm down. The feeding experience is at the center of myriad interactions and feelings that contribute to our sense of security.

The typical feeding experience, associated with predictability and tenderness, was never Mary's, and though we may be born knowing how to eat, we are not born knowing how to love ourselves.

As a consequence, she interpreted the absence of emotional feeding as evidence of something being wrong with her. *(As stated elsewhere, the child always blames herself—not the parents.)* The validity of these feelings of inner ugliness was consolidated in her mind by repeated vicious beatings and eventually by outright abandonment.

It is not coincidental, in my view, that Mary's "feeding experience" parallels her relationship with food today in frightening ways. The abuse continues, but now it is self-administered.

Placement in foster homes and sequences of abuse and rejection drove home the conviction of congenital unworthiness. Later on, when the patterns of abuse and neglect continued, she had a safe place to store them—the same dark room where she hid the conviction of her inner infamy.

Eventually, without the aid of women's magazines or the examples of starving peers, Mary invented the strategies of not eating, of bingeing, and of purging. In one fell stroke, she was able to punish herself for being rotten inside and unlovable; she could fail and thereby confirm her lack of character, and then she could vomit up her ugliness.

When she binges now, she is seeking through food that psychological counterpart of being truly loved and wanted.

This way of coping has come to assume an ever-enlarging presence in her sense of self, to occupy the center of her life. Today it is the central fact of her existence—more necessary to her psychological life than her education, her religion, or even the mental health of her own daughters.

Seen from this perspective, Mary's stubbornness becomes reasonable—as is her need for control, her adamant celibacy, her surface commitment to religion, and the ease with which she lies to herself and others. What is at stake here is survival of self-concept, the metaphor of self that makes survival possible.

To prolong the metaphor, Mary feeds the monster inside her because it is the only one who understands her, the only one who grants her freedom from the acid rage of acid hate. The more energy she expends refusing to feed that monster the metaphoric food of fatness, the less opportunity she has to confront her fear; and on those occasions when she is unable to survive on starvation alone—she does feed the monster. At that point, her self-hatred floods in thousandfold.

When she feeds and purges, she is trying to be a little bad in order to be good again. Her mother need never fear, for Mary will never tell.

Mary thus ratchets back and forth in a trap of her own construction—a double bind in which she cannot win for losing. She hangs in the middle, swinging back and forth over the abyss of non-personness, and terror confronts her whichever way she turns.

She manages only at the cost of unbelievable expenditures of will and courage to maintain her position at the center, but she is slowly draining her life away.

What is the solution for Mary and millions as unhealthy as she—not all of them victims of disorders centered on food? The answer is not an easy one, and it may be, for people whose illness has reached the stage of Mary's, that no answer exists at all.

It is my conviction, though, that assuming responsibility for the conscious construction of self-concept is the cure for eating sicknesses as well as most illnesses of the soul.

Whether I'm right or not, the final answer resides in the realm of self-concept and in the removal of a parasitic appetite, of "a fetus with its own will"—a metaphor that works for anorexia and that was stolen (and quoted out of context) from Susan Sontag.

It is hoped that the succeeding pages will offer some helpful guidance in eliminating those disorders of the hungry heart referred to in this chapter's heading—a title taken from some comments I made in a letter to a friend diagnosed as having a schizoaffective disorder.

The quote follows:

> Feeling sorry for oneself depletes and eventually destroys one's supply of self-love, and one has to turn to others for evidence of self-worth.
>
> This desperate search for self-indemnification from external sources (like one's parents and friends) has the effect, eventually, of depleting these resources as well.
>
> Where does the hungry heart turn for love when it has eaten up the world? It devours itself. The hungry heart must feed itself.

The topic of Chapter 5 is schizophrenia.

CHAPTER FIVE

The Self's Annihilation of Self

In previous chapters, it was proposed that survival drive, the primal metaphorical force, created itself initially through the accidental discovery of particle affinities in a subatomic universe.

In other words, survival drive exists today, albeit in a more evolved form, because of that original process of comparison, the root of all metaphor—and, indeed, the root of everything.

Furthermore, I believe that the process of discovering affinities, as the earliest and most rudimentary form of consciousness, became engrained in nature as a response to what humans characterize as pleasure—a sense of fulfillment born of the act of forming new combinations. This act of a successfully initiated survival strategy is associated, even today, with pleasure.

Eventually, through that process of metaphor Darwin named evolution, the survival process progressed from virtual to actual particle, from energy to gas, to physical and chemical matter, and over time to its manifestation in biological entities.

With the metaphorical process firmly in place, it was but a matter of time until, freed from molecular restraints, survival drive launched itself into the oxygen-free environment of idea where metaphor itself becomes metaphor.

I have suggested that metaphor evolved through three stages: the reflexive, the hylozoic, and the synthetic—the last stage leading to development of the synthetic metaphor of self, a metaphor impregnated (as are all forms of metaphor) with the primal drive to survive and capable of transformations not available to biological life forms.

As stated, pregnant with the desire to survive, the metaphor of self had easy access to subliminal survival devices such as mind blank—running away from predatory doubts and the use of rationalization (formulating easy lies and alibis)—both avoidance gimmicks that made it easy to avoid responsibility for construction of self-concept.

In Chapter 3, I sought to demonstrate that self-concept has consequences for the survival of our physical selves and suggested that metaphor—the subliminal tool of autonomic mirroring—was capable of transforming matter to correspond to self-image. I posited that this process was a possible solution to the mind-body dilemma.

Chapter 4 examined the eating disorders anorexia nervosa, bulimia, and compulsive dieting—diseases that derive, I have argued, from using food as a self-generated distractor standing between the person and her deep-rooted feelings of inadequacy.

An effort was made to show how these illnesses document the mind-body phenomena at work through the agency of autonomic mirroring, a metaphoric process of transference where self-concept illnesses take on a comparable physical form.

With apologies for so comprehensive a review—a summary was deemed necessary for an understanding of how the self-concept was formed and endangered—in this chapter I propose to examine that ultimate consequence of self-concept denial—the annihilation of self by self in that form of that comparison disease called schizophrenia.

Comparison Revisited—Metaphor as Genesis

First, we will look at the role of comparison in psychology: the point was made at the beginning of this project that metaphor is seen as being at the root of all natural phenomena—including matter, language, science, philosophy, history, and psychology.

Consequently, it should not surprise that as one of the behavioral sciences, psychology, is rife with metaphor—as are its various methodologies, to say nothing of the language that describes them.

Psychoanalysis, for instance, is one giant metaphor, proposing that human psychology is a maze of hidden motives that require elucidation for remedial action. The writings of that giant of mind-study, Sigmund Freud, are a tribute to the magic of metaphor.

His infamous Oedipus complex, for instance, is a contorted improvisation based on an ancient literary metaphor of accidental incest—though, in his view, desired and repressed.

He ignores the survival incentives of kingship and prestige (they are not supportive of his thesis), and his entities—id, ego, and superego—are metaphorical constructs devised to support his belief that sex is the secret god of the underworld that is human psychology.

Carl Jung's concept of archetypes, as I perceive it, is an erudite if convoluted attempt to explain the phenomenon that is metaphor. A student and colleague of Freud, his theories share the tragic flaw of psychoanalysis, the absence of groundedness—either in nature or in objective science.

While Jung is to be applauded for his avoidance of Freud's penchant for finding sexuality at the root of all pathologies, his notions of native spiritualism have bothered some readers and, it must be said, embody the fore-mentioned flaw of "ungroundedness."

A more scientific way of looking at metaphor may be found in Gerald Edelman's investigations into the processes of brain function.

His studies—far more grounded in objective scientific research than Freud's or Jung's—have enabled him to arrive at a functional hypothesis as to the source and nature of thought processes. As will be shown, his hypothesis may be seen as a literal description of the metaphorical process as it functions in nature.

More importantly, he suggests that the brain's physical functions are themselves acts based on the mechanism of comparison. Finally, he proposes an origin for self-concept based on what appears to me to be the very metaphorical process described in the present study.

For the source of his hypothesis, he visits Jack Fincher's compendium of brain research called *The Brain: Mystery of Matter and Mind* (Washington, D.C., c MCMLXXXI):

> The brain functions by a constant recycling of impulses among its many circuits. Initial sensory signals are received by groups called feature detectors or "recognizers" that are probably composed of physically related groups of circuits. After the signals are processed by the recognizers, other circuits called recognizers of recognizers (R of R) record the information in less specific forms. This information is then recycled and picked up by other R of R groups or sent to parts of the brain controlling the body's actions.

Fincher continues in his own words:

> He [Edelman] sees the brain "as a seething mass of patterns going on and off." New information from the senses activates recognizer circuits. Their reactions are recognized and recorded by R of R circuits. These processed signals then reenter the system and are read by other R of R groups as if they were exter-

nal signals. This continual reexamining and comparing of recycled information with newly arriving sen-
sory-impulses may be what we call consciousness and
self-awareness. (p. 45)

In the way of an aside, let it be said that the "mass of patterns going
on and off" describes, in my view, the search for affinities in that pleth-
ora of particle substitutes (metaphorical affinities) stored in the brain as
a consequence of experience.

Driven by the survival impulse, these "particles" are congealed
through the act of comparison (the search for affinities) into the metaphors that constitute consciousness—a consequence of "reexamining
and comparing."

As stated, Edelman's hypothesis, as are all theories, is a metaphor in
the sense that he is using language to describe a process that exists in his
mind; furthermore, within the use of that system, he employs explicit
devices of comparison such as "as if" and "comparing." The "R of R"
structures are metaphors capable of recognizing affinities.

Attention is drawn as well to his copious use of prepositions…
grammatical units (metaphors) that serve as indicators of position—a
relational device with a comparison basis.

More importantly, his hypothesis suggests that the brain's physical
functions are themselves acts of comparison. Finally, he proposes an origin for self-concept, which itself describes the process of metaphor.

Specifically, the reference to the "recycling of impulses among its
many circuits" implies the existence of a propulsive process, and that
process is comparison; the existence of "physically related groups of circuits" suggests that the physical structuring of the brain itself—itself a
metaphorical process—involves the use of comparison.

His so-called "recognizers of recognizers" function as the actual
agents of comparison; the sending of information to those parts of the
brain that control actions involves the act of comparison; that "continual

examining and comparing of recycled information" that results in the creation of consciousness—and self-awareness involves, also, the process of comparison—elevated in this instance to another level: the non-physical.

Of especial interest to this writer is the statement, "These processed signals then reenter the system and are read by other R of R groups as if they were external signals."

This literally describes the metaphorical process in that the "processed signals" are used as though they were "real"; moreover, it provides evidence for my conviction that the brain treats mental engrams the same way, regardless of origin.

In other words, self-concept survival is viewed by the brain in the same terms as it views physical survival.

Finally, Edelman's suggestion that impressions are organized according to "physically related groups" describes the consequence of comparison, and also implies recognition of dissimilarities—the positive-negative charge inherent in all nature—showing that in the prosody that is comparison, similarities—whether existing in positive or negative states—are recognized by metaphor as affinity pairs.

Unfortunately, in my view, Edelman does not propose a reason (or purpose) behind these functions—a deficiency I seek to remedy in my concept of survival drive—the source, ultimately, of all forms and substance, including self-concept.

The drive to survive drives everything.

Self-concept comparisons, non-physical though they be, are based on reflections of the physical processes and functions (also metaphors) described by Edelman. I contend that these metaphors remain at the reflexive level until they come under the conscious supervision of self-concept.

It cannot be known for certain that Edelman is conscious of the role of comparison in his hypothesis, but there can be no question of its importance to Dr. Silvano Arieti, a psychiatrist noted for his study of schizophrenia as well as other mental phenomena.

He stresses this importance in ***Creativity: The Magic Synthesis***
(N.Y., N.Y., 1976):

> Some readers may think that in my views on paleo-
> logic thinking...I attribute too much importance to
> the concepts of identity and similarity. But it is exclu-
> sively on *the ability to compare and identify* [my ital-
> ics] that logical thought is based. James wrote: "Logic
> has been defined as the substitution of similar, and
> in general one may say that the perception of like-
> ness and unlikeness generates the whole of rational or
> necessary truth." (James, 1911), p. 118.

Dr. Arieti has explored in some detail the schizophrenic's use of
paleologic thinking (*op. cit.*, p. 67), and more will be made of this subsequently, but the point here is that he recognizes the role of comparison
in mental processes.

He again stresses (*op. cit.*, p. 136) the importance of comparison:

> We have repeatedly seen that one of the mainstays
> of human cognition is the ability to associate sim-
> ilar things and then to distinguish similarity from
> identity.

A poet also sees similarities in the dissimilar, in the process of creating a metaphor. Aristotle wrote,

> The greatest thing by far is to be a master of meta-
> phor; it is the one thing that cannot be learnt from
> others; and it is also a sign of genius, since a good
> metaphor implies an intuitive perception of the simi-
> larity in the dissimilar.' (***Poetics***, 1459a), p. 136.

(The reader is asked to forgive a momentary digression, but I find it regrettable that Aristotle limited the purview of metaphor to the realm of rhetoric. Quantum mechanics has revealed that his definition applies in most respects equally well to subatomic particles and all versions of matter. The intuitive perception referred to is, from my perspective, the action of survival drive.)

The fact that the thinking mode hypothesized by Edelman is based on comparison, the fact of the importance of comparison as stressed by Arieti, or even the proposal that all psychology (including the approach being argued for here) is based on comparison, should not be surprising.

All life is attraction and repulsion. The first atom had it, and the universe is a metaphor of that.

Self-Concept as Metaphor

Self-concept is a metaphor and, like all metaphors, is neither true nor false—just efficient or not. This means that extra care is called for in the selection of those metaphors that govern one's life; this is particularly the case with subjective metaphors—as opposed to scientific ones—where grounding is a factor of results.

As a synthetic metaphor, the concept of self is subject to the curse, and blessing, that is openendedness. Given the pervasiveness of reflexive impulse, it is of crucial importance that individuals intent upon assuming responsibility for self-concept have access to means of grounding their metaphors so as to protect themselves from reflexive subjectivity.

(For a detailed discussion of grounding consult "Self-Concept" in the Dictionary, Appendix II.)

Because they are self-willed and subject to selection from a variety of options, actions are one of the most vital sources of grounding in the metaphor that is self-concept.

Basketball players, for instance, are forever imagining their best move to the basket. They create a metaphor in their minds of the move and the spectacular score that follows. Then, after much practice, they actualize the metaphor to a crescendo of applause and internal approbation.

The athlete, through effort and responsibility (as indicated by willed practice), has created a conscious metaphor (a physical action) that directly contributes to a positive sense of self. Her actions illustrate a process available to us all.

In the real world, it is through actions, including thoughts, that positive contributions to self-concept are possible; and, as stipulated above, the conscious choosing of metaphors is necessary to the construction of a positive sense of self.

We judge our competence by the actions we invest in, and we enhance self-concept by consciously choosing those realworld actions that contribute to a responsibly constructed sense of self. Like my commitment to exercise referred to in Chapter Seven, consciously chosen actions and activities are an investment in self-concept. As indicated by the phrase "if at first we don't succeed, then we try and try again," effort is rewarded by the very fact of trying.

It can be seen, then, that making conscious judgments on the basis of experience and logic enhances the odds of affirming results, thereby assuring survival of the psychological self.

Before actions can contribute to self-concept, however, a presiding sense of agency, a concept of self, must exist. Dr. Michael Gazzaniga, a one-time student of Roger Sperry and subsequently director of the Center for Neuroscience at the University of California-Davis, has concluded that just such a presider exists in the human left brain. His term is "interpreter."

In an interview conducted by Diane Conners (**Omni Magazine**, 16, I, October, 1993, 102 ff), he argues (in agreement with Dr. MacLean) for the relative unintelligence of the human right brain, saying it can solve simple problems but doesn't have the capacity to put them into action.

> It doesn't really see causal relationships. That's why
> we think this interpreter we've seen exclusively in the

left hemisphere is part of our human automatic reflex to see relationships and therefore make interpretations about the world.

Later on, Dr. Gazzaniga states that patients without an intact interpreter "are no longer members of our species," referring to this interpreter's ability to "make inferences" (104). He goes on to define consciousness as "the feeling [we have] about specialized cognitive processes."

In the context of comparison psychology, the interpreter he refers to is self-concept, and it is self-concept that is the source of human consciousness. From my perspective, awareness of feeling *is* consciousness.

Dr. Gazzaniga, contrary to my thinking, believes that consciousness is an instinct. He asserts:

> Everybody's worried about the mechanism of consciousness. But what's the mechanism for why we want to survive? Consciousness is an instinct. You don't wake up and learn it, right? It's there from day one. Like survival. (106)

(That he compares instinct and survival has to strike the reader as paradoxical, to say the least—since, according to comparison psychology, they are the same.)

Keeping in view the importance of recognizing that even the attraction of subatomic particles requires a level of consciousness, I think the answer to his question, as well as to the enigma of consciousness, lies in the proposed evolution of survival drive through the three forms of metaphor hypothesized here: reflexive, hylozoic, and synthetic.

The instinctive consciousness Dr. Gazzaniga refers to is, in the context of comparison psychology, reflexive metaphor, the earliest form of awareness.

The metaphor that is self-concept is viewed, here, as the apogee of evolutionary development—to this point in time, anyway—and is the synthetic metaphor back to which (excepting the hylozoic) all accomplishments of the species may be traced.

As synthetic metaphor, self-concept is a product of survival drive expressed on the phenomenological level, and it is speculated that the process of construction went through stages something like this:

Its survival not being based on physical survival constituents, this burgeoning sense of self came to be more and more absorbed with issues of psychological survival, issues traceable backwards, to known objects in the physical world.

Thus, food, a physical survival imperative, possessed real-world properties that could be translated into psychological feelings such as love, acceptance, and respect—synthetic "things" that "fed" the concept of self and provided emotional equivalences comparable to having a full stomach or a satisfied sexual appetite.

Shelter, aside from contributing to physical survival by providing haven from wintry winds, sweltering heat, and marauding predators, may've also provided the basis for emotionally equivalent metaphors of home and refuge, with all its attendant DIY impulses.

The drive for sex—the reflexive impulse to survival through progeny—may have known similar transformations with lust mitigating into sexual attracttion, with mounting and mating evolving into courtship rituals, and children morphing from being bothersome distractions or bonded servants into cherished possessions.

Such one-on-one equivalences as suggested here may strike the reader as contrived (and they may well be), but the objective in presenting them is to illustrate the affinity "language" of synthetic metaphor when applied to the evolution of a sense of self.

The metaphorical processes involved in creating self-concept are certainly more complex than these comparisons suggest—given the chemistry of metaphor and the brain's ability to discover, faster than the speed of light, affinities not available to the conscious mind.

Still, the mind is self-evidently capable of conscious metaphor, and an empowered self-concept, aware of its limitations but determined to be the best it can be—to act in those ways that contribute positively to a conscious construction of self-concept—is capable of discovering unthought of affinities, of making positive contributions to a world sorely in need of a new direction.

It must be said, however, that the system for developing self-concept was engineered well before existence of abilities susceptible to conscious action.

In the natural order of things, the infant whose needs are satisfied will instinctively feel good about himself; and should these needs not be provided, the inverse will be true (*op. cit.*, Hirschmann and Munter, p. 96.)

Margaret S. Mahler, MD, (***On Human Symbiosis and the Vicissitudes of Individuation***, Vol. I, N.Y., 1968, p. 220) traces the first faint glimmerings of self (early aspects of what she calls the separation-individuation process) to the first six months of infancy, and she sees the process continuing for up to thirty months.

Elsewhere in the same work (p. 42), she describes a more consolidated sense of self:

> It is at the same time, that is, two years and ten months to three years of age that the personal pronoun "I" begins to be used without hesitation and grammatically.

Perhaps the point of self-concept origin is made even more clearly in her quotation of David Beres:

> Only with the development of…the capacity to create a mental representation of the absent object [metaphor], does the child progress…to the delayed

abstract, conceptualized response that is characteristically human (p.115).

She continues in her own voice:

> I consider it [the abstract, conceptualized mental representation] the spark which ignites the ego's capacity for human affect, for human social and emotional development (p. 115).

Viewed from the context of comparison psychology, the awareness of separateness (separation-individuation) implies the existence of some notion of self; and certainly the unhesitating and grammatical use of "I" clearly establishes the existence of a self with wants and desires of its own.

The capacity for "mental representation"—which is another way of describing the capacity for metaphor—is absolutely imperative to the development of a metaphorical self.

This infant self, though, is a fledgling self, dependent upon others for satisfaction of its wants and needs, and incapable of actions taken in the best interests of self-concept.

While groundwork may be laid and much good done in the development of "confident expectation" (Benedek, 1938) or "basic trust" (Erikson, 1950), as cited by Mahler (*op. cit.*, p. 223), the first real test of self-concept competency seems to come with adolescence.

Adolescence may be defined as that period when forces—biological and social—conflux upon the human animal in such a way as to mandate that individuals take responsibility for their concepts of self, a requirement seemingly geared into the system of growing up.

It was, therefore, no coincidence that ancient tribal initiations took place upon the onset of puberty, or that young adolescents then and now strive so vigorously for self-concept actualization.

Adolescence, then, is a period of trial and error, of testing one's limits, having them tested by others, and, from time to time, a period of testing the limits of one's parents and authority figures in general.

Very often, unsurprisingly, parents become the standard against which adolescents measure their own personal worth—oftentimes to parental diminution.

No teacher worthy of the title can forget the almost slavish devotion of young men and women in search of conceptual solidification and self-anxious for guidance to making up their minds as to what they believe and who they are.

It should not be surprising that so potent a period in the lives of young people provokes disagreement among psychologists as to what adolescence is or even if it exists.

The question of adolescence is indeed controversial—the only aspect about which there is consensus being the description of it as the period between puberty and maturity, and the boundaries of maturity keep getting expanded.

Even so, an index-guided tour of the textbook, ***Abnormal Psychology and Modern Life***, Eighth Edition, Carson, Butcher, and Coleman, 1988, Scott, Foresman and Company, reveals that something of significance has to be going on: the first signs of the psychopathic personality are said to appear at adolescence, p. 247; autistic deterioration typically recommences with adolescence (puberty), p. 519; hyperactivity (for unknown reasons, though the onus of assuming responsibility for self may be a factor) ends with adolescence, p. 572; the eating disorders anorexia and bulimia begin in adolescence, pp. 261, 264; migraines make their initial appearance during adolescence, p. 268; the majority of reported first homosexual experiences take place during adolescence, p. 439; and the first symptoms of schizophrenia make their appearance during adolescence, p. 347.

Neuroscientists have established that brain development continues into late adolescence, indicating that even physical maturation processes occur over time.

And J. S. Kasanin, MD, believes that conceptual thinking develops during adolescence ("The Disturbance of Conceptual Thinking in Schizophrenia," *Language and Thought in Schizophrenia*, Ed., J.S. Kasanin, M.D., W.W. Norton & Company, Inc., New York, 1964, p. 46.)

Obviously, then—whether it be a product of hormonal overload, psychosocial conflicts, problems associated with higher levels of personal responsibility, or a combination of all these forces—adolescence is a time of convergence in human development. Where there is so much foment, there is need and opportunity for responsible action.

Dorothy Rogers concludes (*The Psychology of Adolescence*, N.J., 1977): "Finally, because of teenagers' preoccupation with self, adolescence is perhaps the optimum time for making conscious efforts to improve their self-image." (p. 46)

From the perspective of comparison psychology, it boils down to this: adolescence is put-up or shut-up time, that time when youth will either accept responsibility for the quality of their concepts of self or face the consequences of self-engineered misery—consignment to a life where freedom found in individuality remains a vain and impossible dream.

Accepting responsibility for self-concept construction is a teachable process, and adolescence is the time when educators should do their best work. It is also the time when the progression to schizophrenia just may be stopped in its tracks.

The responsibility for self-concept construction does not end with adolescence, though it does get easier with age, and only death can end it.

There are sharks in the water and tigers on the land.

Ego Involvement in Schizophrenia

Schizophrenics are so involved in the struggle to preserve self-concept that they cannot disengage from the conflict.

This is why in the battle for Greece Alexander stood on a hill above the contest. Had he been involved in the actual combat, he would have lost his objectivity. Reinforcements could not have been dispatched to the point of rupture, necessary supplies not held in reserve, or important resources could have been expended on meaningless skirmishes.

In schizophrenia, the general ends up in the trenches, engaged in hand-to-hand combat with self-created demons.

Another metaphor useful in describing what in comparison psychology is seen to be at the root of schizophrenic deterioration is the concept of the schizophregenic mother—not because the concept is valid, but because it illustrates the double-bind element so obviously inherent in schizophrenic illness.

In this largely discredited scenario, the mother is said to present conflicting signals to the infant so that the child is pulled toward and pushed away, in much the way Charlie Brown is denied the football by Lucy in the Shultz comic strip.

The result is that the child is damned if she does and damned if he doesn't—a dilemma illustrated in the use of pronouns in this sentence.

Both metaphors (schizophregenic moms and real-world Lucy's) illustrate the schizophrenic problem mirrored so effectively in the Greek myths of Tantalus and Sisyphus:

Torn between the desire to be fed and the desire to feed, between the desire to be safe and the desire to be brave, between the desire to survive and the drive to be free, the rock of success driven almost to its pinnacle only to see it fall crushingly to the bottom—uncertainty and pain are the only certainties.

The basis for a similar double bind may be found in human chemistry (a possibility not surprising when it is considered that every conceivable metaphor may be retraced [ultimately, and, given appropriate technology] to a survival counterpart in the physical world.)

Such a chemical basis for double bind may be found in Restak's version of what happens when reserpine (a derivation of rauwolfia) is administered to individuals suffering from depression (*op. cit.*, p. 300).

He describes the effect of reserpine as one of exhausting the neurotransmitters, serotonin and norepinephrine, with the consequence that these chemicals are no longer available when called upon—in case of the need for the fight-or-flight response (an explicit physical survival [reflexive] metaphor).

Apparently, the forementioned neurotransmitters—not utilized because the stimulus for their release was elicited through psychological needs, not external threats necessitating physical escape—are then broken down by the enzyme monoamine oxidase.

With serotonin and norepinephrine no longer available, reserpine is freed to attack the effects of hypertension. Unfortunately, the reduction of hypertension, which itself is a consequence of bodily defense against depression, leaves the gates open for the original cause of the depression. The result is a cycle of intensified depression, a double-bind consequence.

A similar process, I propose, is taking place in schizophrenia, with anxiety—for the purpose of this comparison—assuming the role of reserpine.

Let us suppose the self-concept of a schizophrenic is besieged by a constant barrage of negative perceptions generated from both inner and outer worlds.

Aware of this assault upon its ideal state of homeostasis, the brain rushes the cavalry in, say in the form of an adrenergic hormone.

Because no physical fight-or-flight reaction is called for, the adrenergic hormone would not be fully utilized, resulting in something like monoamine oxidase being summoned to break down the excess adrenaline.

Unfortunately, based on this hypothesis, the threatened self-concept would continue to trumpet its need for cavalry, thus necessitating more analgesic, which, in turn, would necessitate more monoamine oxidase, breaking down not only the adrenalic hormone but the summoned analgesics (say norepinephrine and serotonin) as well.

The result would be a pharmacological double bind (very possibly based on the neurotransmitter model presented above) with serious psychological and physiological consequences, as the brain is literally fried by an orgy of self-negating comparisons. It is a pattern easily followed in the real world of self-concept impoverishment.

This possibility is supported by Arieti's quote of Carl Jung (***Interpretation of Schizophrenia***, *op. cit.*) to the effect that

> the emotional disturbance in dementia praecox [Jung's term for schizophrenia] engenders an anomalous metabolism or toxin which injures the brain in a more or less irreparable manner.

Arieti continues with the statement, "This fact is particularly interesting in that, for the first time, the nervous system [and I would add self-concept] itself is considered the victim of a psychosomatic disorder." (p. 28)

Arieti's comment, the reader is reminded, also provides support for the mind-body linkage so important to this study.

Finally, Dr. Goldstein (*op. cit.*, p. 46) has found equivalent schizophrenic symptoms in somatic patients. Dr. Goldstein believes this "may suggest an origin in a disturbed function of some apparatus of the brain, particularly of the frontal lobes and the subcortical ganglia."

Available evidence supports, then, the premise that the process leading to schizophrenia could indeed begin with malfunctioning in the realm of self-concept, an entity most certainly located in the frontal brain regions.

Additional support for the hypothesis that self-concept is involved in schizophrenia may be found in a physiological double bind intimated in the curious discovery that the immune system may be activated against brain tissue in schizophrenics.

In an article in **Psychology Today**, Nov., 1988, 24-25, entitled "Schizophrenia: Does Body Assault Brain'?" Jamie Talan credits Bruce S. Rabin, professor of pathology and psychiatry at the University of Pittsburgh School of Medicine, with the discovery that 20 percent of schizophrenic patients were found to have at least one autoimmune disease.

Furthermore, Rabin found an instance of immune response having been triggered against the hippocampus in 20 percent of patients—this as compared with 2 percent of the healthy comparison group (25).

The hippocampus, "a deeper, older part of the brain which is very much concerned with the...ways we relate to the world around us" is actively involved in comparison—(Restak, *op. cit.*, p. 292). The immune system, like the brain itself, works on the basis of comparison. That which is perceived as alien is attacked.

With respect to the assault upon the hippocampus, it is interesting to speculate as to why this organ is affected instead of, for instance, the amygdala. Dr. Mortimer Miskin (Restak, o*p. cit.*, p. 212) believes the hippocampus stores spatial images while the amygdala stores emotional ones.

According to Dr. Mishkin, the hippocampus is directly concerned with the sensory inputs of touch, vision, sound, and smell, while Dr. MacLean (*op. cit.,* p.. 346) suggests a connection between the hippocampus and the posterior portion of the hypothalamus—the area from which the sympathetic responses of fight, flight, wakefulness, etc., derive.

As discussed previously, these functions parallel the sympathetic as opposed to the parasympathetic branch of the autonomic nervous system, meaning that these functions are related to external survival factors rather than internal, housekeeping matters.

The concept of self, being more closely related to image than to feeling—note how in this context we always refer to our "image of self"—would, under terms of this hypothesis, owe more to functions in the hippocampus than the amygdala.

Should this speculation have value, it would explain why the hippocampus is attacked in schizophrenia. It would also provide support for the theory that schizophrenia is in fact a self-concept disease.

To return to the question of immune system involvement in schizophrenia, Professor Rabin reports that:

> ...researchers also found decreased levels of interleukin-2 and T-suppressor, both of which are intimately involved with fighting infection.

This leads to speculation that schizophrenia might have an actual impact upon the immune system. Finally, Rabin reports that:

> Russian researchers have observed similar immune abnormalities and have treated some schizophrenics with drugs that suppress the immune response. Unpublished reports suggest that newly diagnosed patients then go into depression. (25)

What manner of disease is this, that is treated by defeating the very system created to prevent disease? Why would the schizophrenic experience depresssion from getting better?

That the very system designed to protect the human organism from disease should be turned against the schizophrenic is, in an ironic way, confirmation of the double-bind phenomenon and of the schizophrenic's prejudice that the world is out to get him/her.

However, the answer to the immune system's involvement seems more likely to lie in the fact that a metaphorical illness is being attacked by nonmetaphorical means. The brain perceives the organism to be under attack, dispatches the necessary forces to do battle, and arriving on the scene, finds no enemy at hand.

That the immune system should tire of battling ghosts goes without saying. And obviously, a depleted immune system makes the schizophrenic more vulnerable to illnesses in general.

However, there is more involved that this:

It is a system of metaphor set against metaphor. That self which views itself as unworthy and inadequate—so much so that it invents systems (ie, hallucinations) to avoid confronting itself—ends up (as a consequence of stress or depression, of anxiety or self-loathing) feeding the disease that destroys the very house in which it resides.

Now this is a double bind to end all double binds! From the perspective of comparison psychology, it begins with a decision to hide from ourselves the fact that we find ourselves defective or abhorrent.

(If the victims of eating disorders avail themselves of the mechanism of autonomic mirroring to effect changes in the physical self to correspond with the psychological self they abhor, it follows that victims of other mental illness might very well employ the same mechanism in their assault upon self.)

This, another instance of the pervasiveness of double binds in schizophrenia, suggests that the agency (self-concept) responsible for survival in the world of mind is perversely attacking itself—an instance of metaphor assaulting metaphor and thereby mirroring its own destruction.

I believe schizophrenia to be the ultimate consequence of failure to take responsibility for one's comparisons in the realm of self, and one does not have to look far for evidence of ego involvement in studies of this disease.

In ***Reality Lost and Regained: Autobiography of a Schizophrenic Girl, With Analytic Interpretation*** by Margaret Sechehaye, tr. by Grace Rubin-Rabson, (N.Y., 1951, p. 109), Sechehaye writes:

Quite unlike the situation in neurosis, schizophrenia seems to be primarily an ego sickness. Certainly,
in the psychotic, there is an eruption of unconscious
life into the field of consciousness, an encroachment
possible only in the face of ego breakdown.

Sechehaye not only finds ego involvement in psychosis, her reference to the eruption of "unconscious life" in the presence of ego breakdown supports the concept argued for here of self-concept as arbiter of
experience.

Kurt Goldstein, MD, also believes that ego is affected in schizophrenia.

In the article "Methodological Approach to the Study of Schizophrenic
Thought Disorder," *Language and Thought in Schizophrenia*, (*op. cit.*),
he writes:

The demarcation between the outer world and his
[the schizophrenic's] ego is more or less suspended
or modified in comparison with the normal. (p. 123)

One piece of evidence for this involvement of ego in schizophrenia
is the oft-noted incidence of intrusive "primitive drive material" (see
the Secheheye quote above) in schizophrenic communication.

This belief assumes that self-concept (the arbiter of psychological
survival) is the agent of discipline in a world rampant with stimuli, and
the fact that—in the absence of ego control—primitive drive material
erupts, suggests persuasively that self-concept is the object of assault in
schizophrenia.

When the ego is weakened, or excessively involved in a struggle for
its own survival, loose associations may obtrude into the realm of consciousness and, as happens in dreams, send the patient off on a divergent
tangent.

Not only is obsessive ego involvement apparent in schizophrenia, persuasive evidence exists that employing escapist devices to avoid pain associated with self-concept insecurity may well lead to schizophrenic incongruities.

The way this works is suggested by Norman Cameron, PhD, MD, in "Experimental Analysis of Schizophrenic Thinking," *Language and Thought in Schizophrenia*, *op. cit.*

> When schizophrenic preoccupation reaches a point where it shuts out external influences, as if they were all intrusions, a new relationship develops. It [the new relationship] is found only in severely disorganized and preoccupied individuals. One observes that the intrusive material— our work the theme of the logical sentence—can neither replace the fantasizing or be completely excluded, as it might be in stupor. The resulting compromise is very interesting. On analysis one finds certain elements belonging to the external problem interspersed in the stream of preoccupation which it could not halt.

This "stream of preoccupation" is seen here as a consequence of an obsessive concern with ego survival, and the fact that the "intrusive material" imposed upon the patient's consciousness is "interspersed" in this "stream of preoccupation" implies that attempts to keep the schizophrenic "on line" are thwarted by the patient's absorption with consuming ego survival interests.

Because the schizophrenic's world is rife with things that cry out for meaning, what he or she needs most is the certainty and security of identity. Without these things, the patient is lost in a wilderness world where things cry out for a name.

Unfortunately, the thing that names everything is itself without a name. Adam cannot name the garden flora and fauna because he cannot name himself!

(Several years ago, a schizophrenic friend called me long distance at 4:30 in the morning because his mind was racing compulsively and he was unable to sleep.

I was talking calmly, and I thought effectively—telling him he needed to concentrate on positive elements in his life—when he interrupted and asked if I would mind talking with his sister while he smoked a cigarette.

So intense was his involvement with his own pain or nicotine addiction (very often the same thing!] that all my well-intended efforts had gone for naught, and the likelihood is that he had not heard a word I said!)

Also indicative of ego involvement in schizophrenic symptoms is the fact of excessive self-absorption illustrated above. Dr. Cameron (*op. cit.*) provides an instance of personal conflicts intruding themselves:

> A woman patient could not bring herself to divide the blocks [given her to arrange according to her own system] because for her this involved her separation from her husband and differences over having children; neither could she group them together, because, she said, "They belong together only if they are true." (p. 57)

Not only personal conflicts between husband and the desire for children are involved here. Certainly, her inability to arrange the blocks, and her use of the word "true" indicating order as well as the fact of family disjunction, is indicative of self-concept deterioration. The blocks are made into metaphors of the state of her inner life. She cannot organize them, as she could not organize her life.

Along much the same line, Dr. J. S. Kasanin in "Concluding Remarks," (*op. cit.*, **Language and Thought in Schizophrenia**) recounts an episode in which he asked a schizophrenic patient why she was so unhappy.

> She responded by saying that Durer's "Melancholia" which hung on the wall over her bed depressed her very much. When he asked her why she didn't remove the picture, she responded, "If I do, I'll be it." (p. 126) [This is not only an explicitly metaphorical statement, but one suggesting an act of transference, and the need for psychological survival.]

Dr. Kasanin calls this an instance of a schizophrenic "shifting from one realm to another"—a schizophrenic characteristic.

It is for me, however, something in addition—a revealing instance of the way metaphor works in all minds—schizophrenic or not. She had made the painting (and the blocks) into metaphors that protected her threatened self-image. Removing the painting (or arranging the blocks) would have the effect of defeating her "system"—her aberrant way of seeing (and surviving) in the world.

This same aversion to confrontation is illustrated in the case of Renee, the adolescent schizophrenic whose autobiography has already been mentioned (Sechehaye, *op. cit.*), writes:

> I was glad that Mama [Sechehaye] changed her method at the end of the first year of analysis. In the beginning, she analyzed everything I said, my fear, my guilt. These investigations seemed to me a bill of complaints, quite as though in looking for the cause of the feelings, they became more at fault and more

real. As if to say, "Find out in what instances you are guilty, and why." (p.33)

In addition to indicating the involvement of ego in schizophrenia, it appears likely that the intrusive material so often emphasized in discussions of the illness is evidence of an all-consuming absorption with the feared, perceived, or on-going deterioration of one's concept of self.

One should not disregard Renee's objections to her analyst's questions and probings as being a kind of "bill of complaint." It was as though the analysis of her problems had come to be an attack upon herself—as in fact it was.

At the very moment her concept of self was under siege by agonizing feelings of unworthiness and despair, Dr. Sechehaye was compelling her not only to look directly in the face of, but to participate willingly in the dissecttion of, that very source of pain she was doing all in her power (resorting to schizophrenia!) to avoid.

(That Renee was defensive about the enforced examination of self indicates, as well, the involvement of ego in schizophrenia.)

Another device for avoiding the pain associated with ego disintegration in schizophrenia, in addition to the patient's desire to avoid use of the first-person pronoun, is that the I-ness that reminds the patient of the quicksand on which identity stands, may be found in the employment by schizophrenics of what has been called paleologic language by Arieti in *Creativity: The Magic Synthesis.*

This type of logic, as defined by both E. Von Domarus, MD, ("The Specific Laws of Logic in Schizophrenia," *Language and Thought in Schizophrenia, op. cit.*) and Arieti (*Interpretation of Schizophrenia,* N.Y., 1955, p. 204) describes a language that substitutes predicates for subjects.

In other words, the part of speech that functions according to Aristotelian logic as noun (self) or pronoun—the grammatical substitution for property (self)—is replaced by an adjectival quality, a descriptor, not a thing.

Not only does little Renee (*op. cit.*, Sechehaye, p. 33) not want the first person pronoun "I" used around her, she prefers to think of herself in the third person, as "the little personage."

Seeing herself in this detached, non-subjectival fashion must be seen as self-protective, as a conscious device of avoidance utilized to protect a besieged concept of self—the very site of illness.

This device for avoidance may have been literally localized by Dr. MacLean (*op. cit.*, 128 above) in his suggestion that a visceral kind of "metaphorizing" may be taking place in the limbic brain.

At the point of that reference, it will be recalled, attention was directed to a similarity between that visceral language and paleologic language.

The implications of this similarity are significant for this study. Phylogenetically, the limbic brain evolved earlier than the human forebrain and cerebral cortex—those areas of the modern brain of which Dr. Arieti wrote:

> It is my belief that schizophrenia involves first the functions of the centers which are the last to appear in phylogenesis" (*op. cit.*, **Interpretation of Schizophrenia**, p. 422).

Not only does this statement support my belief that self-concept is indeed a modern creation, but it also suggests that schizophrenia is a disease of self-concept.

If the visceral brain were incapable of synthetic metaphor, this would mean paleologic thinkers did not possess self-concepts, a consideration helpful in explaining the reversion to primitive materials so often referred to in discussions of schizophrenia, as well as the hypothesis being argued for here: that schizophrenia is a self-concept illness.

The absence of self-concept would further explain the paradox so apparent in the cave paintings of Lascaux (**Discover,** July,1990, 61-65)**,** where men are depicted as diminutive, stick-like figures, overshadowed by larger-than-life, vividly portrayed bison, stags, horses, and the lithe massive figure of a white bull-like creature (the extinct aurochs) [61].

In other words, the drawings suggest that the emphasis of the cave-men artists is on physical survival rather than on psychological survival. Self-concept, if existing at all, was still aborning.

(As an intriguing side note, it is interesting to consider the roles of art and survival. Apparently, the cavemen artists believed the depiction of animals magically contributed to successful hunting and therefore to their physical survival. These survival overtones continue in art into modern times, though now—despite the ability to willingly immerse oneself in reflexive energy—the survival interest is more likely to be synthetic than reflexive.

(Art, after all, is creation, and it should surprise no one to find those earliest of metaphors being summoned to the fore in artistic creations.)

So it is that the use of paleologic language becomes, after the pattern used in avoidance of the first-person pronoun, an example of metaphorical regression and evidence of self-concept degeneration: a willing immersion, perhaps, in the non-subjective lake of limbic reasoning where the concept of self does not even exist.

(Such an immersion into prehistoric brain regions, it is believed, would require an immense degree of terror, intense enough to be capable of wrenching control from the dominant cerebral cortex and, perhaps, an instance of what psychiatrists refer to as a schizophrenic break—that moment in time when the loss of self is as terrifying as the fact of death.)

The survival metaphor that is language is thus converted in schizophrenic thinking into a way of escaping the pain of self-concept deterioration. It is another instance of metaphor being used against metaphor (another illustration of double bind!) resorted to in the interest of escaping pain.

It is an escape bought at enormous cost!

J. S. Kasanin, *op. cit.*, p. 129, has pointed out an additional varia-tion on self-concept preservation through the use of language:

> The schizophrenic…has no intention of changing
> his highly individual method of communication and
> seems to enjoy the fact that you do not understand
> him.

Not only does the schizophrenic's use of paleologic thinking protect self-concept and super-add a kind of perverse pleasure in the process (giving the patient some form of power), it may permit construction of an esoteric, Alice-in-Wonderland kind of world where an idiosyncratic version of self-concept can preside and even flourish.

Whatever form of regression (or device of avoidance) is chosen in the interest of psychological survival, schizophrenics have less and less in common with a world where reason and pragmatism preside.

Marilyn Ferguson has written of schizophrenics who develop an extreme distaste for meat (*op. cit.*, ***The Brain Revolution***, p. 210), thereby raising the intriguing possibility that limbic-brained beings were vege-tarians—a likely prospect, certainly, if speculations regarding the rapid growth of the cerebral cortex as a result of meat protein are proven valid.

I refer here to the implications for self-concept in the appearance of Homo sapiens, the carnivore, and the effects of that massive infusion of red-meat protein on the explosive growth of the cerebral cortex.

I am reminded of a schizophrenic friend who fantasizes about being a wolf. He says his sense of smell improves, and he sees better in the dark. And certainly, with respect to self-concept theory, there is greater opportunity for ego enhancement in the successful stalking of the canny wildebeest than in the contemplative munching of a rooted form of jun-gle broccoli!

(This same friend, by the way, informed me some months ago that he had rediscovered a liking for vegetables, raising the question in my mind of whether or not this could be interpreted as a sign of regression.)

Some years ago, I had opportunity to know a young schizophrenic at my place of work. She had already been institutionalized several times, but at this stage of her illness, medication had her illness somewhat under control.

Su-Su was beautiful—desperately in love with Billy Dee Williams (her overly indulgent, wealthy parents had actually arranged a meeting between them!) and, obviously intelligent, she possessed a tuneful voice she was prone to demonstrate at inappropriate times—during breaks between classes and while gliding voluptuously up and down the hallways.

"We Are the World," as I recall, was one of her favorite songs.

Several years after she had left the program, I saw Su-Su again. Sadly, she had grown thin, her once golden skin now turned pasty and dull, her formerly luxuriant hair lifeless and clamped tightly to her head. She had even lost all her teeth.

The hands that held onto mine so tightly were sticky and puffy, and the sickly smell associated with over-medication was very evident.

Su-Su held my hand that day for the longest time—not seeming to want to let it go—all the while telling me of the job she had lined up and the wonderful retirement benefits she was going to have.

Su-Su's mother had died some months before, and I was reminded of that day in the hall outside my office when she said of her mother, "She's an ugly, fat pig!" I had responded, saying that her mother was a good, decent woman everybody loved.

She looked me straight in the face, that day, and, with the greatest conviction said, "She's an ugly, fat pig."

It may have been, psychiatrists say, a literal image.

On this sad day, however, the words she spoke of her mother were kind, and her large eyes welled with pain.

The story of Su-Su is truly a sad one, revealing, I argue, the slow, inexorable paralleled deterioration of self-concept and body so typical of schizophrenia.

It is a telling comment on the nature of the illness that even in that tragic stage of deterioration in which I last saw her, Su-Su's mindset was still centered on survival (physical and psychological) as mirrored in her inflated employment prospects and supposed retirement benefits.

Self-Annihilation: The Schizophrenic Process

It is not enough to assert the involvement of ego in schizophrenia, as it is not sufficient to show the devices of avoidance utilized by the schizophrenic in escaping inordinate pain.

To really account for the illness, it is necessary to discuss the process by which the failure to confront one's inadequacies in the realm of self-concept results in that full-blown mental illness called schizophrenia.

I believe that the schizophrenic process begins with deterioration of the self-concept's capacity for metaphor—the self-concept, itself, being a synthetic metaphor. This, in turn, results in a crisis of confidence with far-reaching consequences.

Evidence of metaphorical impairment in schizophrenia is easily come by. As Arieti stipulates in **Creativity: The Magic Synthesis** (*op. cit.*, p. 138):

> Whereas in the psychopathologic use of the primary process there is no consciousness of abstraction (as a matter of fact the power of abstraction is impaired, and the mind has to find concrete channels), in art the use of the primary process does not eliminate the abstract.

Whatever reservations one may have as to the validity of the "primary process" (and much of the neuroticism attributed to artists may be traced to it), it is apparent Arieti believes the metaphorical ability to be impaired in schizophrenics.

He is not alone. In *The Brain* (N.Y., 1984), Richard Restak, MD, writes that the "splitting of the mind" in schizophrenia "refers not to split personality but to the patient's inability to harmonize feelings and thoughts." (p. 277). To harmonize, I emphasize, is to compare and combine.

Mahler not only recognizes deterioration of the metaphorical capacity, she points to a direct relationship between this capacity and self-concept (*op. cit.*, p. 109):

> The most essential failure of the fragmented ego pertains to the overall mechanisms of integration and synthesis of inside with outside stimuli. There is a failure of repression as well.

The process of synthesizing inner with outside stimuli is, of course, a function of comparison necessary to physical survival, and the failure of that metaphorical system in the realm of ego emphasizes its role in self-concept function as well.

The fact that there is failure of a defensive mechanism as important as represssion indicates, also, that the entity that makes repression possible is either under attack or too diffused to employ it.

(That the capacity for repression [mind blank, in my terminology] should be affected in schizophrenia should not surprise. After all, it is the excessive use of this device—as a means for avoiding self-concept responsibility—that laid, in my opinion, the tracks for the schizophrenic consequence in the first place.)

In addition to deterioration in the metaphorical process, the patient also experiences a growing sense of panic associated with loss of control. Mahler contends on page 230 of the work cited:

The other side of the psychotic conflict [the reference
to instinctual drives is omitted] that results in panic
entails the threat to personal entity and identity, as
well as danger to the sense of separateness, and the
threat of the dissolution of body-ego boundaries.

The threat to personal entity and the fear of dissolution of body-ego
boundaries derive, I believe, from a maddening accumulation of unre-
lated stimuli the patient feels he or she cannot assimilate.

This leads to the perception of diminishing control of self, which,
in turn, is immediately converted into feelings of inadequacy. It is my
contention that the fear of the loss of self is at the root of schizophrenic
panic and that the fear of physical death is metaphorically translated to
this fear of loss of self—insanity being the psychological equivalent of
physical death.

Dr. Arieti believes, along with Dr. Sullivan, that panic lies at the
root of the schizophrenic break. He quotes Dr. Sullivan as having written:

In the history of every case which he studied, he
found a point at which there occurred a disaster
to self-esteem. This even was often experienced by
the patient as a state of panic. (*Interpretation of
Schizophrenia*, *op. cit.*, p. 37)

In the final analysis, one suspects that panic is the result of an overwhelming fear of full-fledged insanity. In fact, Renee writes (*op. cit.*, p.
24), "Madness was finding oneself permanently in an all-embracing
unreality."

She portrays a stark introduction to the world of the schizophrenic
in the dream she recounts in the work already cited, pages 5 and 6. In
her dream she sees a barn, a haystack, and a needle—an otherworldly
recreation of the proverbial statement "lost like a needle in a haystack."

The needle is described as "electrified, austere, and sterile," and in the dream it "sets the hay on fire."

The dream, to this writer, depicts an ego isolated and lost in an unfeeling world (body'?), itself unable to feel.

Interestingly, the needle begins to hum and glow, vibrating [in a fit of anger or panic?] against the unfeeling mass surrounding it until the hay bursts into flame.

Is the hay her insensate body, or is it the unfeeling universe? Very likely, it is both—anger at her malformed, inhuman self and then anger projected outward against a vindictive world.

The ego strikes out, but to what end? The house where the spirit resides is reduced to a heap of ashes.

Another possible consequence of schizophrenic panic is demonstrated in Mahler's description of her case study Stanley:

> There did not seem to exist for him any clear-cut differentiation between the actual object and the mental representation of it." (p. 94)

Subsequently she writes about Stanley's compulsive initiation of the speech and mannerisms of others, concluding (p. 108):

> Two or more things, images, concepts, affect, and perception at one time experienced together, became engram conglomerates [metaphors?], syncretically and therefore forever connected with each other in his memory.

This malfunction in the mechanism of differentiation (comparison!) may also be seen as having derived from schizophrenic panic and a manic desperation to hold onto normalcy.

Because the confidence that comes with a fully integrated sense of self is lost, each aspect of an experience must be assigned equal value. The result is that Stanley mimics the "appropriate" behavior of others because he has no faith in his own.

As ineffective as it may be (and this is one factor in the incongruity of affect so often observed in schizophrenics), in terms of human relationships Stanley's consolidating of experience into "engram conglomerates"—my word for this is metaphors—represents the human way of holding onto a reality under threat of being lost.

The fact that Stanley can bring to bear sufficient force of will to amass this kind of information, indicates the straits to which a fear of mental death can drive one, as well as the force of the psychological drive to survive.

Another aspect of schizophrenic deterioration apparently attributable to fear of loss of self-concept control may be found in Dr. Goldstein's argument that schizophrenics emphasize concrete as opposed to abstract concepts (metaphors) because concrete objects are more amenable to survival needs of the ego:

> The objects which impress the patient are not the same as those which would impress the normal person in the given situation. He experiences only objects to which he can react in the only way of which he is capable, that is, in the concrete way. He does not consider the object as part of an ordered outer world separated from himself, as the normal person does. (*op. cit.*, p.123).

The schizophrenic emphasizes the concrete as a way of avoiding ambivalencies and as a means for pinning down reality. This is because the self-concept is an abstract entity under assault by disembodied fears. The schizophrenic holds fast to concreteness because the grasp on a non-material reality is being threatened. It is also relevant that solid objects are not as easily available to hallucination as synthetic engrams are.

(That the schizophrenic does not "consider the object as part of an ordered outer world separated from himself" is supportive of the fact of ego involvement in schizophrenia. The very process of separation individuation—the process through which the infant becomes aware of self—has been impaired. Significant, too, is the fact of schizophrenics seeking out those aspects of awareness that emphasize the concrete and grounded, the early [original] basis of metaphor—see "grounded metaphor" below.)

The fact that these "objects" are assigned bizarre meanings may be construed, as well, as evidence of a metaphorical wrenching of reality to the needs of a threatened ego.

Everything must be explicable, else everything is chaos. It is a strategy made possible by the open-ended nature of metaphorical reality and one not limited to the world of schizophrenics—as suggested, possibly, in the conservative's emphasis upon money, military preparedness, the right to bear arms, and deficit reduction.

Reference to the world of dreams—a surreal incarnation of survival drive even the "normals" among us will recognize—will illustrate the point.

From the perspective of comparison psychology, the events and characters that occupy our dreams are very nearly irrelevant.

They are seen as events and characters chosen by the neocortex in answer to the random impulses generated by the brain stem and are the metaphorical equivalents of those psychological fears that threaten the survival of self-concept.

If I find myself in a dream taking place in an important social setting—where people whose opinions of me matter or whose presence in my dream confirms my personal status and significance—and I suddenly discover I am naked, the dream is not an omen of an event destined to occur somewhere in my future.

On the contrary, the dream is a metaphor of the world finding out I am not as smart or as adjusted or as well-endowed as I profess to be. Survival drive is at work, here, on the psychological plane, an instance of metaphor if ever there were one!

The issue, then, is not the events or characters in my dream. The issue is the feelings those events elicit. Those feelings do not have to be Oedipal lustings after my mother, but, observed with intent, they can provide me with helpful signposts for my life-time trek toward self-concept self-sufficiency.

It is believed that the schizophrenic's daily existence is essentially a waking dream, and the characters and events in this dream are relevant only to the extent that they can be twisted into conformations that help ensure survival of a threatened ego. The more threatened this self-concept, the more bizarre these metaphors (conformations) become.

Again, as in the dreams of so-called "normals," it is not the events or characters that are relevant, it is the nature of the feelings expressed that matter.

The enormities erupting from the mind of the schizophrenic, it is believed, are always decipherable on one of two planes—as a perceived threat to physical survival or as a feared disintegration of the consolidated sense of self.

What makes a therapeutic intervention so difficult with schizophrenics is the fact that the agent responsible for interpreting reality is under attack by itself—as mentioned, another version of the double bind (and perhaps the fundamental one) that inhabits and excoriates the schizophrenic's world.

The person to be reached, if help is to be provided, is not available to be helped. The schizophrenic's method of survival negates the very possibility of attention, to say nothing of the fact that a debilitating ego capacity makes her/him incapable of taking assertive actions in the interest of self-concept survival.

This deterioration of the very facility that makes sanity possible is accompanied by a sense of panic which results in "engram conglomerates," an intensification of the incongruity of affect, an emphasis upon the concrete as opposed to the abstract, and the assigning of bizarre meanings to objects and concepts in the interest of justifying an increasingly aberrant view of reality.

Ultimately, as Dr. Cameron has stipulated (*op. cit.*), the schizophrenic shuts out all external influences in an effort to hold onto some fragment of reality. The utter dissolution of reality is metaphorically analogous in the schizophrenic's mind to that ultimate dissolution of matter called death.

Also involved in the schizophrenic process, and also a consequence of comparisons made in the realm of self, is the fact of social alienation, a factor in the schizophrenic's ultimate withdrawal from the world.

In the article already cited, Dr. Cameron describes what happens when the schizophrenic's comparison abilities get diverted from existence in a social mileau toward an exclusive, pain-centered obsession with self:

> Ultimately one will find that the disorganized or scattered schizophrenic has somehow managed to get himself isolated from the common social environment. He has become unable any longer to share genuinely in the attitudes and perspectives of those around him, to take their roles [metaphor!] when mutual misunderstanding arises, and so to be able (p. 50) to assume their point of view, grasp their difficulties, and modify his own behavior to meet them. On the other hand, his own asocial development has brought him to a point where no one else seems able to take his role and share his perspective either. (p. 51).

It is apparent, then, that the schizophrenic loses the ability to empathize (a necessary ingredient in the act of human comparison, and an example, possibly, of the deterioration of Dr. Ramachandran's "mirror neurons" (*op. cit.*, pp. 117-135).

Perhaps even more tragic is the fact that this loss of human affect costs the schizophrenic acceptance and membership in society, a loss that confirms "difference" upon every encounter. This isolation inevitably leads to an even greater eccentricity of metaphor and personal affect.

In addition to their loss of personal relationships, schizophrenics suffer farther social alienation as a result of their use of language as a device for psychological survival.

Dr. Sullivan (**The Language of Schizophrenia,** *Language and Thought in Schizophrenia*, *op. cit.*) examines the cultural complexities confronting the schizophrenic—especially from the perspective of language (a metaphorical system)—as follows:

> People acquire language because culture—any culture—that has endured for centuries is now so complex that as soon as one can he must begin to live in an unreal world, unreal because it is shot through with subtle evaluations. (p. 4)

Imagine how much truer this is for the schizophrenic (who perceives "evaluations" everywhere!) than for us so-called "normals!" He continues his discussion of language as a device for security survival! (pp. 7-8):

> The peculiarities of language behavior in the schizophrenic arise from his extreme need of a feeling of personal security. The schizophrenic, early convinced that since it is unobtainable, satisfaction is not the prime consideration of life, uses language exclusively and more or less knowingly in the pursuit of dura-

ble security. A durable feeling of personal security is practically impossible because culture has not been organized to provide it, since all cultures evolve from certain irrational premises of human beings—not only irrational, but pathetically inadequate.... Since language is the most subtle and powerful lever that any culture provides, most linguistic operations of human beings in general, and all linguistic operations of the schizophrenic, have to be oriented toward the pursuit of something quite impossible of attainment: a feeling of security in the presence of strangers. As the schizophrenic, because of the very insecurity which has always characterized him, has tended even more to divorcement from these fellow men with whom he has never felt secure, the language operations at the height of a schizophrenic episode show most perfectly the sheerly magical operations which men effect by language (p. 8).

The "extreme need of personal security" Dr. Sullivan refers to derives from the fact of a self-concept threatened by perceived social judgments—threats directed at the survival of self-concept. The "sheerly magical operations" of schizophrenic language constitute an effort to communicate with others based on a radicalized concept of self.

It is difficult for the so-called "normal" person to appreciate the demoralizing effects of perceived negative social judgments—particularly when accompanied by a paralyzing sense of personal unworthiness on the part of the schizophrenic.

The consequences of that "sheerly magical" use of language makes the failure to communicate (preordained even for "normals") a source of even greater loneliness and alienation for the schizophrenic.

The picture Dr. Sullivan paints of human culture is not a pretty one, and the plight of an insecure schizophrenic seeking some form of serenity in a crazy house of mirrors is horrible indeed.

If he offers any hope, it is in his plea for "consensual validation"—something difficult of attainment in a world made up of "irrational" and "pathetically inadequate" human premises—to say nothing of self-concepts irresponsibly and reflexively constructed.

In introducing the question of "personal security," though, Dr. Sullivan provides support for the concept that underlies this study—the idea that it is the perceived threat to psychological survival that is at the root of schizophrenic madness.

The feeling of security in the presence of strangers—so desired and so denied the schizophrenic—is a metaphor of what the patient sees as normalcy.

The "language operations" Dr. Sullivan refers to may not differ in many respects from the otherworldly mystery of Homer's *Odyssey* (and, indeed, some of the beauty and witchery of the schizophrenic's world seep through her/his language to those of us existing, still, in a consensual reality), but the fact is that schizophrenics cannot communicate with each other either. They are alone, each of them, in a private place they have chosen as an alternative to unending pain.

Their poetic ravings are more a product of the primitive realms in which they reside than in any conscious production of self-concept.

As apparent as it is that schizophrenics make self-defeating choices, it must be said that schizophrenic discomfort is a product of much more than private choices made in the defense of self-concept.

The consequences of social alienation also become factors in self-concept deterioration, and much of the illness that is schizophrenia derives from self-concept choices made under conditions of a socially imposed insistence upon conformity—an imposition the schizophrenic is ill-equipped (to say the least!) to satisfy.

It is regrettable that much of that socially imposed insistence upon conformity on the parts of "normals" among us derives from obedience to "the short and easy way"—to unconscious responses to reflexive survival urges.

Even the negative responses of "normals" to schizophrenic affect is a consequence of unexamined, primitive survival urges, and responsible choices require conscious decisions.

Almost always the human animal chooses the easiest (reflexive) path. An individual seeking to make positive contributions to his sense of self will not permit himself/herself to be turned away by emotional affect in another human being (See Dr. Sullivan's concept of consensual validation, above).

There is one additional factor in schizophrenia that requires comment here. I refer to the deterioration of the physical self, represented in the case of Su-Su discussed above.

This deterioration could be traced to a weakening of the immune system referred to above, and not necessarily attributable to autonomic mirroring. Still, if schizophrenia does, in fact, attack the immune system—the point is moot.

However, should autonomic mirroring have the capability of imprinting the existence of mental illness on the surface of genes—a factor well within the realm of possibility given recent evidence of the effect of environment on genes and the capacity of the mechanism as posited here—this could explain the oft-noted repetition of mental illness in families.

Schizophrenia: Escape Hatch from Pain

As stated, sociological schizophrenia—that form of the illness derived from election rather than genetic impairment or outright trauma—is believed to be a disease of self-concept. It derives from a deterioration in the metaphorical self-concept as a consequence of the patient's long-standing refusal to confront and resolve conflicts in self-perception.

In other words, out of the desire to escape pain in the realm of self, the schizophrenic avails herself/himself of existential escape hatches made possible by the metaphorical nature of reality.

(The descent to paleologic language discussed earlier is one instance of this. Ultimately, it is believed these devices of avoidance obliterate the adjudicator of reality that is self-concept.)

Although schizophrenics suffer unbelievable pain, many authorities see the illness as a coping mechanism—as a last-resort refuge from mental suffering.

Dr. Sullivan, it will be remembered, said schizophrenics' use of language was done "more or less knowingly." Mahler writes of autism (*op. cit.*, p. 124):

> Patients like George sever the ties with unbearable reality.... These patients...regress into autism to maintain their lives and entity in some dedifferentiated, deanimated form.... This is a means of warding off the danger of losing whatever minimal individual entity they may have succeeded in attaining.

And Kasanin writes (*op. cit.*, p. 46) that:

> Schizophrenic reaction comes here [in so-called neurotic schizophrenic cases] only as a last resort, when other neurotic defenses fail...To this group also belong the cases in which there is a frank emotional conflict over certain instinctive drives which are unacceptable to the patient.

With respect to the "instinctive drives," let it be stipulated here that if there are indeed such forces at work in human psychology, it is the self-concept response that makes them "unacceptable" and not any latent qualities for good or evil found within them.

Arieti stipulates as well, in **Interpretations of Schizophrenia** (*op. cit.*, p. 80), that:

> The psychosis may be viewed as the ultimate attempt on the part of the patient to solve his difficulties. From a psychodynamic point of view, it offers many apparent advantages, which vary in each case as to quality, quantity and interrelationship. The most common are the following: the difficulties appear to the patient no longer general in character, but restricted to specific situations. He is not the self-pitied victim of his own general inadequacy and worthlessness, but the victim of the malevolent doing of other people. Whereas before the onset of the psychosis the patient felt that millions of malevolent authorities were justified in having a low opinion of him, now he feels that a few malevolent, powerful people are unfair toward him and cause his troubles.

Finally, Carson, Butcher, and Coleman (*op. cit.*, p. 352) stipulate as follows:

> Although extreme ego-defense mechanisms are commonly observed in schizophrenic patients, it is often unclear to what extent they are a causal factor, as opposed to a reaction to the frightening experience of disorganization. Here it may be emphasized that a schizophrenic breakdown often appears to repre-

sent *a total defensive strategy* [my italics]. In essence, the individual seems to withdraw from the real world and evolve a defensive strategy that makes it possible to distort and "reshape" aversive experiences so that they can be assimilated without further self-devaluation. Even though this defensive system may be illogical and far from satisfactory, it relieves much of the inner tension and anxiety and protects the individual from complete psychological disintegration.

In other words, the schizophrenic state provides the patient with one or more ways of thinking that offer release from the unceasing mental anguish that accompanies the disintegration of identity. It is, of course, a strategy not limited to schizophrenia—as the variety of autoimmune illnesses demonstrate.

The actions described above, though driven by mental anguish of the highest order, are almost certainly conscious and deliberate stratagems—variations on the lower-grade strategies of mind blank discussed above.

These ways of thinking, it should be noted, are all metaphorical ideations whereby the schizophrenic may trick away the pain. Though it may seem cruel to say so, these are all—as is sociological schizophrenia itself—conscious devices for evading responsibility for the conscious construction of the metaphor of self.

It is an avoidable consequence, subject to early (even educational) intervention. Schizophrenia is the supreme consequence of denial of self-concept responsibility.

Self-Concept Illness as Rationale

The very concept of schizophrenia as a form of mental illness has become a controversial one in recent days with some writers denying it exists at all.

One of the reasons for this controversy is the difficulty specialists have had in arriving at a common definition with common symptoms everyone will accede to.

It is believed that the definition of schizophrenia as an illness affecting the metaphorical concept of self may resolve some of the questions and remove certain ambiguities surrounding the issue.

The reader is reminded that self-concept is a metaphoric expression of survival drive, and survival of self requires the maintenance of an inner sense of emotional security; to that end, the human search for equanimity may utilize a variety of evasive tactics.

Some of the agreed-upon characteristics of schizophrenia (see DSM-III-R diagnostic criteria for schizophrenia [Highlight 10.1], ***Abnormal Psychology***. *op. cit.*, p. 328) include paranoia, delusions of persecution, hallucinations, delusions of grandeur, hostility and violent actions, loose associations, autism, adualism, and catatonia.

Taken in order and beginning with paranoia: from the perspective of comparison psychology, paranoia derives from the fear of insanity, from the fear of loss of authority over self-concept. It is a transference device whereby insecurities may be blamed on the malicious intent and behavior of others.

More precisely, it is the assignment to external entities the responsibility for internal fears. It is a device (a distractor) making unnecessary the confronting of perceived inadequacies in the realm of self. The persistent suspicion that the world is "out to get you" also functions as a self-generated distractor that keeps away (for a time) the anxiety accompanying the threatened loss of one's sense of self.

Delusions of persecution are also a form of projection whereby one's perceived failings are made the fault of others.

Because the perception of persecution results in an alteration of the affect one presents to the outer world, people may respond nervously or even impatiently to the victim of persecution delusions. Thus, assumed rejection is immediately perceived as just another instance of persecution.

A former student told me her teachers deliberately tried to break her concentration and cause her to fail. She believed one teacher maliciously brushed against her while proctoring a major examination and that her teacher's persistent coughing was a willed act designed to distract her and cause her to fail.

These sort of delusions of persecution derive from paranoid feelings and make the confrontation of one's inadequacies unnecessary.

They work like distractions, intervening between the patient and her omnipresent pain.

But to continue the **Abnormal Psychology** catalog of symptoms: hallucinations (usually auditory and often self-recriminatory) also function as a displacement device for the patient's feelings of being weak, unlovable, and weird. And a perverse kind of relief is found by transferring the name-calling to another entity rather than oneself.

Typically, hallucinations keep "up a running commentary on the individual's behaviors or thoughts," "accuse them of immoral practices, 'pour filth' in their minds, and call them vile names" (Carson, Butcher, Coleman, *op. cit.*, pp. 329 and 336).

Hallucinations are self-generated acids that devour self-concept. Because they are spoken by "others," because they are not "said" by the hearer, they may represent a last-gasp tactic for avoiding self-concept responsibility.

A schizophrenic friend of mine was recently taken off thorazine by his doctors preparatory to the administering of clozapine. He promptly began to hallucinate and, in answer to the advice of one of the voices in his head, attempted suicide

> *Delusions of persecution are also a form of projection whereby one's perceived failings are made the fault of others.*

It is of great interest to me that the figure urging suicide upon him was John Wilkes Booth—a historical figure with whom he closely identifies and upon whom he has conducted intensive personal research.

Because Booth had the courage (in my friend's mind) to strike out at perceived societal repression, my friend employed Booth's actions for fraudulent enhancement of his own threatened ego. This is, I believe, an instance of self attacking self.

Delusions of grandeur are psychotic attempts to reverse inadequacy upon itself and replace depleted egos with historical ones that are strong, in control, and feared by all—in point of fact, effective "talismen" for the evil impulses patients see in themselves, embodying qualities exactly opposite from the patient's own. Sometimes the delusions are acts of desperation growing out of a perception of total unworthiness.

Hostility and physical violence (forms of problem solving by no means limited to schizophrenics) derive from anger at oneself for not being accepted, successful, or respected.

They are products of desperation that provide momentary relief from the futility of forever trying and forever failing.

One young man of my acquaintance attempted to smuggle a machete into a psychiatric ward. His intent was to find and punish the orderlies who had, some years before, restrained him in such a way as to humiliate him.

For a period of months, unbeknownst to his therapist or family, he had brooded over what he perceived as an insult to his sense of personhood. Ultimately, he came to see the orderlies' treatment of him as a metaphor of all the injustices he'd been subjected to throughout his life—including the curse of mental illness.

Driven to the wall by his illness, unable to get or keep a job, he was defending what little ego he still possessed with the only weapon he had left. Under conditions where a continuous state of inadequacy presides, individuals may be driven to acts of violence, violence born of anger, disillusionment, and loss of hope.

The current spate of mass shootings in movie theaters, schools, churches, grocery stores, shopping malls, and on military bases may be traced to the same kind of self-concept demoralization—as the immersion in primitive, survival-based metaphors would seem to suggest.

Even such carefully planned and executed acts as the bombings at the Boston Marathon—purportedly retaliation originating from a perceived disrespect for the Muslim religion—may be seen as expression of similar motives, with young emigrants resorting to violence out of ego dissatisfaction translated into religious fanaticism and overt acts of violence.

Loose associations, word salads, and the intrusion of primitive drive material in language derive from frantic (and losing) efforts to hang on to a unified sense of self in the face of social and/or personal expectations.

In an article entitled "Associative Thinking in Schizophrenia: A Contextualist Approach," by Rana Gordon, Marshall L. Silverstein, and Martin Barrow (*Journal of Clinical Psychology*, October, 1981. Vol. 38, No.4, 684-696), loose associations and the intrusion of primitive drive matter are discussed from the perspective of contextual meanings.

The study found that 24 percent of the schizophrenic responses and 11 percent of the non-schizophrenic control cohorts fit into what they characterized as "Code Type 8"—a category indicative of "severe associative thought pathology characterized by intrusion of primitive drive material into the associative response." (p. 690)

The statement they cited as typical of Type 8 responses *(the word-pairing was butter-cereal)* is of particular interest to the proposition that schizophrenia is an illness of self-concept.

(Both loose associations and primitive drive materials are represented in the example):

> I put butter in my cereal and butter is a witch and the
> cereal is like an army of people that's going to destroy
> the butter. (p. 688)

Recognizing the risk involved in interpreting schizophrenic metaphor, I would like to suggest that the butter in this highly run-on sentence represents the patient—she perceives herself as being or having the qualities of a witch.

As a witch transforms matter into (and the irony of this insight into the nature of the schizophrenic method should be noted) something else—in this case an army of people. Her creation *(and the fact that it is people is also highly informative)* is bent on destroying her.

The so-called "intrusive material" illustrated here is highly egocentric—a fact, I believe, that also speaks to self-concept involvement in schizophrenia.

Additionally, it is instructive to note that the patient's persecutors were created by her, a suggestion that on some level she recognizes her own complicity in her illness.

Attention is directed to similarities between this metaphor and Renee's needle-lost-in-the-haystack metaphor discussed earlier. In both instances, the self is immured in unfeeling substances, and selves destroy selves.

Word salads are of great interest to this study because they involve the use, or the loss of use, of language—the greatest accomplishment of the metaphoric mind. Frank J. Bruno, PhD, ***The Family Mental Health Encyclopedia*** (N.Y., c1989) defines word salad as:

> A chaotic jumble of words and sentences that make little sense to the listener. Some of the words may be neologisms. The tendency to produce word salads is associated primarily with the schizophrenic disorders. It may also be displayed by patients suffering from neurological disorders.
>
> Here is an example of a word salad produced by a patient suffering from a schizophrenic disorder:

"I you perfect lakaloo insisting past tense science for now trust deeds no no no." (p. 418)

The fact is that language is symbolic and, as has been stated earlier, abstractions are one of the many schizophrenic aversions.

It is interesting that word salads occur in the disorganized type of schizophrenia—see Carson, Butcher, Coleman, (*op. cit.*, p. 336)—that version of the illness for which the prognosis for recovery is most dim.

One suspects that the reason word salads mark a significant stage in deterioration is because language is based on sound—one of the earliest ego differentiation devices the infant has available. In other words, word salads may be viewed as evidence of the deterioration of the metaphorical ability itself.

This makes a kind of sense when one recalls that schizophrenia is a disease of self-concept and that language is mankind's most effective device for organizing reality.

As Dr. Andras Angyal has said, speaking of schizophrenic language,

A faulty end result in any performance may be due either to a defect in the tool or to a defect in using the tool. ("Disturbances of Thinking in Schizophrenia," *op. cit.*, **Language and Thought**, p. 122)

That the tool of language has limitations is obvious to anyone who has tried, for instance, to give expression to the emotions of love.

Here, however, the defect is in the use of the tool—a tool for the survival of the psychological self—that the patient is incapable of using.

It is a competence lost for lack of a firm hand on the helm of self.

Finally, autism (withdrawal from contact with humans), adulism (the inability to distinguish between ego boundaries and the external world), and catatonia (a stop-action sequence designed to slow down impinging stimuli and maintain sanity) can all be construed as escape mechanisms freeing the patient from responsibility for (or his fear of) making ego decisions.

From the perspective of comparison psychology, all these symptoms, then, should be seen as consciously invoked devices for dealing with an ego-splitting illness that grows out of the patient's perception of self as inferior, inadequate, and irretrievably doomed.

As Susie Orbach has argued in a different context (**Hunger Strike**, *op. cit.*, p. 132):

> Self-hate is debilitating. Anyone who suffers it will do almost anything to disguise it. They may turn it into depression, they may seek relief through chemical means, or seek to remake themselves like the anorectic.

Had she added turning to the escape hatch of schizophrenia as another option, she would not have been wrong.

All of those qualities said in **Abnormal Psychology** to be descriptive of schizophrenia may be traced, then, to deterioration of self-concept and, subsequently, to self-detestation. Like all metaphors they are all survival-based—in these cases, on survival of self.

Schizophrenia is, after all, a mind disease, and the mind is the kingdom where self-concept presides.

Before concluding this chapter, I would like to return to the issue of autonomic mirroring addressed here and in previous chapters. Without naming it, Maggie Scarf addresses this very question in her report of an interview with R.D. Laing (**Body, Mind, Behavior**, Washington, DC, p. 174):

> A number of psychiatrists, however, looking to these genetic studies, have come to believe that schizophrenia may very well be a stress disease in which the tar-

get organ is the brain. That is, just as one individual develops peptic ulcers when exposed to too much strain [a now discredited precept]—because his vulnerable organ is his intestine—and another develops hypertension because in that case his vascular system is his bodily weak 'link,' so schizophrenia may represent a disturbance of brain function resulting from too much environmental stress. In this case since the brain is the organ of thinking, the "symptoms" would be impairment of thought processes rather than high blood pressure or something like that. Does this model make sense to you?

In the interview, Dr. Laing goes on to reject her "model," preferring naturally enough his metaphor of a schizophregenic society.

There is, however, a neatness to Ms. Scarf's "model" that makes it tempting, particularly since the process she is suggesting employs the very means of metaphor. Ultimately, however, it is that very neatness that arouses suspicion.

Her "model" does not, for instance, resolve the issue of why people exposed to equal levels of stress do not all develop schizophrenia, nor does she suggest what processes, chemical or otherwise, are responsible for the damage.

(Recent discovery of the existence of four million gene switches [see the *New York Times* article cited above] may well shed light on some of these questions.)

I believe the issue of schizophrenia—to say nothing of the functions of metaphor—is too complex to be resolved by simplified one-on-one relationships, no matter how "neat" the metaphors are or how gratifying they may be. Metaphors, after all, build on other metaphors and, in the world of the schizophrenic, there may well be little or no recognizable logic to their conformation.

Stress has received singular emphasis in the work, but it is believed to be only one of many complex issues impinging upon the cause of schizophrenia.

In my opinion no suggested cause of schizophrenia addresses this complexity better than the concept argued for here—that the agonizing death of mind is traceable to deterioration in the metaphorical self-concept, a deterioration (according to comparison psychology) resulting from the failure to take responsibility for the development of a sound and ego-enhancing sense of self.

Lest those damaged brain structures so vividly portrayed through magnetic resonance imaging (MRI) and computerized axial tomography (CAT) be construed as support for the belief that schizophrenia derives exclusively from brain or chromosomal malformation, let it be said that from the perspective of comparison psychology these impairments could be invoked, just as well, by massive doses of psychotrophic drugs or from hormonal silencers invoked by the individual in the interest of quieting the repeated reminders of self-concept inadequacy.

Along these lines, Andrew Croyden Smith (*Schizophrenia and Madness*, London, 1982) admonishes us to take care when tracing the origin of schizophrenia to strictly physical causes. (He is discussing the once-popular dopamine theory.)

> Frightened people have tense muscles, but apprehension is not a muscular disease, and similar cautionary reflections must apply to the significance of physical changes in the brain of mentally ill patients. (p. 100)

It is, then, with sincere apologies to my good friends at the Alliance for the Mentally Ill (AMI) and to the many advocates of the brain disease hypothesis—see, for instance, Dr. E. Fuller Torrey's blame-erasing treatise, *Surviving Schizophrenia: A Family Manual*, New York, 1983)—

that I return to my oft-stated premise that schizophrenia (of the psycho-logical type) is a disease of self-concept, not of organs in the brain.

To the extent that parents are responsible for non-nurturing environ-ments, to that extent should they accept responsibility for their children's maladjustment rather than searching for guilt-erasing rationalizations.

The stairs that lead to mental illness are many, but the first step to sanity is each individual taking responsibility for her/his theory of self—regardless of circumstances and/or parental failures. Where society (and parents) go wrong is in not teaching the process.

Ultimately, of course, each individual is responsible for construct-ing his/her own sense of self, and scapegoating (by parent or patient) is just another short and easy path to avoiding self-concept responsibility.

If schizophrenia is, indeed, a disease of self-concept, then it behooves us all—parents, adults, and child—to take on at the earliest point of self-awareness responsibility for a willed construction of a positive sense of self. Once schizophrenia takes hold, it is too late for the most sophis-ticated of anti-psychotic concoctions and, regretfully, for comparison psychology as well.

Summary

As has been stated, everything is a product of metaphor, including the production of the human brain and the evolving notion of a sense of self. Schizophrenia is seen as a disease of self-concept created, to some extent, by the human desire to avoid suffering—a metaphorical extrapo-lation of the fact of mortality.

Schizophrenia, as a self-concept disease, establishes both the exis-tence of self-concept and the consequences of our failure to build it responsibly.

Chapter 6 describes the process.

CHAPTER SIX

The Path to Independent Living

This is a difficult chapter to write, given the fact that the person presuming to elucidate the subject suggested in the chapter title has but begun the trek himself. Even so, beginnings adumbrate arrivals.

From the beginning, it will be remembered, it was stipulated that no metaphor is right or wrong, just efficient or not.

And this is true: freedom is not possible in the grasp of tyranny, and yet every dictionary is a despotism, every system a prison, every metaphor a potential entrapment.

The solution to this paradox lies in the recognition that my truth is only true for me—a position fraught with difficulty given the fact that safety is found in stubbornness.

While I may accede to another person's metaphor (as in a dictionary of meanings) for purposes of communication, I cannot bind anyone to my personal truth, and indeed that same connotative freedom must exist for my fellows, else it cannot exist for me—though I hasten to add, agreement is welcomed!

Versions of this democratic modesty are mouthed so often as to approach glibness (or hypocrisy), but the fact is that without tolerance for another person's metaphor we are all held captive to mind-locking bigotry. This does not mean that we have to agree with another person's metaphor, but it does mean we must agree to (and defend) that person's right to hold it—factually wrong, or stupid, as it may turn out to be.

Thus, the statement that no metaphor is true or false, just efficient or not, is a fundamental tenet of comparison psychology, the approach to mind-function espoused here.

Metaphors, like cosmic particles, are made and discarded every day. One needs only look at the one-function telephone as an instance in case. The belief in demigods is another. Thunder, once compelling evidence of a deity's anger, is now a meteorological consequence.

Precepts once immutable are now debatable, and those people intent on there being such things as inviolate truths—commandments engraved in stone and enforced by a heavenly tyrant—are unlikely to be comfortable with what follows.

This is because, from the viewpoint of comparison psychology, we conform others to our metaphors (or accept theirs) out of an unconscious desire for security (psychological survival), for a feeling of acceptance that in the world of mind is the equivalent of that reflexive drive for physical survival in a world made bloody by tooth and claw.

That imprinted universal dictum to stay alive has—thanks to the arrival of self-concept—been modified in humans into a concern for keeping the psychological self alive—that is, self-content, self-confident, secure, and self-directed.

It goes without saying, then, that the laws governing physical survival are vastly different from those governing the world of mind where self-concept presides.

In this new world, strength and agility are only obliquely important, as the need for hunting down food is now metaphorically translated into the need for self-approval.

All too easily is the need for shelter shifted to the need for castles; for the animal fur needed for warmth to ermine for prestige; and having children—all too often an unconscious consequence of lust—comes to be seen as testament to parental brilliance.

What is sorely needed, from the perspective of comparison psychology, is human awareness of how effortlessly primitive survival drive may be allowed to take up residence in the world of self-concept.

We humans may possess the power to remake the world, but many of us continue to let the ancient compulsion to survive physically color and control our mental perceptions, drive our physical actions, and govern our opinions.

To counter this (in my philosophy), individuals must resolve to enshrine in their minds the first imperative of consciousness: a determination to tolerate the perspectives of others as well as campaign for their right to hold them—resisting, in the process, the inherent survival compulsion to sway their opinions into consensus with ours.

It is mandatory that we do so, otherwise the very possibility of freedom is denied us by our selfish insistence upon our own prerogatives. No metaphor (not even this one) is true or false, just efficient or not.

With the advent of self-concept, survival took on overtones above and beyond those of physical survival—eating, drinking, finding shelter, staying alive, and propagating—and the issue of staying alive psychologically—that is, feeling good about the self one perceives and its competency—became the new imperative.

This said, it is important to recognize that while psychological meaning is assigned (subjective) and must be gratuitous, the system that makes possible the making of metaphors is not.

The rule of metaphor governs everything, and though its origin is grounded in physical survival where rejection of its "truths" may be fatal, its governing mechanism is always the same—survival is primary, whether of the physical body or of the ephemeral self.

The governing mechanism is comparison—the universal engine, not only of thought, but of action—beginning with the birth of particle conglomerates and the sense of time their existence makes possible.

As perceived here, the process goes like this: this particle's spin, this molecular construction, this amalgamation of gas and matter—finds compatibility with some random object in its path and shouts *eureka!* That globule of fruit dangling before me is edible or it's not; this person likes me or he doesn't; beauty is skin deep, or it's in the mind.

The method used is always the same: the slots in the metaphorical formula into which we insert our meanings are operant or epiphanant (cause or consequence), and the need to survive (physical or psychological) drives the objects or ideas we place inside them.

Thus, the conclusions I come to about survival, or about the nature of beauty, may or may not be true for you, but the mechanism that underlies metaphor—those cosmic formula, those brain modules (physical structures) that exist for detecting and identifying affinities—we all share in common. We all utilize the same mechanisms; we all compare to survive.

These mechanical structures whose existence underlies the philosophy of comparison psychology are, then, the same for all. The concepts—virtual or literal—placed inside those "slots" are inevitably subjective, but we must all compare (find affinity in objects, place parts of speech into preprepared sockets, and read the meanings of perceived actions) to know anything.

Ultimately, also, we must compare to develop a concept of self; and (as will be shown) it behooves us to choose those comparisons that best serve the interests of preserving our self-created selves.

This means that the very nature of our reality is determined by the quality of our chosen comparisons. While it is possible to "fudge" on the system—see the next chapter heading—the consequences of doing so irresponsibly can be fatal, to our bodies, our concepts of self, and to the nature of our human relationships.

The consequences for not accepting responsibility for our comparisons may have been discussed sufficiently, but it is important to emphasize that it is the exercise of responsibility based on integrity that grounds our metaphors and gives psychological life its viability.

The Open-Endedness of Metaphor

The fact that what is true for me needs not be true for you is one of the great liberating verities in the universe. It means that although the forces allied against our doing so are formidable, we are literally free to create our own phenomenological worlds.

At the same time, this metaphorical open-endedness—our freedom to slot our ideas as we choose—means we also have the freedom to use the system to self-destructive ends, literally deceiving ourselves or others through fabrication of self-deceptive systems.

For instance, many years ago I knew an artist who distributed a statement of his philosophy of art in a brochure accompanying his art show at the college we both worked for. His statement (I regret I did not save it) was a melange of pretentious language that (because it meant anything) ended up saying nothing.

He was young in the art business, but, in my opinion, he was either trying to convince the viewing public he existed on a higher plane than they, or he was obfuscating the fact that he had not yet developed his own rationale for his art at all.

(It is a source of great personal pleasure to me that, having occasion recently to view his latest productions, I found myself greatly impressed with his art. From my perspective, his concept of self has solidified, and he was now creating art for his own purposes, without the overriding [and defensive] need for public acceptance.)

No matter which of the two possibilities spelled out above—snobbery or deception—was operative at that first art show, his philosophy of art appeared to me, then, to be an instance of using the open-endedness of metaphor to obfuscate—a chosen mode of behavior that militates against a concept of self-grounded in integrity. (Either he was lying to himself or he was lying to his viewers—the possibility that his art was over my head not being considered.)

On some level, I believe he would have had to know which of the two cases was true for him and, consequently, he could be fairly charged (viewed from the perspective of comparison psychology) with committing an act of treason in the realm of a responsibly constructed concept of self.

Another damning instance of the use of metaphorical open-endedness run rampant occurs in the field to which I have dedicated much of my creative energies. I refer to poetry.

It is a quality made evident in obituary poems, for instance, where the motivating force behind them and their metaphors seems to be affirmation of immortality—for benefit of the deceased, but especially for the survivors.

These type metaphors are viewed as open-ended—not only because they are based on an affirmation of faith not confirmed by experience—but because their operants are not traceable to an object, idea, or action in the real world.

Some months ago, I had occasion to read an article on metaphor in *Poets & Writers* by Professor Dan Albergotti of Coastal Carolina University ("The Truth of Imagination," 59-60, Jan/Feb 2012). The professor supports his philosophy of metaphor by reference to a poem by Melanie Carter—an example, in my mind, of poetry built upon open-ended metaphors and replete with their ungrounded consequences.

I reserve for later a more detailed discussion of Ms. Carter's poem, but to me Professor Albergotti's article represents what I see as a fairly recent development in literary theory, a penchant for interpreting metaphors based on readers' own idiosyncratic, private meanings—to perceive, in other words, the "good" metaphor as one which speaks to the free-wheeling unconscious, providing an easily arrived at, "unearned" *aha!* (survival) response.

To this generation of readers, it seems, the more the poem invites the reader to bring to bear upon it his own interpretation and personal experiences, the better he/she appreciates the poem. In addition to encouraging sloth, this approach gives readers permission to indulge their emotions regardless of meaning or the poet's intent in writing the poem.

The result is that the poem is transmigrated into a vehicle written for the reader's personal pleasure—not for the earned pleasure found in shared enlightenment, or in the rewards garnered from careful reading or scholarship.

To me, this "modern" approach reeks of the notion that pleasure is its only reason for being, incarnating therein that philosophy underlying the once-popular euphemism, "If it feels good, do it!"

In nature, pleasure follows on the heels of successful consummation, and the experience encourages the seeking out of new combinations and new pleasures. In the Albergotti way of doing things, the pleasure comes before discovery and is found in fraudulently concocted affinities that afford an un-earned emotional response.

It is a short and easy way of prostituting the metaphorical formula to the end of easy pleasure.

As it can be fairly said of nature that its very existence derives from the discovery of affinities in matter, so can it be said of the human brain: its very survival is dependent upon metaphor. When chosen in the best interests of psychological survival, affinities endow sanity; chosen on impulse or at random, the result is irrelevancy, chaos, or insanity.

As nature's metaphors are forever grounded in actual matter—in electric pulses and particles—so may it be said of language-based synthetic metaphors: they are most effective when grounded in the stuff of ideas based on an allegiance to the originating source from which they sprung.

According to this philosophy, all metaphors (and anything capable of being held in the minds of humans or of nature is a metaphor) consist of two fundamental parts, an *operant* and an *epiphanant*.

The *operant* is seen as that word, image, or idea that serves as the base (the point of origin) for the comparison that is a metaphor. It may be one thing or a conglomerate. The *epiphanant*—via the bridge of a verb of being (the verbal equivalent of survival drive in nature)—completes the *aha!* comparison that is the telling mark of all metaphors.

METAMORPHOSOS: A PROPOSED PATH TO INDEPENDENT LIVING

Beauty is Truth

Thus, the scientist in search of a conductor for a laser beam, will select as *operant* a material known to contain conductive properties. Once she finds an effective conductor, the epiphanant (that *aha!* moment of discovery) is confiirmed in the success of the experiment.

To further continue this description of the way metaphor works, let us consider the history of that once towering and dominant tree, the American Chestnut.

This magnificent accomplishment of nature (a metaphor of high honor indeed!) was annihilated years ago by a fungus (*Cryphonectria parasitica*), imported from Asia. Efforts now under way to restore the tree to American forests employ the stratagem of splicing the DNA (*operant*) from blight-resistant Oriental species into native survivors with the hope of restoring the species (epiphanant)—an instance (as it turns out) of a scientific metaphor debunking a literary one—that only God can make a tree!

As it is with scientific metaphors, so should it be in the human language of metaphor.

All metaphors seek that moment of *aha!*ness when connections are made and certainty is achieved; and great poetry kindles this moment through apprehension (and celebration) of the writer's intended meaning—not through happenstance or some accidental tapping into a forgotten memory, genetic or personal—but as an experience of survival achieved through that moment of found-meaning that is survival made metaphor.

In other words, the reader owes it to the poet—who has worked hard for his "money"—to bring to the reading of the metaphor that is the poem the best attention to details he can summon, the best facts of reason, research, and scholarship she can muster—accompanied, always, by the overriding determination to allow the poem the integrity of its own being.

While it is true that no metaphor is right or wrong—just efficient or not—the effective (efficient) metaphor can always be recognized by the fact of certainty grounded in integrity—in the fact of an experienced (and honorable) connectivity between epiphanant and operant.

The philosophy of metaphor sees this connectivity as necessary to grounding—the source of integrity in nature, in writing, and (as I hope to show) in psychology.

Some degree of support for my belief in the importance of grounding as defined here is suggested in the field of embodied cognition, in which the relationship between metaphor and body is argued for and demonstrated.

While it is too early in these investigations for this writer to commit one way or the other to the philosophy championed there, it is certainly true that metaphorical concepts such as "in front," "upness," and "downness" are grounded in human experience and are dependent upon bodily perceptions.

Furthermore, given the concept of evolving metaphor argued for in comparison psychology, it is easy to conceive of certain primitive organs taking onto themselves cognitive survival functions and abilities, carrying some of them over—even into the modern era.

Thus, the heart may be someday shown to possess limited cognitive abilities of its own, and its palpitations induced by powerful emotions may turn out to speak to fears of physical harm or to what the romantics among us characterize as love.

It is conceivable, also, that the evolving human brain took over— for reasons of survival efficiency many older survival functions—meaning that certain early cognitive functions relevant to primitive living were rendered either obsolete or irrelevant.

The viability of this possibility is affirmed by the concept promulgated in quantum mechanics in which individual cosmic particles found affinities in each other, beginning, thereby, the process of creation by metaphor—a process confirming, by the way, the tendency engrained in metaphor to evolve from the platform of previous functions and structures into more efficient expressions of survival drive, as illustrated in the discussion of aural evolution to follow.)

Metaphor, from this perspective, was grounded in the material from which it originated in its earliest permutations, a characteristic that can be found even to the present day as a crucial attribute of efficiency in metaphors, be they reflexive, hylozoic, or synthetic.

There is other support, though, for the importance of grounding in metaphor. The reader is reminded that from the perspective of comparison psychology everything in our universe—elementary particle, physical matter, or idea—owes its existence to metaphor.

One of the strongest elements in Dr. Ramachandran's ***The Tell-Tale Brain*** (*op. cit.*) is his identification of those areas in the brain responsible for implementing the various forms of cognition.

For instance, on page 178, while discussing the inferior parietal lobule (IPL), he writes:

> And since we have two angular gyri, they may have evolved different styles of abstraction: the right for visuospatial and body-based metaphors and the left for more language-based metaphors, including puns.

It may be important to note that, according to Dr. Ramachandran, the angular gyri are unique to Homo sapiens—a fact that lends credence to comparison psychology's argument that survival drive, as the source of all metaphor, is forever at work in evolution, driving it to ever greater levels of survival efficiency.

The point of the quote, however, is to show how survival-based metaphors derive, first, from a physical platform, represented in the gyri, and then evolve to language-based metaphors, including puns—a form of non-physical metaphor, the source of irony, and, I hasten to add, another form of metaphor!

It may be said, then, that the source of metaphor can be found in the physical world, and that even our more evolved metaphors (given scientific acumen sufficient to the task) may be traced to a physical operant for their comparisons.

Charles Darwin

This concept is fundamental to the theory of comparison psychology (and to Darwin's theory of evolution) that all metaphors be traceable to earlier metaphors and that—in the world of linguistic metaphor—the closer the metaphor is to its physical source (its operant) the more effective it is likely to be.

I found support for this concept of grounding in the highly effective use of metaphors in Lee R. Kump's article, "The Last Great Global Warming," (**Scientific American,** July, 2011).

In a surprisingly poetic treatment of a scientific subject—designed doubtlessly to add vigor to the bland objectivity of scientific reporting— he writes of "methane *belches*," (59), "left on the counter to *thaw*," (59), and of "planetary *fever*" (61).

Since methane is regarded as one of the major contributors to global warming, and since in this context it bubbles up from the ocean (and melting arctic ice), it is not difficult to see "*belches*" as having direct linkage to its operant, methane—not to mention the equivalent function of gas in humans and cows.

The same may be said of the metaphor "left on the counter to thaw," which builds on the author's description of permafrost as being like "frozen hamburger in the freezer"—also, by the way, a metaphor with provocative epiphanant possibilities!

He refers to permafrost (as a result of thawing) being "essentially left on the counter to thaw." Here the *epiphanant* exists in the phrase, "left on the counter to thaw," and the direct linkage is to the *operant* hamburger—also a metaphor of permafrost, and a grounded one at that!

The third metaphor, "*fever*," has as its operant "planetary," and the word, "*fever*," the *epiphanant*, conveys the senses of both heat and illness, a telling instance of the way metaphor enriches language by reaching across the universe of meaning for connections.

Another metaphor, more complex than these, came from a speech delivered at the 2011 Democratic National Convention held in Charlotte, NC. "Being a woman no longer qualifies as a pre-existing condition!" the speaker said to arena-rocking applause.

That the sentence is a metaphor, and that it is a highly effective one, is self-evident; it is not, however, one easily analyzed by the system of *operant* and epiphanant proposed above.

This is because the *operant* is here implied, and the *epiphanant* requires knowledge of a particular requirement of the then recently enacted Affordable Care Act.

The implied *operant*—and one should not be surprised at the degrees of subtlety metaphors are capable of!—is "womb"—a grounded *operant*, if ever there were one! The *epiphanant*—and, as in often the case with metaphor, knowledge or scholarship is required for effect—is that provision of the new health law that forbids insurance companies to penalize clients for pre-existing conditions.

Thus, it is that the epiphanant brings to the listener the immediate *aha!* apprehension of the discriminatory history of women, going back to the very origin of the species. Also embedded in the metaphor is the fact that women play roles in the making of the universe that men cannot match.

The metaphor successfully does the one thing that metaphor does best, and much of its success can be traced to its being grounded in nature and knowledge. The metaphor reverberates with meaning, but it is meaning based on the real stuff (the operant) that is grounded in nature.

In this writer's view, all four cited metaphors are successful (efficient) for reason that in each case the operant is a physical entity that possesses clear and direct linkages to its epiphanant.

In other words, the cited metaphors have integrity because their epiphanants are clearly tied to their source of origin, their operant. They are not open-ended and therefore not subject to any interpretation. They are, in other words, grounded—in nature and, thereby, in integrity.

The more metaphors are self-concept related the more complex the *epiphanants* are likely to be. This is a consequence of self-concept metaphors being grounded in conscious thoughts and actions rather than in nature. (For a more detailed discussion of self-concept grounding see Dictionary, page 388 below, under "Self-Concept."

This may be seen, for instance, in **The Tragedy of King Lear**, where the grounding elements in the play (*operants*) consist of characters (and their personality modifiers) and the themes (*epiphanants*) of pride, filial ingratitude, and old-age dementia lurk below the surface— all products of self-concept survival urge. And not to be passed over lightly is Shakespeare's own use of grounding (not plagiarism as critically impugned) in his utilization of historical works like **Holinshed's Chronicles**.

Evidence may be found, also, in **Hamlet, Prince of Denmark**, where grounding is provided in the historical sources, the characters (and their modifier characteristics), who function as operants, while epiphanants are found in Hamlet's search for self-concept actualization, in the existence and issues of lust—Oedipal and otherwise—as expressed in the roles of Gertrude and Ophelia and, one suspects, in the self-concept history of William Shakespeare himself.

At the risk of stating the obvious, the more complex the relationship between *operant* and *epiphanant* the greater the requirement for the grounding that is scholarship. Understanding, after all, is epiphanant.

(A proposed example of one kind of scholarship required for grounding is provided in my subsequent discussion of works by William Blake and Christopher Marlowe.)

I return now to the delayed discussion of the poem by Melanie Carter entitled "Water to Sky." I quote the poem, with words and passages I see as ungrounded, in bold type. (The title, I suggest, is ungrounded as well.)

> For seven days a common hummingbird
> has **trimmed** the air outside my window.
> Hardly more than *a **green seed***, it glides
> from pane to pane presenting its fine throat—
> a **fragment** so soaked through with red
> I think it must have swallowed ***the hook God***
> ***dangles*** into *this **uncertain sea***.
> Is it wrong to say God? Because when this
> bird moves, *its **wings** pluck the **invisible line***
> it is suspended from and the diphthong note
> that quivers through the air sounds like
> **a fiddle string gone out of tune with all**
> **the distance between *here and there***. *My father*
> *must be playing this creature*, this stunning,
> **bloodstone**, caught and reeling.

The first bold-typed word, "trimmed," requires us to see the hummingbird as a pair of scissors or, at best, a string trimmer.

This is hardly a grounded metaphor since a hummingbird resembles not at all either of these possibilities in nature, and nowhere in the poem is such an operant suggested. Certainly, the air is in no way trimmed or altered by the bird. The word "trimmed" is thus a metaphor that requires the reader to search for a possible meaning, a meaning for which no evidence (*operant*) is provided and which, because of the utter absence of guidance, must be seen an instance of ungrounded metaphor.

The second demarcated word, "seed"—particularly a green one!—is in no way justified. Not only does the bird not resemble in any believable way a seed (no *epiphanant* is even suggested), but the writer provides nowhere in the poem a justification for its being seen as one.

Thus, not only is the reader left free to interpret the seed in any way she chooses, he is provided no direction or guidance as to the meaning intended. Therefore, "seed" is an ungrounded metaphor tied to a non-existent *epiphanant*. Indeed, so ambiguous is its referent, it hardly qualifies to be labeled a metaphor at all.

The third bold-typed word, "fragment," is not only missing an *epiphanant*, it gives this reader the impression of having been grabbed from the air at random. Mere polity—to say nothing of English grammar—mandates some kind of grounding referent.

The next phrase, "the hook God dangles," transforms the bird into a fish bloodied from ingesting a hook dangled, not in air but in an "uncertain sea," by a cruel God who fishes, apparently, for the sake of bloodying flying (swimming!) things.

There is no logical basis for the sudden appearance of the "hook" and no suggestion of a reason why God would be "dangling" it.

Though "uncertain sea" has a nice ring to it, what was once air is now inexplicably turned into ocean, the uncertainty in the "uncertain sea" is without *epiphanant* and is in no way qualified or accounted for. Readers are left undirected, at sea, and free to manufacture meanings as they choose, an inevitable consequence of ungrounded metaphors.

In the next selected passage, its "wings" (remember that at one point in the poem the bird was a green seed) "pluck the invisible air" (not an act easily visualized), the hummingbird remains tethered to the hook and its invisible [fishing?] line, but now it is transformed into a musician with winged fingers that pluck invisible strings in invisible air.

The final selected phrase, "a fiddle/ string gone out of tune/ with all the distance between here and there," is for me the most effective metaphor in the poem for reasons of the operant "fiddle string" having gone "out of tune" (something fiddles actually do!) by reason of distance—the latter phrase functioning as an unqualified epiphanant.

The problem with the metaphor, even so, is that "fiddle string" has as its referent "the invisible line" that is not only invisible but imaginary. How it manages to make a sound—even an out-of-tune one—is left to the imagination of the reader, who—without a direct linkage between *operant* and *epiphanant*—is left, proverbially, without "a leg to stand on."

Finally, for reasons we can only guess at, the writer's father takes over the fishing chores and starts "playing" this bird, this seed, this bloodstone—the latter being, apparently, a metaphor of the original bird. Why it should now be a bloodstone is left, without guidance, to the reader's discretion. (Perhaps it is the stone, coated with blood, that locked Christ in the tomb? There are literally no limits!)

One is left free to speculate, also, about the meaning of the poem—apparently the hummingbird ends up being an emissary from her deceased father, but it is hard to identify any precise emotions associated with the act or any connected integrity in the poem's ungrounded metaphors.

As implied earlier, the chemistry of metaphor is sometimes too complex for even the most attentive reader to detect every *operant* or every *epiphanant* in metaphors as rich and complex as those found in a successful poem or play. This is because *epiphanants* become *operants* attracted to other *epiphanants*, and the process of discovering affinities is sometimes faster (indeed!) than the speed of light.

Even so, the law of metaphor is inviolate: every metaphor in nature is grounded, at some point, in a discovered affinity found in a real-world object—else it is an ungrounded, stillborn embryo—a potential without any survival function in nature.

Extended, now, to language (itself a metaphor) an *operant* without a clearly designated *epiphanant* is ungrounded and hardly deserves the appellation "metaphor." In fact, said in the language of comparison psychology, such a "metaphor" lacks integrity; because it means anything, it means nothing.

Responsible writers are in control of their material, and control requires that metaphors be conscious and consistent, that they collaborate to the end of a purposeful (not reader-created) communication. The result may well be magical, but magic is most certainly not involved.

One more instance of grounded metaphor, and its importance to poetic (and psychological) integrity, and I am done. I propose, now, to look at John Keats's "Ode on a Grecian Urn." (For reasons of space, I will not provide a copy of this readily available poem.)

The most evident aspect of grounding in the ode is, of course, the precise description of the urn—be it mythical or not, it matters not—painted with "leaf-fringed legend," with "deities or mortals" in pursuit of "maidens loath," and "that heifer lowing at the skies…"bound with," and her "silken flanks with garlands drest" for sacrifice.

The specific description of the urn (along with its grounding in Grecian lore) makes possible the effectiveness of metaphors such as "foster-child of silence and slow time" and "sylvan historian"—metaphors, in each case, with clearly defined operants.

The motive is to so illuminate the urn through the preciseness of the scenes depicted on it that the reader can visualize the images of the scenes described, thereby providing the basis (the operant) for carrying the weight of the thematic elements—the mutability of all things human—of the poem.

This is no small matter since the objects and events described must provide believable metaphorical correlatives to the themes (epiphanants) that the poem exists to say. Thus, the immutability of youthful love is conveyed in the Bold Lover's unconsummated kiss, forever passionate, forever frozen in time. "For ever [sic!] wilt thou love, and she be fair!"

With one exception, the metaphors that make up the stanzas of the poem are grounded, as well.

For instance, in the third stanza the boughs are "happy" because they cannot shed "or bid the Spring adieu"—real natural objects and an actual season humans know and cherish. Here love, Keats says, is "for ever [sic!] panting, and for ever [sic!] young;"

All breathing "human passion" [far better, to Keats, than the crushing feeling] "That leaves a heart high-sorrowful and cloyed, / A burning forehead, and a parching tongue"—undoubted references to Keats's own ever-present (and painful) symptoms from tuberculosis, the antithesis (epiphanant) of those eternal feelings frozen on the urn.

The same groundedness (the use of tangible figures necessary to metaphorical meanings) is featured in the fourth stanza where the town folk come from the now-vacant village, the "mysterious" priest leading to sacrifice ("at what green altar?") the young and "silken-flanked" heifer, festooned festively with flowered garlands.

The fifth and final stanza literally summarizes the grounding elements that make possible the metaphorical leap to theme (to epiphanant).

The stanza begins with the apotheosis, practically, of the urn, labeling it "O Attic shape!" and specifying raised figures of "marble men," "maidens over-wrought," "forest branches," and "trodden weed"—all figures of the natural world to which Keats then applies the fitting metaphorical extension (epiphanants) of "Cold Pastoral!" (a description pregnant with idyllic implications of an ancient time).

Next, calling the urn "a friend to man" who teaches us (based on its example) the eternality of art, he tells us the abiding truth that art alone can survive the cold of winter, the parched tongue of disease, old age, and death—preserving through the beauty of the urn (and ode) those qualities that make us forever human.

It is the truth—reverence for beauty—to which Keats would have us dedicate our lives. This done, the indignities associated with the fact of mortality would no longer afflict our lives. That is, Keats would say, the only truth we need to know, a truth the metaphor that is comparison psychology can recognize.

I made reference earlier to one metaphor in "Ode on a Grecian Urn" that I regard as ungrounded. It occurs in the first two lines of the second stanza: "Heard melodies are sweet, but those unheard are sweeter."

In my opinion, these lines affirm that melodies heard in the mind are to be preferred over the real thing. Not only does this contradict my theory that grounding is facilitated by the use of real objects—heard music exists in the real world—but unheard music makes any sound you choose, an ungrounded metaphor personified!

An ungrounded metaphor is, by definition, lacking in integrity— the one verity that protects us from anarchy and from the tyranny of the open-ended metaphor!

Art cannot be eternal if it means anything you want it to!

The preference, these days, for shotgun metaphors—*operants* that fly through space in quixotic quests for *epiphanants*—is not, of course, limited to poetry. Metaphors make everything work (survive). And it is at this point that the business of metaphor takes on life-or-death ramifications.

There are, for instance, ungrounded metaphors aplenty in the "general-practitioner" metaphor that presides over the reflexive-based self-concept metaphor. Self-concepts can and often do grow like Topsy, leaving personalities to sputter and spurt like untended gardens.

Many adherents of so-called general-practitioner metaphors—those formulations that bubble up at the behest of society and accidents of nature—spend vast sums of money on clothing and cars, convinced that appearance (where is the epiphanant?) is all that matters; willing victims of television advertisements, they opt for fountain-of-youth facelifts that promise recipients awe in the eyes of others and a new-found sense of inner worth; and who among us can ever forget that one-time tennis star announcing to the camera with an affirming grunt, "Image is everything!"

From this writer's perspective, such individuals are willing victims of an unexamined survival impulse, and they are investing in feeling good about themselves based on the operant of appearance and the epiphanants of perceived acceptance, of admiration, or a recovered sense of self-respect—hypothetical quotients of a subjective metaphor devoid of any proven basis in reality, of any kind of conscious grounding in the makeup of their metaphor of self.

Their deceptions may impress others, but in their heart of hearts they have to know they are lying; and this knowledge cannot but have deleterious consequences for their concepts of self and sense of integrity—to say nothing of foregone opportunities to make profound and lasting contributions to the world around them.

It is the same formula expressed in the desire to drive fancy cars, to keep up with the Joneses, and in bragging about our children's accomplishments. We glow in reflected energy, but it is an unearned and unwarranted glow—a glow not grounded in conscious actions or chosen choices.

We are, of course, free to use metaphor as we choose, but if we exercise that freedom reflexively (without conscious grounding), it is at dear cost to our sense of earned integrity—the one essential element in the construction of a solid, efficacious sense of self.

Finally, thanks to electronic wizardry, we now have social networks where we can project to the world the idealized (ungrounded) image of self we wish the world to see, where we can amass "friends" like scalps on a warrior's belt—never making any of the sacrifices true friendships require—and where we can publish our inanities without censorship or consequence—short of being "unfriended."

We have "electronicized" self-concept, making possible a prefabricated world where reality (and feeling good about oneself) is a simple matter of keystrokes, where consciously positive investments in self-construction are not only unnecessary but practicably impossible.

No wonder we are alone and lonely. We are carelessly tinkering with the very roots of relationships—all consequences of our unwillingness to invest in those actions and sacrifices necessary to real friendships and a grounded sense of self.

Accounting for much of the popularity of Facebook and like systems is the tendency of people to employ the inherent open-endedness of metaphor to hide from self-concept insecurities—an unconscious expression of the reflexive impulse to survive applied to the psychological self.

These people choose a short and easy way (the ephemeral stuff of Facebook "liking") in order to avoid the difficult work of conscience—of being responsible for self-generated, constructive metaphors of self.

Sad to say, they may end up feeling good about themselves at the end of a session or as a result of supportive comments; but the feeling they carry is a counterfeit one, one untried by their standing strong and taking action in the face of circumstances that require a willed and conscious investment in real-life exigencies, in self-concept sufficiency.

In their passionate professions of undying love and everlasting friendship, in their public displays of religious piety, in their angry postings of political views (subliminal pleas for psychological security found in unanimity), and in their hostile putdowns of people who dare to differ with them—we may well be witnessing the modern phenomenon of lonely people, devoid of self-concept sufficiency, seeking the affirmation of ghosts.

Thus, it is that we utilize the inherent open-endness of metaphor to supply the reflexive needs of physical and psychological survival without regard (or knowledge) of consequence, and from that time on—actions have consequences—the vaginal walls of Eden have been breached, and the iniquitous serpent slithers into the garden—at our personal (and all-too-often willing) invitation!

Small wonder, then, that, as tropic plants do, we unfold our petals to the sun of public approbation. It is a conditioned response that evokes the infant memory of Eden innocence.

Viewed from the perspective of comparison psychology, if our metaphors fail (lack grounded epiphanants) we have to know whose fault it really is. Like Pogo, we will have searched out the enemy and found it to be us.

Now guilt, the inevitable consequence of lying to ourselves—the *real* original sin—is our ever-present, nagging companion. We can silence it—for a time with, with opiates, with religion, with Facebook, and Trumpian certainties like the Big Lie—but ultimately its hissing sibilance will slither into consciousness and Eden will demand again its tuppence—we will know our nakedness and be ashamed.

If we truly know the serpent is an invited guest, what do we do: lay out the best towels, complain about the extra work, rename the beast, or face (and learn from) the consequences of our chosen metaphors? The choice is ours, as inevitably are the consequences.

(All too often our response is to kill the messenger!)

That we should desire the approbation of our fellows is not surprising; there are primal precedents for it being so. At the same time, public approbation can be withdrawn at any time, and should it become our only source of internal sustenance we could be left like seaside shells cast up empty by a vast, unfeeling tide.

It is, of course, a practicable possibility that an individual could live her/his entire life basking in the reflected glow of the opinion of one's fellows. The open-endedness of metaphor mandates that it be so.

Still, the questions remain: When dependency is extended beyond childhood—when we lackadaisically invite the serpent in—is psychological maturity a possibility? "What does it profit a man if he gains the whole world and..." ends up empty, denied of that personal sense of integrity that grounds his being?

This perpetuation of dependency into adulthood is, of course, but one consequence of manipulating others for unearned ego needs.

It explains why the schizophrenic, deprived of self-love and desperate for a sense of worth, has no alternative but to manipulate—endlessly bleeding parents and friends for evidence of human worth.

A similar extrapolation of the dependency metaphor may account for the purported early success of that late radical movement, ISIS (Islamic State in Iraq and Syria), in recruiting to its cause scores of alienated youths.

Suffering from the lack of a consolidated sense of self—all too often the consequence of ghetto impoverishment—and persuaded that their unhappiness is a consequence of malevolent forces outside themselves, these youth are easy converts to a black-and-white doctrine that sees the United States of America as the Great Satan bent on the utter destruction of Islam.

Once this conviction becomes the presiding epiphanant of their metaphor of self, all observed incidents become supportive of this "truth," and it is a small cost to pay—indeed an affirmation of rightness—to die for one's beliefs, the newly discovered grounding core of their being. It is, of course, a sad and ironic perversion of survival drive.

If the ISIS (and Taliban) motifs have about them a ring of familiarity, readers should not be surprised. Variations on the theme are heard in the core concepts of the NRA, the Tea Party movement, the omnipresent "Dark State," and the KKK (see reference to "great repository metaphors" in Chapter Two, page 52.

Some years ago, I completed the reading of Dr. Norman Brown's **Love's Body** (New York, N.Y. c1966)—a marvelously learned and poetic work in which he speaks of aphorism as "the road of excess which leads to the palace of wisdom." (p. 187)

As much as I admire and respect Dr. Brown, in this instance I must respectfully demur. Aphorisms, all too often, rely on the notion of an absolute truth, and the "truth" that hides behind the veil—what he calls the "four-fold vision" of William Blake—reeks with the musty smell of thanatopsis.

Others have promised the ultimate security that comes with God-like revelation. Carlos Castaneda's perception of a magical reality made available to us through the portals of peyote is a temptingly beautiful one, and the dream of power is a wonderful survival aphrodisiac—particularly for the oppressed.

Even Dr. Brown's vision of freedom from repression, earned through celebration of the pornographic grunginess he sees as undergirding psychoanalysis, offers up the Dionysian version of freedom.

The point should be made, in passing, that Dr. Brown's interpretation of Blake's vision is not the same as mine.

In my view, William Blake knew about metaphor in the sense being discussed here long before anyone else. In fact, what is often seen as mystical and visionary in Blake is oftentmes a renunciation of those very qualities.

The fact is that what all mystical philosophies (and there are many of them!) have in common is their seeking to overthrow the reality principle, replacing one propagandistic reality with a revolutionary new one emblazoned with the one final, unvarnished, real, and ultimate truth.

The truth is there is no final truth, and those philosophical systems that seek to find it founder on the search (and need) for one.

Ultimately, the need for absolute truth is the fear of death transmogrified into a survival system. All philosophies that would adduce the contrary abuse the open-endedness of metaphor in the interest of survival in a mythical hereafter.

Though I may not be able to prove it, the world is "the real world yet," and *caveat emptor* is no empty warning. We are responsible for our metaphors, as we are their consequences.

The previous chapter dealt at length with that form of mental illness called schizophrenia. This illness was chosen because it represents the culminating consequence, in this writer's view, of the failure (or inability) of individuals to accept responsibility for the metaphor of self.

Schizophrenia also represents another use of the open-endedness of metaphor and, like the various forms of mysticism, constitutes a stretching of the boundaries of metaphor for reasons of survival.

If, for instance, mysticism may be defined as belief in realities not subject to perceptual or intellectual proof, so, too, may schizophrenia.

Like the mystic, the schizophrenic believes in sounds and sights not subject to impartial verification; the schizophrenic formulates a private, esoteric version of reality based on the authority of personal experience only.

However, unlike the mystic's world view—though concocted for the same reason—the schizophrenic view of reality derives from loss of a coherent image of self rather than the deliberate construction of an alter one; and, in a desperate attempt to hold onto self, the schizophrenic sometimes reverts to a kind of mysticism not unlike Ezekiel's famous wheel—a vision of self in torment described as a burning, revolving ellipse eternally reverting upon itself.

(It is in the schizophrenic's desperate attempt to deal with the tortured state of self [and his/her existence in a phantasmagorical world of primitive impulse] that she/he sometimes crosses the line from egocentric babble into the realm of poetic expression.

(Sadly, the tortured state of self is the only subject on which he/she can focus unsplintered attention, and that way self-pity lies.)

And, in the same way the schizophrenic is seeking surcease from pain, the mystic may well be seeking relief from an insecurity that comes from the lack of meaning and the absence of a consolidated sense of self.

Even as the schizophrenic seeks order in a dissolving universe (through strategies such as hallucinations), the mystic seeks order in apparent chaos through use of visions and open-ended metaphoric systems derived there-from.

As with the schizophrenic's reality, the mystic's truth is verifiable by personal experience only.

At the risk of over-simplification it can be said: the schizophrenic's struggle is for psychological survival in a realm where the loss of self is the metaphorical equivalent of dying, while the mystic's system is a proposed solution to the conundrum of mortality and an effort, as well, to save the phenomenal self of the practitioner.

Both systems take advantage of metaphoric open-endedness in the interest of survival; and both systems purchase self-deceptive solutions at the price of personal integrity. Both are short and easy ways to psychological survival, traceable—ultimately—to their fear of death.

The Boundaries of Metaphor

I shudder at the thought that my Calvinistic upbringing may unconsciously contaminate this discussion of boundaries, but a discussion of freedom inevitably dictates the discussion of limits.

Elsewhere I have referred to metaphors of warmth and tenderness having the possible effect of directing the infant's attention away from the distractions (and terror) of an outer world, and undoubtedly this is an evolutionary adaptation serving the ends of physical survival. It is an adaptation with psychological implications as well.

We now have access to a technology whereby this natural way of defining reality could be changed. We could, for instance, direct the infant's attention to other factors. Do we want to? How much tinkering with survival drive do we dare undertake?

We could, if we chose, place all newborn infants in giant, antiseptic feeding wards and hook them up to rubberized milk dispensers. We could even arrange that there not be enough milk for all, thus requiring subjects to compete for access to the dispensers.

Some would make it; some would not, and those who survived would certainly be the "fittest;" however, they would have no knowledge of enfolding and holding.

Would they be autistic? Only if we insist on their joining our reality. Allow these infants to grow up together, preventing all contact with an outer world, and they will develop their own survival system—their own language, their own tribal mores, their own value system and religion, and, yes, their own self-concepts.

What manner of beings will they be? Certainly, they would be larger than we are, and stronger; most assuredly they would be self-centered, and aggressive; and if they owed loyalty to or felt gratitude toward anything, it would be the rubberized milk dispensers and their version of the disembodied entity that supplies it once a day—albeit niggardly.

The greater question is how would they resemble us? Would they be willing to experiment with the freedom of others in the name of science, of knowledge? What of empathy? With no knowledge of holding and enfolding, would their motivation be survival at all costs? What would their boundaries be?

These are questions better left to future Huxleys and other authors of fictional worlds, but this extended metaphor illustrates the kind of activities the open-endedness of metaphor makes possible—Hitler's "final solution"—that Jews are the genetic strain polluting the Aryan genome—being another instance in kind.

What is there to prevent our conducting experiments with survival drive? Good sense, law, and the Christian ethic did not prevent our extending the boundaries of the metaphor of atomic weaponry and employing it, not once but twice.

Conscience did not prevent Iraqi rulers from spraying death-dealing chemicals on their own people and invading and incorporating (albeit temporarily) the tiny sheikdom, Kuwait. It did not prevent genocide in Serbia, nor the dive-bombing and strafing (possible gassing) of one's own citizens in Syria.

The question of boundaries, then, is a crucial one, and as the demand for individual freedom becomes more rooted in the human mind, as religion and law exercise less control over the actions of people, as citizens insist that laws exist to benefit them and not their so-called leaders, the more necessary a standard of responsible behavior based on individual freedom will become.

Comparison psychology, it is believed, can provide some useful direction.

It will be recalled that self-concept is a metaphor (whether responsibly constructed or not) of our own making—consolidated in adolescence, and perfected (ideally) during maturity. It is a metaphorical structure based on psychological survival, self-centered and self-created.

Whereas in religious mysticism emphasis is placed on a denial of self—since self-love is viewed there as the antithesis of good, as an affront to the philosophy of survival of the masses at the expense of freedom for the few—in comparison psychology, pride in the self-constructed self is mandated.

It is to that end that responsible actions are taken.

While many religions place responsibility for goodness on obedience to the law, self-abnegation, revealed truth, and a benevolent superbeing, comparison psychology insists the self-concept is (or ought to be) self-created, the responsibility for its development rests with the individual, and acceptance of this responsibility lights the one path to human freedom.

The first step on this proposed pathway to freedom lies in our recognition that we are all susceptible to an unconscious enslavement to survival drive, that pragmatic elements of physical survival may govern our behavior and relationships with our fellows. Nowhere is there a law requiring that we be aware of our internal motivations.

The short and easy way predicts that we will flow like rivers—circumventing what barriers (disease, famine, accidents) we can—that we will engage in breeding frenzies and end up—bloated, soporific, and moronic—floating like spilling seedpods of survival—senseless, without boundaries, to the sea.

This, it is suggested, would have been the destiny of humankind had it not been for that accidental discovery, inherent in the search for survival efficiency, of the metaphor of psychological (self-concept) survival, a metaphor owing its existence to application of that model of evolution described by Darwin in **On the Origin of Species**.

As has been discussed, that great metaphorical shift—the application of the laws of the quantum, of chemistry, and biological methods to conscious mental processes—made possible the development of metaphors not exclusively dedicated to survival of the physical self.

This diversion of survival drive into the realm of the synthetic metaphor of self-concept was a fortuitous discovery, for it not only facilitated survival of survival drive, through the dominance of an advanced species, but it made possible the engineering of an entirely new version of survival—based not on the survival of organisms, but on the survival of self.

This version of survival drive, while metaphorical and responsible for the transformation of this planet and planets yet to be colonized, still functions under exegesis of survival drive—a circumstance that allows us to remain subject to subliminal manipulations. Oblivious to its force—it can control us still.

(This is the terror of subliminal survival drive. Unconscious of its existence, our hidden fear of death transforms free-form figures into institutional monsters thirsting for our blood and for our very souls.)

For evidence of the omnipresence of survival drive in our lives, consider the following: we give it other names, clothe it in expensive linens, crown it with gold and jewels, perfume it with myrrh and frankincense, house it in palaces, and bow down and worship it.

We establish governments at its behest, build up massive supplies of armaments for it, create an industrial-military complex for it, go to war for it, and (irony of ironies!) willingly die for it.

We give birth to children for it, name our progeny for it, build houses, erect picket fences, and plant gardens for it; we drive SUVs named for it along freeways named for it, into cities named for it, where we work for money earned for it, in factories named for it, with smoke-stacks pouring out putrid poisons, all in the name of it—an omnipresent, inbred and largely unrecognized primitive drive to stay alive, physically and psychologically.

And we say that we are free!

If, as stated, the first step on the pathway to freedom is recognition that we are (all too many of us) unconscious vassals of an unrecognized drive to survive, the second step is to take those actions necessary to free ourselves from subservience to its blind, unthinking emissaries— governmental functionaries, priests and potentates, admen and soulless corporations.

We must, in a word, be consciously aware of survival drive and all its many manifestations. We do so by taking thought, by setting bound-aries, by rejecting servitude.

As stated often, metaphor is an equal-opportunity employer— meaning we are free to employ it in any way we choose. Many people opt to "go with the flow" and set no boundaries, leaving the development of self-concept to the default position—permitting unquestioned survival drive to do the job for them.

And, make no mistake, survival drive will cooperate; for its pri-mary mission is to assure its own survival, and the making of babies—the unthinking abeyance to its instinctive impulse—is its primum mobile. Making money and building debt are among its worthiest disciples.

On the other hand, people—recognizing the consequences to free-dom of robotic living—possess the wherewithal to select those actions that best contribute to a conscious construction of self-concept—the one force-to-action instrument in the universe that makes individual free-dom possible.

In comparison psychology, it is proposed that each human can assert control over reflexive metaphors by choosing those actions and ideas—conscious thoughts being the same as action—that best contribute to the responsible construction of a positive sense of self.

The best boundaries are those we set for ourselves.

The Responsible Use of Metaphor

The phrase, taking responsibility for one's metaphors, has been used so often in this document as to have taken on the character of slogan, but the fact is we will only be free from subliminal promptings when we have learned to take responsibility for our metaphors—most specifically in that realm where actions really matter, in mindful construction of the metaphor that is self-concept.

One impetus for taking this responsibility might lie in our recognition that ultimately conscious sentience is the only path to freedom.

In fact, the progression from virtual particles to real ones, from gas to solid rock, from mineral to rooted plant, from floating plant to footed fish, from reptile, bird, and simian, all the way to Homo sapiens is a saga of movement away from the teeming mass toward the independent, mobile individual.

Evolution documents it: Freedom of the individual is human destiny.

Once this fact and its implications for self-actualization are recognized, it is possible to see that the next and most important step on the path to freedom lies in the world of the synthetic mind.

It was stated best in the oft-quoted words William Shakespeare put in the mouth of that consummate hypocrite, Polonius—who, not coincidentally, is the oiliest of all employers of the open-endedness of metaphor: (**Hamlet, Prince of Denmark**, I, ii, 11. 77-80):

And this above all: to thine own self be true,

And it must follow, as the night the day,
Thou canst not then be false to any man.

In comparison psychology this integrity to self is grounded in action, on the self-willed determination to build no instinctive systems of psychological security, to recognize that it is through our perception of self that we weave out the pattern of our lives, and that it is the quality of art brought to the process that grounds us and determines who we are.

This is no little thing. As we are untrue to ourselves—as we hide behind the webby fabrications we weave to conceal ourselves from ourselves—so do we lose touch with integrity, that necessary element to the process of becoming the self-guided, responsible individual we aspire to being.

Without integrity, we become (Coleridge might say) procrastinators and equivocators, while the ghost that is our borning-self, wanders the parapets of life, lost and in awful pain.

And thus, to paraphrase Prince Hamlet, it is that "enterprise[s] of great pitch and moment"—the responsible creation of a unified sense of self—wander hither, thither across a thready tapestry of conflicting patterns, and "lose the name of [conscious] action."

As said, this is no little thing, for it is through success in achieving this goal of a unified self that we derive the sense of earned merit necessary to the fueling of those creative ventures that give this phantasmagorical experience called life meaning.

As we can enhance the integrity of self by accepting our mortality (a mandatory step if we are to rest confident in the conviction that our metaphors are not contaminated by an unconscious fear of dying), so can we mold our self-concepts by holding firm to our determination to be honest with ourselves (and others), and to abjure—as the death it is!—lying to ourselves about our motives.

A suggested instance of not being true to one's own self (not accepting responsibility for one's metaphors) may be found in the case of my artist friend alluded to above who, though now deceased, achieved a maturity grounded in integrity and a mastery in his field that may well survive us both.

As people can elect to hide from themselves responsibility for honest effort in the world of real-life performance, so may they choose the escape hatch of mental illness as a way of avoiding a complication they doubt their ability to survive.

This version of escape-hatch, here called mental illness, is not (according to the philosophy of metaphor) always a random act of a lost and disoriented soul. On the contrary, it may be a calculated ploy—the creation and adoption of a system designed to save the individual from the anarchy of absolute nonentity, disintegration of one's sense of self.

Some years ago, I had as a student an Army veteran, self-named Ringo, who informed me—not reluctantly—that he had been diagnosed by military psychiatrists as paranoid schizophrenic. He was highly intelligent, as indicated by his vocabulary and his poetry, and his illness was sufficiently under control, thanks to medication, for him to function reasonably well in an academic setting.

In a wide-ranging counseling session one day, he talked openly about his system for coping.

Once, he said, while hospitalized at a veterans' hospital in Bethesda, MD, he decided to walk nude to the hospital foyer to get a pack of cigarettes.

When a nurse informed him he was behaving inappropriately, he responded by telling her that the label she and her fellow operatives had tagged him with allowed him to behave in any way he chose. "After all, you have classified me as crazy, and crazy people act crazy."

He went on to recount a comment he made to his current psychiatrist: "My world is my own. I don't like your world. I can make my world whatever I choose."

Next, he told me about his dog, a German shepherd he had trained to attack anyone—even Ringo himself. "I've allowed him," he said, "to revert to his natural self."

Finally, we talked about hostility and its effect on his sense of self—how it had the effect of eliminating from his life the opportunity for anything like joy.

His response: "Seeing the bastards dead is my idea of joy!"

Analysis of the above statements, as well as other unreported aspects of our conversation, persuades me that Ringo was indeed schizophrenic. He had devised a way of thinking whereby he could exist on his own terms in his own world.

He had, in other words, built a metaphorical system in which he was free to hate, to blame, a mode of coping from which he could safely hatch his monomaniacal dreams of ultimate revenge against a cruel universe. In this system, his suffering could no longer be blamed on him.

Furthermore, he had literally transformed his dog into an image of himself, using against this animal the methods he perceived his father and society as having used upon him.

The dog's freedom was literally the same as his master's!

When his dog attacked him, "Ringo" was actually glad.

In the meantime, the second knuckle on his right hand was a mass of scarred and clotted tissue from incessant gnawing, and he suffered from a virulent form of disabling arthritis—both forms of self-cannibalism descriptive, as seen by me, of his metaphor of self: a locked-up victim of a self-created escapist system.

The following is one of his poems, published with his permission:

The Spider of Life

Like a spider in a web
Eyes piercing like steel
Cutting to the very soul

Slowly dissolving what is good
Leaving only the piercing pains
Of a life slowly grinding to a halt.
The fly twisting, squirming to get free,
The more he struggles the more
Entangled he becomes.
The spider of life sits idly by
Laughing and enjoying the show.
Tired, so tired, the fly
Grows less and less
Concerned about being trapped
And slowly agonizingly drifts
Toward the comfort of everlasting sleep,
An end which will free him
From his earthly bonds.
The spider licks his lips.

—Ringo

The poem is a bit careless of syntax, and it is not clear where the suffering of Ringo begins and the fly's starts, but the poem successfully captures the sense of imprisonment Ringo suffers.

Unable to live with an image of himself as a person self-perceived as blighted from birth, "Ringo" had, in my opinion, created a substitute system in which some form of self-concept could survive. It is a tragic divarication onto the path of metaphoric open-endedness and a turn away from responsibility for constructing a functioning concept of self.

It is an example of how the human knowledge of physical mortality can be distorted into self-hatred and self-repugnance so intense as to become its metaphorical equivalent—the death of self itself.

Thanks to his system, "Ringo" was alive but dangling in the jaws of grisly death.

My artist friend's way of coping with his feelings of inadequacy was certainly less extreme than Ringo's. On the contrary, his is the system adopted by most of us.

Still, had my friend continued his selected system of coping, it would have morphed into an avoidance system with crippling consequences for his level of being, both as a person and an artist.

But existing somewhere within the boundaries of these two systems—hiding behind language, as my friend the artist did, or inventing a psychosis whereby one's anger at oneself may be diverted onto the world—there exists yet another strategy of avoidance.

I have a special friend, a university graduate in psychology, who writes beautiful poetry and once painted truly exceptional pictures. Despite these artistic traits, and because in recent times she is subject to extended periods of immobilizing depression and anxiety, her creativity has virtually disappeared.

What follows are the facts of her psychological biography as I understand them.

She was reared by introverted parents who, because of their own problems, were unable to provide those consistent levels of "enfolding and holding" infants require (and deserve) to feel good about themselves.

Because she did not receive consistent reflections of worth and affection from her parents, in the way of all children she came to perceive herself as devoid of lovableness and to blame herself for the lacking, thus developing intense feelings of unworthiness, feelings she tried (as a child) to submerge in games of private play.

This decision to submerge one's feelings (whether through mind blank or private play) is a reflexive path readily accessible to children, and in her case it seems to have provided a way of avoiding stress.

It was a system that in the passage of time would normally have been discarded in the interest of more rewarding ways of functioning; however, in the case of my friend, a series of unfortunate circumstances conspired in such a way as to encourage continued use of this defensive system.

In the same way survival drive will spread to the limits of its potential, filling every crack and crevice within an environment, so was my friend's early system a metaphor capable of expansion—though, as it turned out, only within the narrow limits of a system founded on introversion.

Within the confines of this system, she could, for instance, learn to speak, write, and cipher. She could understand systems of science, draw and paint, and run and jump and shout.

Unfortunately, the system allowed no room for people other than immediate family members, and, as it turned out, even some of them were excluded.

It was suggested above that circumstances configured themselves in such a way as to encourage her continued use of a system slanted in the direction of introversion. These circumstances included, as mentioned, highly introverted parents.

In addition, the family residence was in a rural farming community, on land owned by a highly introverted and controlling paternal grandfather. Playmates were practically non-existent, though she speaks vaguely of one early girlfriend and more definitively of a male first cousin.

Otherwise, her relationships revolved around family members, primarily her paternal grandmother (whom she loved unconditionally) and an only brother who early on exhibited schizophrenic symptoms.

(Her father was a distant, father-dominated figure and her mother a classic model of the traditional schizophregenic parent.)

The first years in school generally provide the basis for transition to non-familial relationships as friendships develop; cliques are formed; and invitations are tendered to sleepovers, to church picnics, and other community outings that provide children with opportunity to see and be seen, to make those comparisons and draw those self-concept conclusions that have the effect of integrating them into a larger community.

My friend had few of these opportunities as, even in the classroom, she continued her introverted ways. When speaking of those early years, she never failed to mention how she could not wait to get home from school to continue her private games in an abandoned store on the family premises.

Though she said little about her time in the primary grades (she and her brother, were transferred to a private Christian academy during her second year), she did make reference to a physical education teacher who treated her unfairly and to the fact that she was always the last person chosen for team sports.

From the beginning, she and her brother had seen their transfer to the Christian academy as a disaster; and they conspired together to utterly detest their classmates, who they perceived as elitist snobs.

Possibly because of this, and probably because of a presenting affect born of separateness and introversion, both sister and brother were ostracized by their classmates and treated with outright cruelty and even ridicule.

It is not appropriate at this time to inquire into why children are capable of inflicting unremitting pain on people seen as outsiders—for this, one should visit William Golding's ***Lord of the Flies***—but, as painful as the primary grades were for my friend, adolescence transformed her life at high school into a nightmare straight from hell.

Once during lunch, for instance, she took—in hopes of acceptance—an empty chair at a table occupied, not coincidentally, by a group of popular girls. Without any apparent signal, the students rose in unison and moved to another table. From that time on, she ate alone.

She tried in those early years to be friendly and to gain acceptance—once even summoning up the courage to try out for the cheerleading squad—but her efforts, as always, were rebuffed. Needless to say, there were for her no dates or prom nights.

Eventually, and inevitably, her long-standing feelings of unworthiness—so much a part of her original concept of self and repressed so long by introspection and self-imposed loneliness—resurfaced with a vengeance.

Now introversion, to which she could once retreat and hide, became the very site of her suffering. What had once been hidden was now made known to her in all its horrifying putrescence.

Confirmations of unworthiness seemed then to scream at her from every corner of her life. Even her home had become a house of horrors, with her brother acting out his fears in threats of rape and mayhem, and what smatterings of attention she had once received from parents were now deflected onto her increasingly dysfunctional brother.

Everywhere she looked, there were people making judgments, and finally the evidence was irrefutable: the external world had confirmed her worse fears, and she was unalterably flawed and despised—even by perfect strangers!

No one can survive for long under these kind of pressures, and ultimately psychological survival will mandate a different system.

Logically, speaking from the perspective of comparison psychology, any new method (metaphor) of coping will have retained vestigial characteristics of its predecessor (operant), but to be successful it must provide space for some degree of expansion beyond the limits of the outmoded (ineffective) one.

It was then, with all the qualities of revelation—as Lucifer sprung from the mind of God—that a full-blown metaphorical system blossomed into being.

Thanks to it, she could now understand the reason for her isolation, her feelings of unworthiness, her unceasing suffering. She had been, from birth, a victim of unreasonable and unfair persecution.

Her brother, whom she alternately loved and despised, and who was now enmeshed the bitter toiles of full-blown schizophrenia, provided an enthusiastic chorus of confirmation.

As can be seen, this new-found system continued the advantages of introversion—in that reality remains internal and personal—but it had the added virtue of releasing vast stores of repressed hostility originally directed inward. Now there were persecutors everywhere!

Like all systems designed to circumvent pain, however, this one possessed its own negative side effects.

Among these side effects is a self-imposed isolation in a world where standards of normalcy are set and enforced by the perpetrators of the perceived persecution. In a classic expression of double bind, the people she hates are the very people she must please if she is ever to be accepted as normal.

Thus, the first of what turns out to be many double binds is set in motion. She is damned if she does (becomes a wimp if she bows down to her enemies); and she is damned (by self-consignment to a living hell of perpetual anxiety) if she doesn't.

Thus, confined within this restricted system, she orbits between the gravities of two extremes: resistance—with its consequence of incessant anxiety—or wimpdom, with its aftermaths of failure and self-loathing.

Historically she has opted alternately for anxiety and, after heroic resistance, for wimpdom. And the consequences to self-image, needless to say, are dreadful.

In the meantime—consigned to ever-recurring double binds—she takes prescription medication for anxiety, insists she cannot bear the anxiety without the medicines, and then blames herself for having the anxiety in the first place.

Inevitably her anxiety is intensified by self-blame. She takes more medicine, exceeding the recommended dosage and doing so out of a feeling of anxiety-produced persecution, and then complains that she is doing serious damage to her brain and will end up stupid and incompetent.

Thus, it is that—as with the metaphorical system she has created to avoid self-concept inadequacy—the medicine becomes a self-fulfilling prophecy, leading back, as all self-concept metaphors do, to self-concept.

Pain becomes a consequence of the effort to avoid pain, and she has come full circle. In so doing she has cut herself off from all feelings except anger and pain, thereby created a greater pain, a large aspect of which is her inability to feel those normal and reaffirming emotions common to healthy human beings.

Having said this, having characterized her pain as growing out conscious choices in the interests of avoiding pain, it must be said there is no intent on my part to assign blame. Indeed, the pain she feels is very, very real, and the bravery she brings to battling it is nothing short of heroic.

It is a sad consequence of the fact that the uninformed are prone to non-affirming choices. It is a consequence comparison psychology is designed and exists to prevent.

Let me try to be more specific, though. That feeling of unworthiness she was hiding from when she resorted to private play in the shadowy recesses of her grandfather's old store was more than a childish creation born of feelings of rejection.

What she was feeling was a fear as ancient as protoplasm—terror framed in terms of rotting death and engrained archetypically in her genes for centuries. As with all of us, it was nearby and immediately accessible.

In other words, her fear of rejection—or more precisely her dread of what it means—reached back, metaphorically, to the earliest origins of matter and that dream of ghastly death that impels (indeed created!) survival drive. It is metaphor in action, but metaphor unsupervised.

Even more significant: every failure, every fleeting twinge of self-doubt, every perceived slighting by a friend was attracted magnetically to that bed-plate of her (and our) being where it clusters, festers, yes, and ferments to her (and our) eternal pain.

It is for these reasons that breaking out of our self-protective systems is no simple task. Like a spider's egg sac, positioned in the protected center, our cocooned selves are encased and bound by a thousand silken filaments spun from the saliva of self-pity and rationalization—all designed to immure the metaphor that is self from pain. More to the point, it is a system easily accesssed.

My friend is trapped in a system of her own making—a system where double binds multiply and incapacitate. There is, in truth, no short and easy way.

In Chapter 7, I propose some specific options that, metaphorically speaking, lead up the marble steps to the portals of the temple where effervesce the wellspring waters of human freedom. Would that my friend could follow them!

CHAPTER SEVEN

Comparison Psychology:
A Decalogue for Freedom

To break out of an established psychological system—itself a metaphor and a product of survival drive—is difficult, to put it mildly! This is because, for escape to occur, survival drive must be set against itself—one metaphor imbued with survival drive directed against another propelled by the same compulsion.

This is an instance (in this document) of the infamous double bind prefigured in the conflict within matter, between solid and liquid, cold and hot, entropy and energy, health and illness, life and death.

This said, escape is not impossible, as the very process of metaphor leaping from inorganic to organic, from reflexive to hylozoic, from hylozoic to synthetic, demonstrates.

The question, though, is one of process, and the reader is reminded that while there are no ordained truths, as seen through the eyes of comparison psychology the process whereby knowledge is accessed is always the same: All human effort—scientific, psychological, or philosophical—involves study of energy fields produced by survival drive.

Therefore, while in the world of mind what we see as true has no reality other than what we assign it in the interest of survival, the process whereby we preserve self-concept is the same in all of us. We compare to survive, and in the psychological realm that is self-concept, all comparisons are, or ought to be to the extent possible, conscious.

This being said, the process by which one emancipates oneself from a system grown familiar by long usage will require a strength of will that must be found within the individual or it will not be found at all.

To that end, it is important to understand that the kind of will being discussed here can only be derived by consciously applying the drive for physical survival to the will for psychological self-sufficiency.

As it happens, self-concept will strengthen as positive results accumulate, but as there is no alternative to beginning, so is there no alternative to gritting one's teeth and bearing down hard.

In other words, one must train oneself to be always on the alert for motives. Once instinctive survival drive is detected in one's thought processes or actions (and in the world of self-concept actions and thoughts are the same), the decision must be made to retract (or purify) the survival-driven response and begin again.

Fortunately, the act of identifying the reflexive process is oftentimes sufficient to its rejection.

In comparison psychology, this analysis of motive is mandated by the imperative of integrity—defined, here, as the determined refusal to lie to ourselves about our motives, to always strive to ground our behavior in responsible action, and to avoid, as the plague it is, the easy, self-sacrificing response—that martyrdom of self demanded by social systems and many religions.

An unconsciously constructed self-concept is, by definition, an accidental one, one ungrounded in integrity and vulnerable, thereby, to the consequences of incoherence.

In addition to one's vow of integrity in all actions, another effective means to self-concept development is the accumulation of knowledge—knowledge whose possession adds to our understanding of the world around us and, not coincidentally, adds depth of substance to our concept of self. (It is a form of grounding.)

As it is in the world of cybernetics, where the analysis of data makes possible the discovery of relationships, so is it in the world of mind. Every bit of information acquired and stored in the brain is available for that compulsive activity of mind—the search for those satisfied comparisons (epiphanants) that constitutes survival.

This search for affinities is, of course, an expression of survival drive, the consequence of which is metaphor. The more bytes of information stored in the brain, the greater the odds of discovered affinities, the greater the stability of self, and the more certain the growth of self-confidence.

Ultimately, this is why—next to the requirement for parental responsibility for self-concept instruction—the provision of a quality education is society's primary responsibility. In pursuit of responsibility, comparison psychology stipulates the following: no task is too small, no act of learning irrelevant, and no failure to learn acceptable.

Every task, every skill, every accomplishment must be seen as a once-in-a-lifetime opportunity for investment in self-concept, and it follows, thus, that failure is not an option.

Time is metaphor, and no artificial limits should be set for academic success, and no one—regardless of ability or disability—should ever be allowed to fail.

Learning—the conscious search for the *aha!* experience—must be made pleasurable, and blame, impatience, and punishment cannot be tolerated.

Eventually, of course, the time comes when every person must accept responsibility for mastering assignments, for seeing this mastery as both an opportunity for a conscious investment in self-concept and for the construction of a self-built pathway to personal freedom and human fulfillment.

It is, therefore, fundamental to the concept of comparison psychology that freedom born of governed consequence is possible, and it is from the conviction that knowledge is truly freeing that the following "decalogue" is presented—not in the spirit of prescription, but as tentative prompting.

Ultimately we must, each of us, find our own way.

I.   Freedom begins with acceptance of the fact that death is unavoidable.

II.   The conscious construction of self-concept is the first responsibility of maturity.

III.   All comparisons in the realm of self-concept should be conscious.

IV.   The sense of earned merit derived from the responsible use of metaphor makes the creation of a unified sense of self possible.

V.   Assertiveness in the interest of self-concept is not only not a crime, it is an act necessary to human freedom.

VI.   Guilt is to self-concept as acid is to flesh.

VII.   The pandemic use of metaphoric open-endedness in defense of self is the psychological equivalent of suicide.

VIII.   Conforming another person to one's personal need is the ultimate act of evil.

IX.   The reversal of self-survival needs against the self is the origin of sickness in the world.

X.   The path to freedom lies in the conscious creation of liberating metaphors.

A discussion (and amplification) of each "Decalogue" follows:

I. Freedom begins with acceptance of the fact that death is unavoidable.

One morning while I was driving to work, a large rabbit sprang from the weeds alongside the roadside and dove directly into the front wheel of my car.

There was a sodden thud and, in one of those impromptu acts of perfect skill, I looked into my rear view mirror in time to witness the rabbit gathering his limbs as though to rise.

Then, in a pausing moment of acquiescence—almost as though he had remembered something—he crumpled gently to the ground.

It is that final gesture, that limb-folding acceptance of the inevitability of death, that is forever etched in my memory.

In the exuberance of the morning, in full knowledge of his youth, strength, virility—the thought of dying was nowhere in the realm of possibility and, even after the whirring silver wheels of my Mustang sent him tumbling absurdly through the morning air, the idea of death was incomprehensible to him. He assumed his muscles would respond as they always had, and he began the act of rising from the grass.

But, ah, the fact of ebbing life, of death irrefutable: no frantic wailing there, no incoherent sobs, no plaintive cries that death relent; no mournful gathering of rabbit relatives; only an unquestioning acquiescence to the law of dissipated energy.

There is a lesson in this story of this rabbit, a lesson of grace and acceptance Homo sapiens has yet to learn. From the perspective of comparison psychology, it is a lesson that must be learned if the species is ever to be free.

Before getting to lessons, though, it is important to stress that in the fact of death, we have the antithesis of survival drive, its opposite.

This opposition, mirrored not only in life but in all of nature, mandates that the urge to survive be subliminal, for if in fact death is inescapable, then life risks becoming irrational.

What being, sane of mind and memory, would struggle blindly against inevitable extinction, a mere agent of fertilization?

This is not a question that perplexes the rabbit, but it bothers us. Thus we make up logical explanations, open-ended constructions that serve the purpose of hiding from us the certainty of our death.

The fact is, however, that so long as we allow ourselves the subterfuge of self-deception, so long do we remain in bondage to our fictions—sacrificing a grounded integrity to the selfish (and foolish) interest of feeling immortal—so long do we stay entrapped.

Furthermore, the fact is, unlike the rabbit from whose mind the knowledge of the great obliterator is hidden, we humans, by reason of language, know all about it.

We commit it to memory in epic poems, write it out in squiggly hieroglyphics on the walls of pyramids, even engrave it on the burnished walls of orbiters launched into outer space. It is our pre-eminent, most-enduring obsession.

We are, however, uncomfortable with this knowledge, and, as stated, feel the need to put it—this negativity pulsating at the end of every comparison—someplace.

It is not surprising, then, that human beings—the masters of duplicity and the carriers, par excellence, of survival drive—should find a way.

It is hypothesized that the first step to obfuscation of mortality required the invention of a subliminal counterpart to survival drive itself, a space outside the parameters of consciousness where the very knowledge of death can be deposited and forgotten.

It its earliest form, this metaphorical space probably owed its origin to the reflexive act of physically removing oneself from proximity to danger—something easily accomplished in a mental world by choosing to think of something else.

From this reflex we evolved those dependency strategies of displacement referred to as repository metaphors, mind blank, and scapegoating.

But death, the bleating antithesis to survival drive, would not be quiet. Lurking predators saw to that; parents died against their children's wishes; and war and the perennial stench of rotting flesh were everywhere.

The more the fear of dying was submerged, the more it magnetically attracted to itself all manner of forbidden flux. Guilt took up residence there, as did feelings of inadequacy, and all the while, from every side, the dong, dong, dong of mutability rang out interminably.

Ultimately this fear of death was joined by its psychological correlative, the fear and fact of insanity—since insanity, like death, represents the loss of control in the realm of self. This linkage leads inevitably to our many strategies undertaken in defense of self.

Furthermore, the fear of insanity having been made the metaphorical equivalent of death, the feared dissolution of self is now accompanied by the shrieking invocation of historic death fears embedded in our cells going back to the very origins of protoplasmic life.

This compounded horror necessitates the creation of even more complex systems of avoidance, among them being autonomic mirroring, the various neuroses, psychoses, etc. As a result, we are trapped in systems of our own making—systems geared by survival drive and within which we seek to hide from ourselves the final fact of our mortality.

This is complicated further by the creation of dependency metaphors prefigured in the concept of a sustaining father, immortal parent, or parents, who cannot die and who, given sufficient loyalty, will generously bestow life everlasting upon their favorites.

Such dependency metaphors also include the accumulation of wealth (the metaphorical correlative of undeath), the anthropomorphizing of nature, and belief in reincarnation. Obsessed with these, persuaded of their validity, we can displace for a little time the thought of our demise.

To this end, then, we devise for ourselves deceptive systems whereby the knowledge of certain death is kept at a distance, if not gainsaid outright.

It is, from the perspective of comparison psychology, an act of self-deception that strikes directly at the heart of personal integrity—the one necessary ingredient (as iterated many times!) of a responsibly constructed sense of self.

It follows therefrom that accepting the inescapable fact of mortality—recognizing and accepting the extreme lengths to which an irrational fear may drive us—and committing ourselves to the creation of no self-deceptive systems, will free us from the self-based charge of hypocrisy, preserve our sense of integrity, and prepare us to willingly follow the steps necessary for individual freedom.

When we lie, we know it; and committing ourselves to wish-it-were-true hypothesies—out of a genetically instilled reflexive drive to survive—constitutes the ultimate hypocrisy and dooms to death an honest (and necessary) commitment to integrity in the realm of self.

Thus it can be seen: freedom begins with acceptance of the fact that death is unavoidable.

II. The conscious construction of self-concept is the first responsibility of maturity.

There was once a college chaplain who would address the student body on his favorite subject—maturity. He would firm his lips into a thin, straight line; stare sternly down upon the assembled students, and proclaim maturity the end goal of all education.

This mannerism of lip, accompanied by a Jovian demeanor, led eventually to one professor's sardonic definition of maturity as the way one holds his mouth.

The chaplain's concept of maturity, based on a firmly held notion of what right thinking was and what appropriate behavior consists of, is most assuredly not the version of maturity being proposed here.

Maturity is, in fact, the way one holds one's mind.

It was said earlier that the child has easy access to reflexive metaphors, and a child's dependency is a fact of its life; and, needless to say, self-concept construction is not a prime survival issue during infancy.

However, with the advent of adolescence—with increasing pressures for self-sufficiency, and with socially mandated expectations for adulthood—self-concept becomes a crucial survival issue. In fact, to continue the dependencies of infancy is to remain an infant in an adult frame.

It is not surprising, then, that at this point in life (the very point in life where responsibility for constructing a personal sense of self is thrust upon adolescents) that the various forms and rites of initiation are invoked in all human societies—ancient and modern.

It's as though every action taken in the exuberance of youth is in some way an insult to adult survival—that somehow it is mandated from on high that behavioral standards must be set and enforced by adults.

It is, of course, the drive for psychological survival—a fact largely unrecognized and subliminally driven—that motivates adult enforcers to initiate and enforce those practices responsible for establishing tribal policy.

(And not to be ignored is the self-righteous joy the enforcers of these rites of passage feel.)

The following letter to the editor (***Raleigh*** [NC] ***News and Observer***, 26A, 10/17/93) provides a case in point:

> The contents of your recent news article concerning sanctioned "sleepovers" at UNC-Chapel Hill were appalling. Then your front page lead story the next day, "Social ills beg for answers," asks for help from universities. What a contrast!
>
> We are not so naive as to think that students are not sleeping with each other or that underage drinking does not go on at the university, just as children will test rules and authority at any age; however, we strongly oppose the condoning and endorsement of this kind of behavior.
>
> School administrations and fraternities/sororities are working together to foster acceptable, responsible actions by students with regard to drinking.

This process was begun not only because of concern for the students but for the liability involved with safety. Money talks!

We suggest, with the new sleep-over ruling, that the university be held liable for all contracted sexual diseases, date rapes, pregnancies and abortions. That should give some food for thought.

Also, if alumni, parents and friends who give aid to UNC-Chapel Hill will withhold their monetary support, someone is going to notice, and it won't be the children who are running the school.

Jim and Harriet Hill

It is tempting to let the letter speak for itself, but too many years in the classroom turns one pedagogical.

The pervasive tone (attention should be paid to grammar and style!) of the letter is paternalistic, sarcastic, and authoritarian, and the underlying expression of physical survival drive leaps out in such well-worn phrases as "money talks" and "food for thought."

The pragmatism always associated with physical survival drive is particularly apparent in the idea that the university should be held "liable" for all cases of sexual diseases, date rapes, pregnancies, and abortions.

This impossible standard (literally a form of blackmail) is the message of a subliminal survival drive frozen into certainty: "Live according to my mandates or be damned forever to (the equivalent of) lakes of burning fire!"

Most offensive to me are the references to "children" and the clause "and it won't be the *children* who are running the school."

Were Jim and Harriet to have their way, freedom would be an insurance package, and the world would be peopled by carbon-copy children!

The concept of maturity proposed by the Hills is exactly the opposite of the concept I would have applied; for if maturity owes anything to intellectual integrity, the standards of measurement must belong to and be the responsibility of those persons whose task it will be to live with the consequences of actions taken.

Next to that early holding and enfolding discussed already, conveying this message of freedom and personal responsibility for construction of self-concept to our offspring is not only the primary parental responsibility; it is (or should be) the mandate guiding all institutions of higher learning.

No person—chaplain or priest, parent or president—has the right to conform anyone to that person's version of truth or personal tastes. To do so, for whatever reason, is the highest form of tyranny.

Even so, driven as we are by the unconscious motivator, we expend our greatest efforts in assuring that our children be recreated in our images, that we survive—not only in these carriers of our genes, but in our moral attitudes passed down through generations.

Not only is this act of molding destructive to the concept of personal freedom—for who can be really free when locked inside a preconceived program that being a role model requires?—it also represents a blatant instance of one person or people applying their rules of survival (be they moral or physical, it is all the same!) to another in contradiction of the professed parental goals we have for our children—that of self-concept enhancement and survival competence.

This is why it behooves us to give thought to the day-by-day business of constructing our own self-concepts—something that will happen whether we think about it or not.

The responsible construction of self-concept requires our taking conscious thought as to the effect each action taken—or contemplated and not taken—will have on the way we feel about ourselves. This involves doing all we can to make sure that everything we do is an investment in feeling positive about the selves we have constructed.

To assume that such self-imposed attentiveness to our inner motives has the effect of turning us into conforming prigs—unfeeling automatons without capacity for experiencing pleasure and excitement in our lives—is to fall victim to an unwarranted assumption this book is written to disprove.

There is no pleasure attainable like that coming from a realized sense of self—a state of mind that liberates the individual to confident adventure; to the delight of humor found in irony; and to the testing of joyous possibilities in language, music, and the fine arts.

Ideally, then, the process of constructing self-concept should begin early— by adolescence at the latest. For those of us beginning late, the task will be hard, but we can begin where we are—recognizing that systems invented to protect self-concept hold us captive at the very stage where we adopted them.

Since self-assessment must begin the process, some questions— bringing to bear upon them a commitment to absolute honesty—such as these might prove helpful:

1. Are my life principles my own, or they copied?
2. If my principles were willingly adopted, were they adopted out of sloth or cowardice?
3. Am I obsessive about money and matters of physical security?
4. Do I swallow my convictions in the interests of friendship, job security, or promotions?
5. Am I beset by feelings of unworthiness or incompetence?
6. Do I take shortcuts at work or lie to my supervisor?
7. Am I a habitual user of escapist substances?
8. Do I make and violate love commitments?
9. Do I suffer feelings of guilt when I do something exclusively for me?
10. Is the need for reflective affirmation (the approval of others) a dominant factor in my life?

These questions are by no means exhaustive, and the responses given are issues of individual integrity; however, from the perspective of comparison psychology, a preponderance of affirmative answers suggests a dependent personality—one that would profit from self-assertiveness in the realm of self-concept.

Those individuals are most free who are most independent (secure in their knowledge of self), and this kind of freedom can never come from conformity.

III. All comparisons in the realm of self-concept should be conscious.

Comparison psychology holds that, to the extent possible, comparisons should be conscious in the interests of self-concept construction; to know that we are in fact free of reflexive influence, our comparisons ought to be weighed constructs, subject to analysis for instinctive motivation.

Even so, it is important to recognize that decisions consciously made do not necessarily mean that what is built is a responsible construction. Sometimes immaturity intervenes, and sometimes we are simply afraid. As no self-concept is fully formed at birth, so do all self-concepts waver.

Furthermore, the speed with which the human brain discovers affinities surpasses, at times, the power of will to isolate and evaluate. This said, we can be responsible for those metaphors we are aware of.

As stated, self-concept was an outgrowth of humans having to assume responsibility for actions taken in the interests of personal survival and of their need (an inevitable corollary) to make sense of a chaotic world teeming with conflicting stimuli. As such, self-concept must be seen as the agent of psychological survival, and it is in the best interests of our psychology that it be a conscious construct.

As it is in the physical world, so is comparison the means of survival in the phenomenal one.

For instance, in the same way that the hylozoic metaphors of herding and farming require specific and even long-range comparison strategies to assure the physical survival of an agrarian people, so, too, do self-concept metaphors require a like attention.

As a haphazard farmer will eventually starve, so will inattention to the needs of self-concept (such as the engrained habit of motive analysis) lead to an impotent and insecure self—and, at the extreme spectrum, to insanity.

For survival strategies to work—on physical or psychological levels—they must be conscious, they must be remembered, and they must be practical. As one would not troll for minnows with a trawler's net, so should one not stalk Moby Dick with a frogging gig.

And, because these metaphors are conscious and may be practical, we are empowered to make comparisons that are in our best survival interests—be those interests physical or psychological. We can, with practice and from a position of confidence, learn to compare in ways that enhance the quality of our survival, including our concepts of self.

Even the failure to live up to our self-created standards is an opportunity to learn from, and not feel guilty about, mistakes. It's an opportunity to bring the full power of survival drive, expressed in the exertion of will, to the conscious creation of self-concept.

One way of determining whether our metaphors serve our best psychological interests is to evaluate them as to whether they derive from confidence or from insecurity—whether or not their underlying motive can be seen to be driven by reflexive survival drive.

If our our actions (or thoughts) are assertive and have the effect of making us feel good about who we are, we may be assured of having compared from a position of strength.

If, on the other hand, we find ourselves equivocating and floundering in the shallows of uncertainty, resorting to tactics like mind blank, we can be sure our metaphors are generated by feelings of insecurity and uncertainty. Such awareness can inform us that we have work to do and of predictable consequences should the work remain undone.

Bringing to bear awareness of this process has the effect of strengthening self-concept and preparing us for future challenges, and needless to say it is not possible to know, as it is not possible to modify, those metaphors which has not been consciously evaluated.

Perhaps an example will clarify:

I must have been seven years old, or eight, and I was working in the fields with some teenage cousins of mine, the Yarboroughs.

Today I can't recall what work we were doing, perhaps chopping cotton, but at some point in the morning one of the older cousins asked me (I being the youngest and least able) to go to the house and check the time—12:00 noon being the time when "dinner" was served.

I remember distinctly that sinking-in-the-belly feeling of inadequacy, not yet having learned to tell time, and my embarrassed determination not to reveal my ignorance. I remember, too, that long walk alongside the fence row to their residence—dreading, every step of the way, the prospect of having to reveal my ignorance to the family.

When I arrived at the house, there was no one home, and my hopes of tricking an adult into telling me the time were dashed. I remember wandering into the living room and hopelessly looking up at the clock on the mantle, only to discover its face was inscribed in Roman numerals.

It was with a flash of insight and a feeling of relief that I ran back to the field, telling my cousins I could not tell time by their clock. I recall their being miffed, but my inadequacy had been hidden (in my mind anyway) by the less-painful strategy of substituting one ignorance for another.

An analysis of this simple story provides some measure of support for the concepts being argued for here.

First of all, it is apparent I was not coming from a position of strength with respect to self-concept. Obviously I believed that my not being able to tell time was evidence of stupidity.

It is also apparent that my decision to hide my lack of knowledge from my cousins was a conscious one—a decision leading to a long and wasted trek.

It is also suggestive that I left on this quixotic mission with the blind and wistful hope that some miracle might occur, making it unnecessary for me to reveal my ignorance.

That a "miracle" occurred—in the sense that the clock happened to have a Roman face—does not account for anything; for the fact is my "revelation" grew out of a desperate desire to protect self-concept.

My wasted perambulation was, in other words, a consequence of inadequacy and most certainly not in the best interest of ridding the field of weeds or enhancing my concept of self.

(Of course, nobody was around in those days to instruct me in the tenets of comparison psychology.)

Another thing: at some point in time I learned to tell time, and even a great many of my Roman numerals, but I do not recall this experience having evoked a determination to either learn how to tell time or to master my Roman numerals—inactions I now see as missed opportunities to exercise responsibility in the realm of self.

The fact is this: a positive response is never derived from a defensive one, and I made no conscious effort to evaluate my conduct or profit from my ignorance. On the contrary, my strategy seems to have been to blank the entire episode.

As a result, I denied myself opportunity for an act of honesty (I will never know now how my cousins would have responded to an open admission of ignorance), and I deprived myself of the opportunity to make a conscious investment in my own integrity, re-enforcing my inadequacy.

From the perspective of maturity it can be stated: it is not possible to know, as it is not possible to modify (or learn from), that mental state which has not been evaluated.

One final point: deducing whether or not factors in our physical world are conducive or aversive to our physical survival is the most rudimentary form of comparison and is, as has been said, employed by all life forms.

It is understandable, then, that physical survival strategies should be carried over, adapted metaphorically, into our human efforts to secure the survival of our psychological selves.

Thus, we "run from" threats to self-concept (scapegoating) or to sanctuary ("mother" and various forms of dependency metaphors already discussed), or, alternatively, we resort to acts of physical violence or intimidation (name calling, swearing, gesturing, flushing red, grinding teeth, deep breathing, or verbal threats.)

Even the decision to respond with physical force—knowing thereby the visceral gratification that accompanies successful conquest of an enemy—comes from a conscious choice—to say nothing of a retrograde one—and constitutes the application of a physical survival tactic to a synthetic issue.

While it is understandable that we would revert to those easily accessible metaphorical structures wired into the system—submission to gravity being easier than resistance to it—it is by no means a necessary or honorable submission.

An instance in case may be found in the fact that, while the primate mind is not easily diverted from its eating and mating mandates, the growing worldwide acceptance of ecological responsibility for the planet provides some reason for optimism that re-education of ourselves (and taking the long view) is indeed possible, and ego enhancing besides.

It is important to note, as well, that when we resort to escapist tactics of the sort discussed above (the reflexive responses of flushing and deep breathing excepted) the decision to opt for an escapist solution is still apt to be a conscious one.

Furthermore, the fact that we may "choose" one or several of these responses could be seen as evidence of the fact of choice. If we can elect to choose one of them, we can elect to choose none of them. We need not be slaves—the National Rifle Association's commitment to weaponry aside!—to a defensive, unexamined survival impulse.

Let there be no doubt about it: whether we like it or not, we always choose our courses of action, because the act of not choosing (responding reflexively) is still a choice.

It is possible, then, to choose to be in charge of our responses, to respond in ways that contribute to our feeling good about our inner selves.

To do otherwise is not in the best interest of self-concept survival and eliminates the dividends a positive sense of self brings.

While it is not written in stone that every response be consciously chosen, it is imperative that those responses of which we are aware be put to the test of whether or not they are a conscious contribution to the development of a positive sense of self.

Most of us are familiar with that haunting feeling of emptiness brought about by a sense of inadequacy, and it is not uncommon to respond to such feelings by consciously structuring our worlds—physically and psychologically—so as to protect self-concept.

We can elect to do this consciously—through responsible job performance, ethical commitments to friends and lovers, and through a determined commitment to practice integrity with ourselves and others—or, failing this, we could elect to respond to our feelings of inadequacy by projecting an outward image of confidence, hoping that the appearance will become (or be seen as) the reality.

The greater the sense of inadequacy, however, the more feverish and flamboyant the projection and the less satisfying that strategy is likely to be.

Mary, the anorectic discussed in Chapter 4, projected a smiling persona—her smile being so entrancing and childlike that strangers would stop and talk with her on the street.

Earlier I referred to a student whose response to inferiority included the affectations of wearing a fedora and carrying an eagle-headed cane. While admittedly an extreme version of ego protection, variations on this device are available to all of us.

Susie Orbach (*op. cit.*, p. 89) discusses what she calls, after D.W. Winnecott, a "false self." Believing anorectics develop this self in an attempt to please a rejecting mother, she writes:

> Inevitably the false self that is taken on is alienated self, but at the same time it is the self the person comes to be in touch with, for the unnurtured real self has been split off and repressed.

What Ms. Orbach describes as a false self is better seen, I believe, as a desperate projection of an image that pleases, that works better in securing survival needs for a self perceived as being under attack.

It is not, from the perspective of comparison psychology, accurate to call this projection a false self since it is a projection the self recognizes, by necessity, as false.

(Comparison psychology—arguing from the premise of there being one self—defective or empowered, weak or actualized—does not concur in the concept of a repressed "real self" or in the currently popular idiom of "the inner child.")

This is why, generally speaking, the term "mind blank" is preferred to "repression." When an individual perceives stimuli as threatening to physical or psychological survival, that person may opt to "run away" rather than confront.

When one runs away from psychological threats, one does so by not thinking about them, by blanking the mind, or by concentrating on something else. The self-concept inadequacy so dealt with continues to exist, however, and will reappear when activated by similar stimuli.

Because the vulnerability was "run from" and not confronted or "repaired," similar stimuli will activate the same response, accompanied this time by memory of the first, the second, and the third—on and on until—no longer able to ignore the baying hounds of self-recrimination—the neurosis (the implanted neural pathway) or psychosis takes up residence in the realm of self.

The term *repression*, then, implies a bearing down, a locking up, an inhibition of forbidden thoughts or actions. It conjures up images of a heavy metal lid barely keeping under control a bubbling, boiling mess percolating in a seething cauldron.

Mind blank, on the other hand, invokes the image of a human being acting (however misguidedly) out of the desire to preserve and protect. It is an understandable—though not responsible—act of human will consciously taken in defense of self.

(This discussion of my preference for the term "mind blank" over repression illuminates, I believe, one of the important differences between comparison psychology and psychoanalysis, a difference defined for me by the distinctions drawn by Camille Paglia.

I refer, now, to the terms, *daemonic* and *Apollonian*, terms she uses to distinguish between chthonic [Dionysian] nature and the human [what she calls "masculine"] will to creativity.

It is instructive to note the similarities between her language and the quality of imagery often associated with learned discussions of the Freudian unconscious.

Notable in her work, **Sexual Personae: Art and Decadence from Nefertiti to Emily Dickinson**, [New York, 1990], pp. 5-6, for instance, are phrases such as "but earth's bowels, not its surface" [p. 5]. And, speaking of the Dionysian, "It is…the blind grinding of subterranean force, [p. 5] the long slow suck, the murk and ooze," [p. 6] "maw that spat him [man] forth and would devour him anew." [p. 9]

(She describes [p. 11] the human fetus as "a benign tumor, a vampire who steals in order to live." The so-called miracle of birth is 'nature getting her own way.'")

(This is language fraught with the energy of reflexive metaphor. It is effective because it speaks to the unnamed mystery and terror [the fear of death] that lurks within us all. At the same time, it encourages grandiloquent efforts, such as Paglia's, to justify pornography, bestiality, and sadomasochism.

(Comparison psychology is unabashedly Apollonian in the Paglian sense. It is, in other words, based on the idea that synthetic self-concept and not superego holds the reins of human posterity. It is optimistic, affirming the possibility of humans existing in a world of sunlight and purpose where survival is a factor of choice, not a stew of chaotic and unbounded survival forces.)

But to return, after an overly long digression, to the projections we use to protect self-concept: a consequence of these ways of coping will—according to the tenets of comparison psychology—result in an abrogation of that earned sense of merit necessary to a unified and positive sense of self. There are doubtlessly an unlimited number of such strategies available to us.

Whatever the strategy, if it involves avoidance, the consequence will lead to an unrealized and incoherent concept of self—the result of which is likely to be puerility.

William Wordsworth spoke of these consequences when he wrote: "We have given our hearts away, a sordid boon!" And T.S. Eliot (in the words of Prufrock from the poem by that name) intoned the same epitaph, "I have measured out my life with coffee spoons."

But our lives are ours, to conduct as we see fit.

I conduct the business of my daily life cloaked in the color of skin called white—a circumstance of genetics for which I take no credit—and (unlike the case with my black friends) it is not possible for me to know the daily dose of rancor experienced from exposure to racial prejudice.

It is, therefore, with some degree of fear and trembling that I approach this next example (and I apologize, beforehand, for the length of this exposition—a fact that likely provides some insight into the reasons for the confessed trepidation.)

The topic of the immediate discussion, the reader is reminded, is that all comparisons in the realm of self-concept should be conscious.

There is a black man (I will call him Bishop) whom I came to know through a work relationship—a man with whom over a period of years I have worked hard at trying to make a friend.

Unfortunately, as I have gotten to know him better, I have found much with which I can identify but very little I can share. It is not just that he will not let me know him, there is a blockage between us as real as rock and as impermeable as steel.

The following analysis derives from my effort to understand this blockage and the anger I perceive welling beneath it. I am intrigued, as well, by the fact that his persona has the effect of evoking a response of visceral hostility in me and in other whites with whom he works.

My analysis of Bishop (and my need for analysis may suggest inadequacy on my part) finds he has structured his life into five interlocking circles—each circle (metaphor) spiraling out from the previous one in such a way as to be descriptive—not only of the way open-ended metaphors work—but of the very process involved in formulating an image of self not tested by reality.

These interlocking circles I call: racial hegemony, psychological protectiveness, personal privacy, theological dogmatism, and autonomy in the work place. Each of these proposed circles is remarkable for its closed-endedness.

Racial Hegemony

In this first of circles, racial hegemony, everything seems to grow out of Bishop's conviction that only another black can understand what being black is like.

There is, according to him, a black way of speaking (a dialect) that communicates only to other blacks, a family lifestyle that is uniquely black and that manifests itself (as I interpret it) in a circle-the-wagons mentality when any member is threatened; and there is also black brother and sisterhood, black music, and black food.

Whites may dance around the periphery of this world, but in his opinion they can never understand its essence.

It is understandable that racial discrimination in a predominantly white society will have the effect of driving minorities to introversion and self-protectiveness; and racism—perhaps the ultimate expression of white self-protectiveness and the kind of response this book is written to eliminate—has no place in a world truly liberated from prejudice; but the fact is that hegemony has the ironic effect of assuring Bishop's alienation from a world in which he must work and prosper to survive.

More tragic, though, is the consequence that this philosophy creates a close-ended system—negating the very possibilities of empathy, insight, or understanding on the part of blacks and non-blacks alike. It creates a gulf born of a gulf—a perfect example of a double-binding defensive metaphorical system.

From the perspective of comparison psychology, Bishop's philosophy is a defensive system deriving from a position of weakness. Ultimately it is a form of pragmatism that affirms the preeminence of physical survival, and in effect says we have no control over our lives and are all victims of environment.

Racial hegemony, then, like any form of exclusion, has about it the quality of defensiveness, making it possible to intellectually justify these attitudes while, in fact, they likely originate from anger, another word for fear, another word for defensiveness.

Consequently, it is not possible for Bishop to know with certainty whether his withdrawal into hegemony was for defensive reasons or because the white power structure actually excluded him.

This uncertainty (this metaphorical open-endedness) strikes at the root of the necessary sense of earned merit that a unified sense of self requires.

Ironically, the effect of Bishop's defensive insistence upon hegemony—born though it be of personal pain experienced from white racism—is the very one the racist aims for. Not only is he cut off from acceptance by the white majority, this majority now sees him as angry and intolerant and, furthermore, feels justified in so seeing him.

A defensive system—an unconscious comparison—always bites the hand that feeds it—regardless of its color!

(In the interest of brevity the next three circles perceived as defining Bishop's way of seeing are subsumed under the headings of psychological protectiveness, lifestyle privacy, and theological dogmatism.)

Psychological Protectiveness

Bishop is insistent that no one—another black, or even his closest black friend—has the right to know his personal business. This *protectiveness* extends to feelings on any subject but public ones and means he need not share his innermost thoughts with anyone.

In the meantime, his tone of voice and the manner in which he presents his beliefs comes across as angry, arrogant, and dogmatic. His white colleagues see him as militant and close minded.

(The one exception to this seemingly iron-clad rule that no one know his personal business or his inside thoughts is his discussion among blacks about whites, a willingness apparently predicated upon the assumption of prejudices experienced in common.)

Many black men (and women) endure everyday dehumanizing prejudice at their places of work and, as a result of this perceived (and in many instances actual) insult to their man or womanhood, cannot at night—in the privacy of their own homes and out of shame and embarrassment—even tell their pain to their significant other!

286

Again, it is worthy of note that anger at the white establishment for advancement denied may be colored by anger at oneself for not having stood up to racial bigotry and may serve, itself, as the basis for a sublimated anger at the world based on feelings of personal inadequacy.

(It is possible—given the puissance of mind blank and a pervasive negative sense of self—to have adopted a defensive perspective on life without being aware of it; however, it is the unexamined life [metaphor] that allows sublimated anger at the world to eviscerate our power to be psychologically free.)

While "lifestyle privacy," is a logical outgrowth of its predecessors (if whatever goes on in the privacy of the human heart is protected, the same may be applied to one's private life) it is possible, for the first time, to see evidence of the imprimatur of an internal need on the external world.

One's outer life becomes a reflection of one's inner being, and whatever goes on in the home must also be protected territory. Even Bishop's external relationships—with his colleagues at work, with fellow church members, and with his next-door neighbors—are marked by a correct and cordial distance.

Hardly anyone outside of family visits in the home and, over the years, even family members seem to have gone their separate ways.

While Bishop speaks nostalgically of warmer times—of home-cooked meals, his closeness to his grandmother, his brothers, and an up-and-down respect for his father (whom he quotes as saying, "If you're gonna get cut, you'd better do the cutting first—not stand around waiting for the knifing"—sentiments he says he agrees with), the fact is that returning to the equivalent of those times would be seen by him as confirmation of failure to advance.

Like racial hegemony and psychological protectiveness, "lifestyle privacy" has been adapted to the need for self-concept protection, a perception supported by the fact that even here—when issues of racial injustice arise—they are discussed only from the perspectives of illegality or moral turpitude, never from the perspective of personal pain.

The side effect of anger is apparent as well.

Isolation, it strikes me, is the identifying characteristic of Bishop's life.

Theological Dogmatism

Some may regard it bizarre that "theological dogmatism" is lumped here with psychological and lifestyle privacy, but Bishop's approach to religion has taken on intriguing characteristics of his personality.

While his religious philosophy is grounded in the doctrines of charismatic Christianity—and his religious discussions inevitably emphasize its teachings—there is little evidence of contrition or of Christian empathy in the persona he presents to the world.

In those charismatic faiths I am familiar with, religious and self-concept issues seem to be tied together—often overlaid with a strong component of guilt (one of the great advantages of a born-again Christianity being the consequence of instant identity)—in Bishop's case, however, he and his Christianity seem to exist in separate spheres entirely.

Bishop's religion—as with racial hegemony, psychological protectiveness, and lifestyle privacy—functions as a cloak he wears to keep the world from asking questions, as a shield he carries to insure his privacy.

Given the outward show of wearing his feelings on his sleeve, Bishop's admitting to vulnerability of any type would likely threaten his carefully constructed and protected citadel of self. In any event, he never does it.

It is supportive of this argument that Bishop's church membership has that same quality of separateness in a crowd. The membership is exclusively Afro-American, with high-church pretensions, and—while his acts of Christian charity are his own and not to be judged by me—he most certainly doesn't "hide them under a bushel."

Even though he sings in the choir and is a church deacon, he apparently has no close friends in the congregation, and while his church membership provides the appearance of community concern, he still manages an at-arms-length involvement that, as the other circles, seems to be designed for self-protection.

The effects of anger and dogmatism come across here, as well, with theological discussions rapidly deteriorating into loud and angry debates.

Autonomy in the Workplace

This fifth circle into which I see Bishop as having segmented his life—and it should be pointed out that this circle has also taken on qualities of the unconsolidated ego it has been designed to protect—is deserving of detailed discussion, for it, unlike his other realms of being, is subject to a significant intrusion—the exigencies of supervision. I refer, of course, to his world of work.

The fact of this intrusion presents a real challenge to privacy and requires that Bishop gather to himself all available weapons of protection. This means (and he told me this) that he must thoroughly assess those who hold any degree of power over him.

To this end, and by his own declaration, Bishop has made a careful study of each of his supervisors, saying, "You need this kind of knowledge to survive."

This careful study of those who have power over him informs him as to their attitudes toward him. Interestingly, it does not matter to him whether these attitudes are perceived as racist or not, for, whatever the attitudes, they will serve as information needed to secure his survival in the work place.

Truth be told, his system was designed with anticipated malice in mind, and he neither likes his supervisors nor expects that they like him.

Once Bishop has learned what the attitudes of his superiors are, he conditions his conduct upon that knowledge, striking a careful balance between ingratiation and straightforward address. Always he is prepared to evoke the cloak of affirmative action.

He is vain about "knowing the system," fights openly for salary equity, and once told a supervisor who had advised him he was lucky to have the job he had, "You can only control my salary here. I can make as much as I want if I choose to leave"—a self-protective assertion that remains untested so long as he stays.

Not surprisingly, over the years his place of work, like his home, has taken on the qualities of his psychological system. For instance, his department receives its funds from sources outside the institution. This has the effect of isolating (and protecting) him—barring illegal activities—from fiscal oversight by the institution.

Furthermore, since the funds are targeted for a specific population, the departmental services he directs address primarily the needs of a disadvantaged population. This has the effect of detaching his department from comprehensive institutional functions—an effect, in my opinion, the institution does not object to.

Finally, Bishop's staff is exclusively black, an anomaly that has not gone unnoticed within the institution. This has resulted in even further isolation and its concomitant anger.

Even a cursory analysis of this fifth circle, his work world, will indicate the existence of those qualities evident in the other circles. His work world is hegemonic, autonomous, private, and protected territory. His anger, so prevalent in the other circles, is also evident here—in his adversarial relationships with his colleagues and in his dogmatic argumentativeness.

It may be seen, then, that Bishop has created a system wherein he can maintain an image of self that is untested by reality. He has done so, however, at the expense of relationships with his fellows and at the cost of a sublimated anger that discolors and infects his public and private existence.

Bishop's projected image of himself as an in-charge person who contributes to the welfare of his community, who tolerates no unfair treatment, and who has figured out the meaning of everything is, in my opinion, chimera—a psychological version of political correctness created to hide a hidden sense of personal inadequacy.

What Bishop has done is neither evil nor unfamiliar.

Most of us, our self-concepts being haphazard, catch-as-catch-can constructions, have sought to structure our environments in the interests of physical and psychological survival much as Bishop has.

The problem is that self-concepts structured in this fashion lack the "unity" this former professor of English taught as the necessary quality of a good essay.

In other words, each "sentence" in the human essay that is psychological survival is not directed to proof of the thesis: "Empowerment comes from a responsible construction of self-concept."

The result of this lack of unity is a chaotic, ineffective system, a sense of self that is protected at the cost of unity and, as such, must receive a failing grade.

So long as Bishop continues to live within the closed circles he has fashioned out of defensiveness, he will have blocked off access to that sense of self based on earned merit (as opposed to one defensively manifested) the possession of which makes possible the creation of a unified and empowered self-concept.

Should his system abort, he would be left floundering in a sea of insecurity, and—within a set of circles, a significant human potential already showing signs of a parabolic wobble—would be sent spinning, sucked forever inward by the gravitational pull of a protected inadequacy.

It is apparent, at least from this writer's perspective, that Bishop has not taken conscious responsibility for his metaphors in construction of his concept of self, and that, as stated earlier, a defensive system always bites the hand that feeds it.

IV. The sense of earned merit derived from the responsible use of metaphor makes the creation of a unified sense of self possible.

The natural tendency of metaphor is to revert to the instinctive, that imprimatur of physical survival drive here called reflexive metaphor. From the perspective of comparison psychology, it is to this automatic proclivity that much of the evil in the world may be traced.

This instinctive response to perceived difference is responsible for racism, sexism, and homophobia—to say nothing of hate groups, and outright physical violence. A self-concept driven by impulse has more in common with our primitive ancestors than with astronauts and musicians, philosophers and scientists, poets and painters dominated by synthetic metaphors. And, if these reflexively driven people feel good about themselves, it is likely a consequence of herd acceptance, not conscious thought.

It is, of course, due to conscious thought—to a willed selection from available metaphorical choices—that even the possibility of a sense of earned merit exists. And, as previously said, feeling good about the person we perceive is (to the world of self) the synthetic equivalent of survival realized. It is tantamount to absurdity to feel good about oneself when accepting credit for an action traceable to instinct.

In support of my argument, I turn now to Frederick, the subject of a case study in Chapter Two. Frederick was a good man and a good friend, his family and mine spending time at the beach and exchanging home visits on a regular basis. Our friendship endured for over twenty years. I was saddened by his divorce, the inevitable distancing, and his subsequent spate of marriages.

It would be easy to trace Frederick's problems to some nascent form of bipolar illness, but it is apparent that early on he did not commit himself to actions contributing to an earned sense of merit—otherwise, for instance, he would've persisted in his graduate studies and in his position as a banking executive; and he would have worked at being a stabilizing influence at home.

"Of all sad words of tongue or pen, the saddest of these: It might have been."

But it is to Newt Gringrich—the arch enemy of the concepts argued for here—that I turn, thanks to McKay Coppins, staff writer of **The Atlantic** and author of the article, "Newt Gingrich Says You're Welcome," (November, 2018).

According to Mr. Coppins, Newt has long been a fan of the natural sciences, actually having aspired as a youth to being a zookeper. In this interview—conducted, interestingly, in the Philadelphia Zoo—he paraphrases the primatologist, Frans de Waal as believing "that human politics, in all its brutality and ugliness, is "…part of an evolutionary heritage we share with our close relatives…'" a view, he says, with which Mr. Gingrich agrees.

In fact, he quotes Mr. Gingrich as opining, "There is a lot we can learn from the natural world…" going on to say that Gingrich spent the day teaching him about politics and human behavior.

For instance, he [Gingrich] stipulated that the crocodile's evolutionary stability has assured their survival for 90 million years, and the lion society (the male protects and the female hunts) is the exact opposite of the "feminist vision of the world." In a paean to pragmatism., he concludes, "but it's a fact."

It's a dog-eat-dog world out there where, according to Gingrich, who sees "the animal kingdom from which we evolved for what it really is": "A very competitive, challenging world, at every level."

Of politics, Mr. Coppins quotes Gingrich as saying it is "a cutthroat war for power." And he goes on to assert, regarding his comment on the viciousness of the animal world, "It's not viciousness, it's natural."

One final quote, and I am done.

> In [Donald] Trump, Gingrich has found the apotheosis of the *primate* (my italics) politics. He has been

practicing his entire life—nasty, vicious, and uncon-cerned with those pesky 'Boy Scout' words, as he fights in the Darwinian struggle that is American life today.

In his insistence on primal values, it is easy to see how Mr. Gingrich's approach to living and politics is antithetical to my philosophy of self-concept construction as a conscious (and responsible) selection of self-enhancing metaphors. He would return us to Tennyson's anarchic world of "red in tooth and claw" and, furthermore, he would have us feel good about it.

Any "sense of earned merit" in the world of Newt Gingrich would not only be a product of herd mentality, it would be a direct path to the death of civilization.

Welcome, savages, to the "orgified" world of reflexive metaphor.

V. Assertiveness in the interest of self-concept is not only not a crime, it is an act necessary to human freedom.

It is an interesting fact of civilized life that self-centeredness (unearned pride) is seen as one of the deadliest of sins, and everywhere possible society brings to bear forces designed to deter it.

A cursory examination of the word "pride" in Roget's **Thesaurus** (first edition), for instance, reveals forty-seven nouns (eight of which are not clearly pejorative), thirty-five verbs (four of which do not convey a negative connotation), and fifty adjectives (six of which do not assign blame).

In other words, of the 132 words or phrases listed under pride, only 18 of them do not connote negativity.

Wherever such unanimity is found, the ubiquitous force that is survival drive cannot be far behind; and it is easy to see how such name-calling negativity serves the ends of survival drive as articulated in nature and society.

In nature, the ends of physical survival are best served by those in-built mental strategies here called reflexive. In estrus, for instance, the need for impregnation is clearly indicated.

When pursued by a hawk, the sparrow instinctively seeks shelter in branches; and the roar of the bull alligator in springtime informs all competitors to stay out of his territory and away from his females.

Society may itself be seen as a reflexive survival mechanism, and as such it is designed to encourage conformity and discourage individualism, to promulgate work ethics and armed patriotism, and to oppose notions such as welfare and abortion—the adoption of interests of the part being always subjugated to the well-being (survival) of the whole.

It is not just a matter, either, of fear that behavior of the one will detract from the survival of the mass—though the individual who dares to stand apart always evokes non-acceptance, ostracism, and profound distaste—there is the buried fear that members of the mass might come to prefer the practices of the few—that those things which are new and unproven will somehow be preferred over that which encourages the status quo—the safe and comfortable.

Also, it is apparent that the presence of socially enforced unanimity is a factor in securing that psychological unanimity (think survival) so valued by society, and it may well underlie that impetus for community consensus—so evident when an individual dares to resist established social traditions such as those found in religion and politics—think Martin Luther and his black namesake, King.

Because society is itself a representation of an unchallenged, largely unconscious drive to survive, it may serve as an example of the way unthinking (reflexive) responses to environmental stimuli can create double-binding systems in individuals and groups—as represented, perhaps, in responses to protests for equal rights on the part of gays, lesbians, and transvestites.

This said, there are instances when, by thinking, individual humans have managed to free themselves from society's reflexive promptings;

recent social developments offer promise that some populations within the species may be on the path to freeing themselves from that kind of reflexive thinking (an inflection point?) typically fostered and encouraged by social systems.

One example that comes to mind was the enthusiasm with which the antiwar and anti-establishment movements of the sixties swept the country, in the as-yet-to-be-finished feminist accomplishments of the eighties, and in our grudging progress in race relations.

Additional bases for hope are suggested in the dissolution of the socialist states of East Germany and the USSR, and by the expansion (reluctant though it be) of democratic systems throughout the civilized world.

One cannot help but feel pride in the relative ease with which the rights of gays were accepted in the military, and by the approval in an ever-increasing number of states of equality in marriage rights for gays, lesbians, and transvestites.

Also showing some glimmer of promise for social enlightenment may be found in the comments of Michael Shermer (**Scientific American**, 10/11/90) regarding the modern reduction in homicides—by rates of 110 murders per 100,000 in fourteenth-century Oxford, compared to less than 1 per 100,000 in mid-twentieth-century London. He credits this reduction to "the readiness to control one's emotions."

I, of course, credit highlighted progress to the developing power of synthetic metaphor to the evolving of self-concept and the increasing number of individuals willing to assert control over their reflexive compulsions.

Unfortunately, recent decisions of the U.S Supreme Court suggest a return to regressive reflexive metaphors.

Additional reasons for optimism are promised but not affirmed in the assertiveness for personal freedom as represented in the so-called "African Spring"—the movements in Tunisia, Egypt, and Libya. Similar efforts flourished fora time in Syria and even Iraq, only to find the movements stymied by fanatical forces opposed to individual freedoms.

Efforts, failed though they be, to establish a caliph on the borders between Iraq and Syria are explicit reminders of the extremes to which people will go when driven by primitive survival drive and its need for absolutism and power—the affirmation of power and survival, physical and psychological.

The gains made—though few and fleeting—indicate to me that the die is cast, the battle lines are set. Seen from the perspective of comparison psychology, it is only a matter of time until people recognize the issues at stake and refuse to tolerate the forces of tyranny.

The fore-mentioned religious fanatics, the up-in-arms NRA protesters and other right-to-bear-arms fanatics, a Supreme Court's affirmation of the people-rights of corporations, and a Congress dead set on building anew a city built atop a seventeenth-century hill and a frozen view of the Constitution, all will crumble before the onslaught of coming freedom.

There will always be resistance. The comfort found in the status quo is addictive, and nowhere is this more than true than in the realm of personality. However, the path is clear. The only path to real and lasting freedom is our acceptance of the responsibility for the conscious construction of self concept. Failing our willingness to take this step, there are powers out there more willing and ready to make our decisions for us.

Viewed from the perspective of comparison psychology, the steps involved in the process of self-actualization are spelled out in the adventure novel *Angel Eyes* by Eric V. Lustbader (N. Y., 1991), p. 280):

> "Thought takes time," the Man of One Tree had told her [Honno] early on in her stay [on the island of One Tree].
>
> "And it takes effort, because you must decide which thoughts will improve you, which will impair you. You must think of your mind as a garden that needs constant attention. You must study and discuss your studies to

feed it, you must regularly seek the silence and isolation essential for periodic weeding, enabling the memory of features at the next deeper level. The richer one's experience, the greater the variety of patterns that person can use as pathways to general principles."

It is impressive that two individuals—separated by so much time and distance—should come up with precepts so similar in philosophy as those shared by Mr. Lustbader and me; but, speaking for myself, I can only express my gratitude for the philosophical support the novel provides and assure the reader that the concepts shared in common existed in comparison psychology long before 1991.

This said, attention is directed, first, to the reference to time and thought. Time—when measured by the hands on a clock, the days and weeks on a calendar, genealogical or geological history—is a strictly metaphorical concept; however, when measured on the finite clock of the number of possible actions within the span of a lifetime, it takes on a finite quality.

Actions (and conscious thought is always an action) are a necessary constituent in self-concept construction; they are real; they must be chosen consciously—as positive investments in the construction of one's image of self; and, as affinities are made possible by study, so is time energized by actions and thought taken in the best interests of self-concept.

The construction of self-concept is a process involving both time and conscious thought, operations entrenched and made habitual by practice.

That the process is enabled by taking conscious thought is emphasized by the fact that Honno's master requires her to evaluate each thought on whether it will *impair* or *improve*—a requirement, oft-stated in this document, as necessary to taking responsibility for one's metaphors.

Note, also, that Honno is instructed to *study* and *feed* the garden that is her mind—also essential to the process of storing knowledge in the interest of metaphorical creativity as well as showing assertiveness in one's own best self-interest. Of particular interest is the following passage:

> The richer one's experience, the greater the variety of patterns that person can use as pathways to general principles.

I interpret this to mean that study (and by implication carefully chosen actions) are necessary to metaphor and to the development of a realized self-concept—the "general principles" being metaphors arrived at as a result of conscious study leading to synaptic storage and the consequent proximity of ideas—the more knowledge, *the greater the probability of discovered affinities.*

The references to "silence" and "isolation" resonated with me in that I, too, sought both qualities in my removal to the farming community of Bailey, NC—as necessary elements in my campaign for uninterrupted serenity and self-concept assertiveness—the presence of distractions being obvious deterrents to psychological equilibrium and a threat to its very survival.

Assertiveness in one's self-interest—in addition to the properties of silence and isolation—also requires the willed application of consciousness.

Work done by Professor William K. Estes, PhD, of Harvard University, supports the importance of learning (an act of consciousness) in an article found in *Psychology Today* (September-October 1993, Vol. 26, No.5, 18).

He is said (by the article's unnamed author) "to have established that learning expertise exists on multiple levels, the most superficial [of which] is pattern recognition."

He continues:

> Estes's own studies of learning show that every instance of experience is recorded in memory as a pattern of specific features, each of which becomes a category enabling the memory of features at the next

deeper level. The richer one's experience, the greater
the variety of patterns that person can use as pathways to general principles.

While the reference to pattern recognition being "superficial" is
confusing—comparison being seen here as the very basis of metaphor—
the article's references to richness of experience and the variety of patterns support the concept of metaphor being argued for here, as "the
memory of features" makes possible the discovery of patterns and the
epiphanant act of metaphor. The more we know, the more we can dive
into experience and mine new and more complex metaphors.

An individual's determination to be assertive in the interest of a
developed concept of self through a conscious enabling of "richness of
experience" is an important step on the path to psychological freedom.

In addition to Honno's studies to enrich (implant operants) in the
garden that is mind, referred to above, it is important to emphasize that
Honno's work on self-concept included extended and exhausting practice sessions in the martial arts—an important emphasis on the close
relationship (indeed an imperative one) existing between the physical
and the metaphorical.

In fact, it may be said that the very grounding of that psychological
metaphor that is self-concept is dependent upon conscious actions taken
in the name of integrity.

In further support of my conviction that the conscious selection of
actions and ideas are necessary to a consolidated sense of self, I now cite
a column by Terry O'Keefe published in *The Asheville Citizen-Times*
(7/09/12, E3).

He writes of "two decision-making systems" in the brain, one of
which is the anterior cingulate cortex (ACC), which he says "houses a
sophisticated pattern-recognition system." (The other is the prefrontal
cortex, the "house" of conscious thought.)

He says, of the ACC, "Even if we can't directly access these [dopamine] neurons, we can *train* them." [My italics.] He goes on to suggest that this "training" has to be a conscious effort. Though his emphasis is on the correcting of errors, the process is precisely that one proposed by me and enjoined on Honno by her master.

This suggests, convincingly I believe, that willed consciousness in the realm of self-concept development is not only possible but mandatory—as the following personal experience purports to illustrate.

Twenty-five years ago, at the end of an unsatisfactory marriage, I stumbled on a pathway similar, in many ways, to Honno's. (An earlier reference, the reader is reminded, was made to my moving to the farming community of Bailey, NC.)

In what was contrived as a willed and conscious change of lifestyle, I set out to apply my philosophy of metaphor to my daily life—on planes both physical and psychological.

To that end, I sought to apply my concept of physical and psychological self-sufficiency to my way of living. I purchased a house in the country, complete with a sizable garden plot, and I practiced intensive physical conditioning exercises and ran two miles every other day.

In alliance with my goal of physical self-sufficiency (and in the interests of life sufficiency) I quit smoking; hung a clothesline between two sapling oaks in my backyard; and purchased a wood stove, a chain saw, a wood-splitting maul, and a 1957 Chevrolet Apache pickup for the collecting and transporting of firewood.

In this return to self-sufficient living, I was setting in place the physical conditions I hoped would facilitate a metaphorical shift—a translation of physical self-sufficiency into self-concept actualization—eliminating, as by-product, my lifelong perception of myself as a practicality klutz.

I enjoyed success in gardening and in heating my house with firewood, and in continuing my exercise regimen, but in five years my mission of self-sufficiency was sorely tested by the loss of funding for my job as coordinator of a youth employment and training program and by a demoralizing stretch of unemployment.

In addition, because of circumstances beyond my control, my two youngest daughters came to live with me.

Not deterred from my goal of physical and psychological self-sufficiency—though with some sacrifice of serenity and privacy—I continued work on this book, continued seeking employment according to the stringent requirements of the NC Employment Security Commission—and managed to survive, in the meantime, on savings and unemployment insurance.

Eventually, savings having been depleted, I made a decision that turned out to have unexpected ramifications for my search for self-concept sufficiency.

I remember carrying the envelope requesting early retirement to my mailbox as though it were yesterday. I had struggled with the decision, knowing it could have negative impacts on my lifetime dream of early retirement and full-time writing.

So, the complications behind mailing that envelope were considerable, but what stands out in memory was the sudden surge of sheer pleasure I experienced on my way back from the mailbox to my house.

It was—as I was aware at the time—a far more intense feeling than the situation seemed to warrant. There was not a great deal of money involved—certainly not enough to eliminate the financial stress we were experiencing—and I had elected the option stipulating that all payments end upon my death—not, within itself, an obvious cause for elation.

Needless to say, I was intrigued by my emotional response and, over the succeeding months, spent considerable time analyzing and trying to understand it.

Eventually I came to see it as a moment of epiphany growing out of my opting for that retirement provision whereby monthly disbursements would increase during my lifetime but end upon my dying.

I eventually concluded that in making an assertive decision about life and death, I had acted in my own best survival interests—psychologically and physically—thereby experiencing that *aha!* moment of certainty that accompanies the effective metaphor.

Though it is a conviction I cannot prove, I believe it was at that moment my work on self-concept philosophy fell into place. In a word, I was, I believe, experiencing the epiphany of self-sufficiency I had been seeking.

I believe it was no coincidence that I found employment within the month and remained employed until my retirement nine years later.

Now, utilizing the very process of metaphor and at the risk of some degree of grandiosity, I would like to compare cases—the episode involving Honno from **Angel Eyes** with that personal example described above.

Like Honno, I had studied hard, collecting information on self-concept theory, working on this document, and continuing my campaign for physical fitness and personal assertiveness—all in the interest of self-concept.

Even as Honno faithfully adhered to the teachings of her master in a tragically successful effort to erase the consequences of the label *hinoeuma* (husband killer) from her self-image, so had I acted assertively. I provided for my children's physical and emotional needs; worked hard to erase feelings of guilt for a failed marriage; and strove for physical self-sufficiency by gardening, cutting and gathering my own firewood, and thrice-weekly physical conditioning activities—all conscious actions I believe contributed to the epiphany already described.

(From the perspective of comparison psychology, it is not possible for metaphorical linkages to occur unless there be modifiable "objects" in the field of comparison—see my discussion of grounded metaphor above, pages 233-236, see also Metaphor. p. 80.)

It was (and is) a process, interestingly, involving some of the same metaphorical processes as those described in autonomic mirroring—where diseases are created that mirror psychological states.

That this mirror effect can be accomplished by the conscious evoking of autonomic functions is one area where meaningful personal input into the human experience and the development of self-concept may be possible.

In other words, as one consequence of comparison psychology and its practice, one can consciously set up proximity conditions in the "garden that is mind" so as to facilitate self-concept actualization of the sort suggested in that personal experience described above.

The process involved is, of course, the very method of metaphor—in this case facilitated by the conscious juxtaposing of chosen elements adducing to a chosen end.

I would like to end this section with a definition of freedom as seen from the perspective of comparison psychology.

Media, these days, run red with angry battles conducted in the name of freedom—be it in Iraq, Egypt, Libya, Mali, Somali, or Syria. One feels great sympathy for oppressed people denied access to the bare essentials of physical and psychological survival, but this is not the meaning of freedom sought for in comparison psychology, where freedom exists in the mind or it does not exist at all.

Freedom from physical impediments to survival is (or ought to be) a natural right—the one legitimate justification for the existence of governments.

However, granted the fact that no human should be denied the right to the pursuit of happiness—unimpeded by stupid laws, power-hungry individuals, or self-service governments—the fact is that no matter how free we are from tyranny, from poverty, from meteorological disasters, or from people telling us what we can and cannot do—perfect freedom in a physical world is not achievable. If these things do not get us, death most certainly will!

This is not to say that freedom from want and sickness and tyranny is not desirable—indeed, in a world uncontaminated by unconscious survival drive, access to these things would exist as givens—but, if real freedom is ever to be attained, it will exist in the mind unfettered by mental disease and the variety of hypocrisies invented by humans to obscure and sublimate their fear of dying.

It is to this view of freedom that comparison psychology and its theory of responsibility for self-concept is dedicated.

We are born without input into our genetic makeup and without choice of parentage, geography, or economic standing.

While some few of us may have been born to wealthy parents who could provide for our every whim, and while some three hundred million of us (or so) were born in the United States of America—some with parents who urged them to study, work hard, and save money—others were born without these benefits.

This said, there is one thing—regardless of birth circumstance—that each of us does have access to: the right to assertively construct our own concepts of self in such a way that not only are the blessings of life, liberty, and the pursuit of happiness available for the taking, but—most important—we can lay claim to an empowering sense of worth and competence that a self-sufficient concept of self makes possible.

Assertiveness in the interest of self-concept is not only not a crime, it is necessary if we are ever to be truly free.

VI. Guilt is to self-concept as acid is to flesh.

It is hard to conceive of a more useless emotion than guilt, and yet it is a factor—in varying degrees—in every human's psychology, one inevitably traced to self-concept inadequacies.

Freud, not coincidentally a Victorian, traced guilt to the failure of the recalcitrant child (id) to please the dictatorial parent (superego), and saw it as triple plated onto the human psyche as a consequence of that ultimate reversal of power—the seduction of the parent in the people of Electra and Oedipus.

Sex is obviously the boogieman.

World religions have made much of guilt as well, primarily through their emphasis on the failure of the created to please their creator. Their discussions of sin and disobedience seem designed to encourage reformation through the laying on of guilt. Come judgment day, they teach, the guilty goats will be separated from the pious sheep.

Sin is obviously the boogieman.

Parents have been known to use guilt in conforming behavior, and these same parents have seen it used by their children—and against them; our courts pronounce it, as a consequence of failure to conform. Students who fail to study (or retain for regurgitation prescribed instruction) find it documented in the grades they are given.

Failure to conform is the obvious boogieman.

Whatever guilt is found, its roots are embedded in physical survival traceable to that earliest, most primitive, form of survival drive—that pragmatic directive to survive and reproduce at all cost. Failure to perform as "instructed" constitutes a violation of that prime directive, and punishment in the form of guilt rapidly ensues.

As a consequence of this natural pragmatism, the agent whose psychological survival is threatened (recall the infant denied holding and enfolding?) inevitably traces its cause to itself.

Susie Orbach (*op. cit.*, p. 88) addresses this issue:

> Unable to condemn the caretaker, who is still much needed, the developing person takes into itself the idea that it is not the response of the caretakers needs that are inappropriate, but rather the needs itself expresses that are causing the problem. Thus, it berates itself for its needs and attempts to bury them, creating a fantasy world in which negatively experienced aspects of the caretaker, the bad object, are reconstructed.

I find the references to a fantasy world—perchance she means non-literal?—in the last sentence confusing since, by her own statement, Ms. Orbach traces the child's problems to perception of itself as "the bad object." Even so, she places her finger directly on the survival issue.

Thus, it is to the thought "There must be something wrong with me, else I would be getting fed" that comparison psychology traces the origin of guilt. As it is with food, so is it with guilt—the consequence of our inability to feel good about the self we perceive. It is an implanted seed—the source of defensiveness?—destined (if not designed) to be fed by failure.

It rears its ugly head on that day we experience hunger and are not fed.

This hunger sets off the warning system, implanted in the circuitry of the brain, of an imminent threat to survival. The resultant feelings of insecurity are immediately translated by the helpless infant into a fear that food will not be provided, and the result is that piercing midnight scream all parents know.

Even though the infant be fed immediately, that moment of screaming panic is forever seared into brain pathways and will serve forever as the metaphorical template for feelings of inadequacy with death-plated perceptions of oneself as unloved, and, inductively, unlovable.

Even though traceable to infancy, the manifestations of guilt, like all metaphors, are rapidly turned into an adult consequence.

I once had occasion, at a training seminar, to unkindly characterize buzzards as the ultimate pragmatists—creatures committed to the primacy of survival regardless of their means of getting it.

I went on to lament the human use of this mandate to justify all manners of evil and to plead that finding funding be secondary to our working for people.

This tension—between a pragmatic insistence on the preservation of flesh and my plea (hopefully owed to a more evolved expression of survival drive) for humanistic idealism—symptomizes the dilemma of

Homo sapiens trapped between a mechanistic urge to maintain the gene pool and the evolutionary mandate to widen the boundaries of psychological survival in the realm of self.

It is the biblical replay of the saga of Genesis: Eve tendering Adam the apple of knowledge (and he, sometimes later, trying to save himself by blaming her), the pragmatic Cain slaying the poetic Abel, and the consequence always the same—the inner apprehension of a horrendous and monstrous guilt (or sin, for they are synonyms).

We are, then, locked in a double-bind dilemma—damned if we do and damned if we don't. If we ignore the mandate to survive and multiply—opting for abortion, for instance—survival drive (and anti-abortion forces) will shower us with guilt. If we submit to the urge to survive for the sake of surviving, our self-concepts will suffer injury.

Guilt derives, in the first instance, from a perceived failure to honor the primal mandate—the directive to go forth and multiply—a coercive (albeit necessary) device of the pragmatic drive to survive.

In the second instance, frustrated survival drive serves as the grounding element (the operant) to which every act of inadequacy surges, around which inadequacy feelings cluster.

Ultimately, guilt takes on the same qualities as our fear of death—our inability to please survival drive in the realm of self being tantamount to our fear of physical death—and the machinery of double bind is put in place—the fact of death being the consummate heresy in the church of survival drive.

We can deal with guilt, then, if we recognize it as a conscious, double-bind construction growing reflexively out of our electing not to confront the instance responsible for our feelings of inadequacy.

Psychological double binds are always self-created, in the interest of protecting self-concept, and it behooves us to reject guilt on the purely selfish grounds that this way "leads the way to dusty death."

We are not obliged to serve up our own psychology on the plastic platter of engrained pragmatism.

(Driven—poor humans—by the compulsion to survive physically while burdened simultaneously with a nagging sense of disobedience to their better selves, they blow the seeds of self-determination into the winds of happenstance. Small wonder, then, that schizophrenia is a modern illness; that pro-life and pro-choice advocates clash.

(Small wonder that the NRA rises up in arms (!) when the right to kill in self-defense is threatened; that conservative political parties vie with their liberal opposite numbers; that religious fundamentalists battle their progressive counterparts.

(Small wonder that classical capitalism [in the interest of preserving capital—its metaphor for physical survival makes war on social programs for the poor; that "survival of the nation" is used to justify Water- and Contragates; that the HIV stigma can be invoked to deny entry visas; and that polluters of the environment may be protected in the interest of a thing called money.

(Small wonder that pragmatism of the body should devour survival) of the self.)

I have a friend convinced she is responsible for her mother's death from cancer. She holds that had she loved her mother as she should have, her mother would not have felt guilty about her mothering skills and would not, as a result, have immobilized her immune system. That's a long way around, in this writer's view, for a guilt trip.

(No matter that her mother tied her in her crib for hours, or threatened to commit suicide by driving off a bridge with her and her brother as passengers!)

No amount of logic can dispel this illogic because the feeling of emotional undernourishment, "metaphorized" as guilt and inadequacy, has become the dominant fact of my friend's psychological life. Every failure—many of them self-conditioned—serves but to confirm that dominant fact.

Now things have reached the point where her sense of failure begets actual failures, and her feelings of guilt and unworthiness so dominate that—as the hungry infant—the guilt and inadequacy demand to be fed, and the only food that nourishes is failure.

One of the great problems with guilt, from a counseling point of view, is that efforts to point out the fact that mental illness is a consequence of personal choices made in the interest of preserving self-concept inevitably result in the client's feeling attacked (see Renee and her "bill of complaints," Chapter 5, page 189-190).

This is because the feeling of inadequacy is so pervasive that defensiveness has become chronic.

In an effort to get around this problem, I once suggested the metaphor of a toolbox to a client. I stipulated that staying alive psychologically had evolved to the point in modern times of being a version of the primal survival mandate and assuring this form of survival was a matter of selecting a tool from the toolbox to achieve this end.

If we selected the wrong tool for the job, we could just put that tool back and select another. None of the tools in the box was evil, I said, just effective or ineffective.

It is understandable that mistakes can be made—the implement closest to hand is always the most likely to be chosen. The only error is to persist in using a tool that cannot do the job.

(Needless to say, my metaphor did not sway my client, so total was her investment in guilt as an integral part of who she was.)

To leave one metaphor and return to another: We cannot correct the past (the memory of our failures is always with us), but we need not remain enslaved to an ancient appetite. Guilt is a great incompetence.

We can, instead, expend our energies in completing the transition from an unwitting pragmatism (a tool incipient with teeth designed to bite its user) to the conscious use of a tool better selected for the task of liberating the metaphorical self. The selected tool—responsible thought or responsible action—will always contribute to a positive sense of self.

Guilt is to self-concept as acid is to flesh.

VII. The pandemic use of metaphoric open-endedness in defense of self is the psychological equivalent of suicide.

While the problem with pragmatism is that it narrows the meaning of life, it may appear to the careful reader that the problem with comparison psychology is that it is option crazy.

The fact is, though, that this is not the case—as stipulated in the fact that all effective metaphors are grounded in conscious thoughts or actions taken in the best interest of survival of self-concept; consequently, it may be said that the very fact of chosen comparison keeps us close to home.

From the perspective of logic alone—to say nothing of integrity—it is impossible to accept responsibility for one's self-concept and flit off, willy-nilly, in pursuit of every temptation, of every brand of counseling, of any philosophical will-o'-the-wisp that swims into view.

Furthermore, the discipline required to develop self-concept must be self-generated, if it is to stand a chance of working.

This means the individual's choices are limited by the very requirement that, if self-concept is going to empower the individual, it must be grounded in personal integrity—on the determination to invest in those actions and ideas that are in that person's best psychological interest.

Finally, the precepts of comparison psychology are inevitably more liberating than pragmatically based disciplines because the philosophy, when adhered to, eliminates the options of scapegoating and coercion.

The fact is that it is the survival-first principle of pragmatism that locks us into unforgiving systems that mandate defensive living. And it is our need to escape the confines of these trapping systems that is responsible for our destructive use of metaphoric open-endedness.

As has been stated often in this study, there is no such thing as a value-added metaphor. Metaphors are neither good nor bad, just efficient or not, and, because self-concept metaphors allow for open-endedness, it is possible to put them to any use we desire.

Problems come when we utilize this quality defensively—without conscious evaluation—in reflexive protection of self-concept.

Years ago, while employed as dean of students at a small church-related college, I had opportunity to teach and counsel a young woman I will call Hannah. She was tall and overweight with raven-black hair and olive skin.

To my knowledge (though it must have been evident to anyone who thought about it), I was one of the few people at the college who knew Hannah was Jewish, a circumstance she kept secret even from her roommate.

Hannah was a brilliant student, a talented art major, and a fanatical practitioner of Transcendental Meditation ™. Her closest male friend, who lived one thousand miles away in Florida, was also an adept in meditation. In fact, it was through a course in TM that they met.

One fall day, during one of Stephen's few visits to the college, he and Hannah walked the two miles to my residence to ask permission to roll in the leaves in our back yard.

I remember finding the request unconventional and a bit zany but perfectly in character.

(Not only did Hannah want to impress her dean and professor with her originality—there was a world of leaves on campus—but she may have hoped for a kind of subliminal and magical transfusion of feeling while acting out a fantasy in her counselor's backyard.)

In any event, Hannah and Stephen rolled up and down the back terrace, emitting youthful squeaks and screams, for perhaps an hour. What I found most remarkable about the activity was how completely asexual and scripted the play seemed to be.

It was a year later that Hannah confided information that brought the bemusing activity just described into focus. She was, she informed me, incapable of passion and was, in fact, frigid. Her friend, Stephen, she said had the same problem.

The rolling-in-the-leaves episode, had indeed been a scripted event, a quixotic attempt to evoke in each other what they perceived as appropriate youthful feelings.

As I recall, we explored, over months, possible reasons for her anomie—among them that her frigidity might be a consequence of her intense commitment to TM; that she might be ashamed of her Jewishness; or that the thought of bringing another Jewish baby into the world was more than she could stomach. Initially, she responded with anger and denial.

Ultimately, though, she agreed to inform her roommate and friends that she was Jewish. She also committed herself to embracing her heritage and learning to celebrate rather than reject it.

Some years after graduation, Hannah wrote me from Israel. She was living in a kibbutz with her Hasidic husband, a rabbinical student, and was, as I recall, expecting their second child. Her letter was replete with references to motherhood and the joys of obedience to her husband.

I wrote back, immediately, expressing some surprise at the complete reversal of her independent views. Her husband responded to my letter, informing me it was a husband's responsibility to guide his wife's thinking!

Hannah's use of the open-endedness of metaphor was apparent in her initial disavowal of her Jewish heritage—a disavowal expressing itself in her selection of a Methodist college—in her immersion in a Far Eastern mythos (the TM movement), and in her efforts to keep secret from her classmates the fact of her Jewishness.

This use of the innate flexibility (open-endedness) of metaphor is also evident in her denial of feeling as expressed in her frigidity and even in her paintings—which returned again and again to the motif of unnaturally detached and serene matriarchs with Far-Eastern features.

Even her speedy conversion to ultra-Orthodox Judaism, along with her surprisingly quick acquiescence to roles of wife and mother, indicate she was using the flexibility of metaphor to war against some troubling aspect of self.

For me, the most telling aspect of Hannah's story is compended in the leaf-rolling episode; for here (based on my understanding of her psychology) we have an instance of hollowness needing to be filled, of sterility seeking the fruitfulness denied, of the disenfranchised spirit searching vainly for its soul—the metamorphosis of Eliot's hollow men measuring out their lives not with coffee spoons but with fictionalized versions of what being human consists of.

This is perhaps the most horrifying consequence of using the inherent flexibility of self-concept metaphors for protection of self-concept: we end up with no self-concept to protect.

Similarly, a young carpentry student I knew, ashamed of her blackness, pretended there was no such thing as racism, ending up with life existing just beyond her fingertips. Poor schizophrenic Su-Su (discussed in Chapter 5), possessing no actual competencies, finally settled for a room in a nursing home.

Hannah ended up (God forbid!) as a compliant and fertile seed bed for survival drive, her genuinely wonderful attributes tragically wasted because she settled for easy solutions rather than confronting and conquering her inadequacies.

There are other instances of the use of metaphorical open-endedness—not the least of them being in that religion, which promises immortality in the hereafter—a promise that to my knowledge no one (save Christ) has returned from the grave to confirm.

Finally, it can be said here—and much more will be made of this subsequently—that ultimately the best path to the avoidance of open-ended metaphors is found in the fact of conscious actions chosen to the end of a positive construction of self-concept. Unconscious actions are (or ought to be) non sequiturs.

The pandemic use of metaphoric open-endedness in an unconscious defense of self is the psychological equivalent of suicide.

VIII. Conforming another person to one's personal needs is the ultimate act of evil.

Hardly more than 160 years ago, people living in the very county from which I wrote these lines thought there was nothing wrong with owning human beings, and less than forty-five years ago, the minister in a local Baptist church was speaking from the pulpit about "niggers."

Once, almost every day for a number of years, I worked with abused women who had been physically beaten and psychologically abused by their husbands or lovers. Always the story was the same:

> It is all your fault. If you would do what you're sup-posed to, I wouldn't have to beat you.

> You're always looking at other men. Soon as I leave for work, you start running around on me.

> I work my fingers to the bone for you; and you can't even manage to have dinner ready when I get home.

> This house is a pigsty! The children deserve a mother. I regret my part in bringing them into this mess.

> It seems to me you'd have time to wash their clothes, at least.

> As much money as I give you, you'd think you could buy them some decent clothes or get something in the house that's fit to eat.

> I have to finish the job your dumb-ass parents never started—raising you!

These are statements meant to annihilate egos, to humiliate targeted indiviuals, and to assure complete power and control over the victims—women to whom they once pledged everlasting love and whom they now seek to subjugate—out of their feelings of inadequacy born of failure to build a sense of self they could respect.

They manufacture excuses, abuse their partners, and never even see the underlying cause behind their actions. They are imposing dominance out of weakness, using others to fill out their empty metaphors of self.

(This assault on women's egos, I hasten to add, does not excuse women from responsibility for their predicaments or for the state of their self-concepts. They are thinking beings, endowed with the option of making decisions in their own best interest.

(All too often, it pains me to say, women have crumpled before the abuse, buying into submissiveness in exchange for safety and security for themselves and their children—a purchase for which they pay a devastating price, a cost no self-respecting society or self-sufficient woman should ever tolerate: the abdication of responsibility for one's sense of self.)

The abuser's objective, of course, is to conform his victim to "the needs of another"—himself—and, as such, his abusive acts constitute that act of evil characterized above as "ultimate." As is the case with most evils, it derives from an unexamined need to survive psychologically—a need the abuser is either oblivious to or too inadequate to even consider.

This drive to survive psychologically, not within itself a bad thing, derives in this case from the abuser's need to confirm his internal and hoped-for vision of self and to resist the devastating possibility that this image so desperately (and violently) sought is, in fact, not true.

Males seem especially vulnerable to this deep-rooted fear of inadequacy, given society's insistence on their being in charge, strong, and dominant. It is an assigned role that benefits a survival-driven organism (society), not the carriers of the burden.

Perhaps the world's greatest—and least understood—advocate of human freedom was William Blake, who knew (really knew) about metaphor before anyone else. No man ever suffered more for his vision, and nowhere in any art form is metaphor made more alive and grounded.

His insight into the prejudices—and prejudice is always an expression of primitive survival drive—that bind up humankind and cost us our freedom is made evident in his poem "The Little Black Boy."

Here he demonstrates in one scathing line how racial prejudice (a comparison deriving, as stated, from reflexive survival drive's engrained fear of difference) conforms the one to another person's need for the security found in similitude: "And be like him [the white boy], and he will then love me."

Once transported in Blake's poem to heaven, where both boys—black and white—have been freed from their clouds of flesh, the existence of love is still predicated upon the safe fact of sameness, as demonstrated in the lines about leaning "in joy upon our father's knee."

In "The Chimney Sweeper," Blake takes economics (in the guise of child labor) to task, informing us (through Tom) that conforming ourselves to the needs of our employer, and forgetting our own, will ensure that we have God for our father "and never want joy." A heretical conclusion (from the viewpoint of comparison psychology) if ever there were one!

Furthermore, there's real advantage (read irony) in sacrificing such irrelevant personal vanities as curly white hair:

Hush, Tom! never mind it,
For when your head's bare
You know that the soot
Cannot spoil your white hair.

(How reminiscent of our southern plantation owners' advice to their slaves: "Work hard, and do what you're told, and you'll wear shoes and walk them golden streets!")

Finally, Tom's conditioning complete, he went blithely off to work knowing "if all do their duty they need not fear harm."

Again, in "The Garden of Love," Blake illustrates the willingness of the priests of institutionalized religion to conform the world through use of prescriptive "thou shalt nots."

It is in "London," however, that the consequences of prostituting others to the needs of our easy security—be those needs psychological equanimity or economic profit—is presented with devastating clarity:

> I wander thro' each charter'd street,
> Near where the charter'd Thames does flow,
> And mark in every face I meet
> Marks of weakness, marks of woe.
> In every cry of every Man,
> In every Infant's cry of fear,
> In every voice, in every ban,
> The mind-forg'd manacles I hear.
> How the Chimney sweeper's cry
> Every black'ning church appalls;
> And the hapless Soldier's sigh
> Runs in blood down Palace walls.
> But most thro' midnight streets I hear
> How the youthful Harlot's curse
> Blasts the newborn Infant's tear,
> And blights with plagues the Marriage hearse.

The poem speaks for itself, but in the context of the argument presented here it is important to note the use of "charter'd," the apt coinage for defensive metaphors—"mind-forg'd manacles," the church's acquiescence to child labor (the chimney sweeper's cry that blackens church walls), the soldier who dies at the mandate of government, and the youthful harlot who curses her inconvenient pregnancy to the detriment of the child.

The plague that blights the marriage hearse may be either literal or figurative, or both, but certainly prostitution—and what it makes of love—illustrates the levels of depravity to which members of the human race may sink in enslaving others to their personal appetites.

The term, "marriage hearse" is ambiguous—it indicates that the marriage died either because the husband sought prostitutes; because marriage has been "charter'd" to business, church, state, or lust; because the institution itself has been made a vehicle for the dead in spirit—carting everyone off to the graveyard on the easy wheels of self-willing co-optation; or because sexually transmitted diseases can kill both partners.

Whatever the intended meaning, the metaphors are all grounded in real-term possibility and constitute an indictment of the consequences of survival-based ownership.

The reader will recall this section began with a discussion of the institution of slavery—an obvious instance of conforming others to self-serving needs; it went on to a discussion of racial prejudice, a subtle form of slavery—characterizing persons for psychological needs and mandating, as well, their economic servitude.

Finally, a colloquy of typical accusations from abusive males—each of them, it will be noted, designed to subjugate another to one's personal will—was presented.

These topics, it is proposed, represent instances of humans subjugating others to satisfy their need for personal and psychological security.

The excerpts from Blake's poetry, along with the citation, entire, of "London," his famous indictment of human exploitation, drive home the history and the consequences of conforming others to one's personal need.

We cannot own another person without having relinquished control of who we are to the needs of physical or psychological security. Victims of unexamined motives, we have made ourselves—as well as others—willing slaves to a physical and unquestioned drive to survive.

Conforming another person to one's personal needs is the ultimate act of evil.

IX. The reversal of self-survival needs against the self is the origin of sickness in the world.

The self is a metaphorical creation produced consciously (or not) by choices made in a real world. Since it is our own creation, we are responsible for its character.

There is a point, however, when sickness becomes the dominant fact of being, and when this happens the survival of the sickness becomes the reason for survival, and at this point the very survival of the individual as an authentic entity is at question.

Dr. Oliver Sacks discusses in **The Man Who Mistook His Wife for a Hat** (New York, 1985), a patient who calls himself "Witty Ticcy Ray." Ray is a victim of that most cruel of human illnesses, Tourette's Syndrome.

In this illness—suggesting from my perspective (see the italicized passage below) the involvement of self-concept—the patient is subject to sudden explosions of tics, coughs, snorts, and verbal filth over which he or she has no control.

Interestingly, the symptoms do not present themselves (at least in the case of Ray) during *"post-coital quiescence or in sleep or when he swam or sang or worked, evenly and rhythmically"* [my italics] (*op. cit.*, p.363). Each of these italicized instances, it is proposed, grew out of situations where Ray was at ease mentally and not stressed by fighting to preserve a threatened self-concept (see anxiety in dictionary).

At one point in his essay, Dr. Sacks quotes Ray as saying, "Suppose you *could* take away the tics. What would be left? I consist of tics—there is nothing else." (*op. cit.*, p. 98)

In fact, after three months of extensive and successful therapy, accompanied by light doses of Haldol (*op. cit.*, p. 99), Ray deliberately dropped his dosage on weekends to return to his "normal" self (*op. cit.*, p. 101).

A victim of Tourette's since four years of age, Ray's sense of self, though strong enough to permit a seemingly normal life, is inextricably bound up with his illness. However terrible the disease, Ray's election of feelings of inferiority because of it is an instance of using the self against the self.

Similar aberrations of personality may be observed in people who perceive paraplegia as the salient fact of their being, in battered women who come to see themselves as permanent victims, and in members of minority populations who respond to racial prejudice by accepting the characterization of others and thinking of themselves as inferior.

The fact that not all members of these populations respond in this way may serve as evidence of the existence of an element of choice in self-perception and a refusal to give in to the death wish that constitutes a rejection of self.

It is proposed, then, that a person whose perception of self is dominated by a sense of psychological unworthiness may level the weapon of self-loathing against himself/herself in much the way the immune system, through the agent of stress, may be turned against its host (see Chapter 5, pp. 216-217).

These individuals, consumed by a conviction of unworthiness, find escape from their suffering in a variety of ways. Some will escape through use of dependency metaphors, others through the devices of rationalization, scape-goating, psychosomatic illnesses, and (through the instrument of autonomic mirroring) actual physical illnesses.

Some few will hide their suffering under smoke screens of neuroses, gaining quixotic surcease from pain in confessions of their abnormality. Others, unable to hide from the banshee of self-recrimination, cross into the never-never land of psychosis, abandoning all hope of normalcy.

It was, perhaps, a little thing—that first white lie we told ourselves—but it is a seed with growth potential. As our evasions multiply—attracted magnetically to the original site of evasion—and we come to recognize our illnesses as integral parts of who we are, it becomes increasingly difficult to separate self-image from sicknesses.

Eventually, as in the case of Witty Ticcy Ray, the reality of our illness becomes an inextricable part of self-image, and it, itself a metaphor, comes to be imbued with the drive to survive, inevitably at the expense of self-concept survival.

It is thus the infamous double bind begins, as the symbol of our value in the world wrestles with its evil twin, negation. Torn in two directions, it is not surprising a schism should occur. Indeed, the break was preordained when the decision was made to survive at the risk of integrity.

In what may appear to be an abrupt change of direction (but which I hope to show it not to be), I would like now to discuss *The Tragical History of Doctor Faustus*, written by that contemporary of Shakespeare's, Christopher Marlowe.

This play is a remarkable, though damaged, masterpiece and a wonderful tribute, I believe, to the determination of Renaissance man to escape the physical bonds of human limitations, to aspire to human divinity.

I had opportunity to teach the play to college sophomores, and I came, over time, to see the tragedy, not so much as a reworking of the mediexval morality play as a kind of inversion of that resource—as a device, a *deux ex machina*, whereby Marlowe could explore the Renaissance concept of love of knowledge and beauty as the path to true spirituality.

I came to perceive Marlowe—the university wit, the reputed atheist, the artful agent of political intrigue and espionage—as having found great pleasure in taking to task not just superstition and magic, but also Catholicism and the entire underpinnings of organized religion.

Viewed from this perspective, the concepts of necromancy—of heaven and hell, of divinities and devils—come to be seen as foils against which Marlowe could play the Renaissance concept of spirituality existing on an earthly plane and being found in the love of beauty and knowledge.

The notorious tampering with the play by Thomas Nash and other scribblers (see prefatory comments to the play in **British Literature: From Beowulf to Sheridan**, Hazleton Spencer, ed., second edition, Boston, 1963, p. 343) gives me leave to make some imaginative leaps of my own, but, even so, there are surviving passages in the play that are arguably supportive of this thesis.

See, for instance, Mephistophilis's definition of hell as having no limits and not being circumscribed in one place: "[F]or where we are is hell, /And where hell is there must we ever be" [Act II, Scene i, 11. 119-120]. These lines are clearly supportive of hell as metaphor, not an actual place. See also his response to Faustus in the same act, Scene ii, 11. 5-7:

> Think'st thou heaven is such a glorious thing?
> I tell thee 'tis not half so fair as thou,
> Or any man that breathes on earth.

These lines emphasize the Renaissance principle of divinity existing in humanity, and (though spoken by a castaway from heaven—a being who can speak from experience!)—the lines, viewed through the skeptical eyes of Marlowe, cast doubts on the excellence (and even existence) of heaven.

I will leave it to the reader's judgment as to the worth of my thesis—and I remind the reader, again, of the cardinal truth of metaphor: no metaphor is right or wrong, just effective or not—but the proposed thesis (as far moved from critical canon as it appears to be) is too supportive of the concepts argued for in comparison psychology not to be put to use.

For readers not familiar with the plot of the play, it will be sufficient to point out that it reworks the legend of one John Faustus, doctor of medicine and infamous conjurer, who sold his soul to the devil in exchange for twenty-four years as a spirit (see Act II, Scene i, 11. 95-96: "First that Faustus may be a spirit in form and substance.")

At the beginning of the play, Faustus uses his newfound powers in what must be regarded as dedicated humanistic research. He studies astronomy, history, botany, and geography. He delights in debate (rhetoric) and acts of human friendship, and he demonstrates great reverence for the arts. In short, he sets out to accomplish (through the use of magic) the Renaissance ideal of humanistic perfection.

(Again, the reader is reminded of the importance of study and learning to the sowing and discovery of affinities in comparison psychology.)

As the end of his twenty-four years approached, Faustus (who I believe always intended to abrogate, through his strength of will, the terms of his agreement) was unable to resist Lucifer (maintain his integrity?) and forfeited his soul because of his inability to bear physical pain—a metaphor, as seen here, of the incriminating consequences of the fear of death.

It can be seen, again and again—and always at the point where repentance is urged upon Faustus—that Mephistophilis can only control Faustus by afflicting pain on the physical body, a telling metaphor of self-doubt and the human fear of dying—crippling human flaws when seen from the perspective of comparison psychology and the importance it places on integrity.

(For passages seen as supporting this argument, see, also, II, ii, 11. 80; V, i, 1. 69; V, ii, 11. 47-48; V., ii, 11. 80-81, V., ii, 1. 100, and Mephistophilis's statement about the Old Man's great faith: "But what I may afflict his body with! I will attempt." V., i., 11. 81-82.)

It is a likely consequence of the tampering referred to earlier that Faustus, in the above lines, is referred to as an "old Man" with "great faith." This is seen as having to be a consequence of tampering since Faustus's contract with Lucifer clearly specified that he be made a spirit and, thus, not subject to aging. And the very pact Faustus made with

Lucifer denies the major tenets of Christianity and its emphasis on faith. The validity of pain seen as a metaphor of self-doubt, death, and human frailty remains.

Looked at, then, from the perspective of comparison psychology, Faustus's tragedy was not that he sold his soul or that he was unable to repent. His tragedy grew out of his inability to withstand the onslaught of physical pain—a metaphor (as stated) of human mortality (frailty), self-doubt, human servitude to survival of the physical self—and from the lack of will sufficient to withstand his fear of dying.

It can be seen, as well, that the closer Faustus comes to expiration of his twenty-four years and execution of the pact, the more his determination to experience all the wonders that life holds flags, and the more he turns to venal things.

He cannot keep his mind on the divinities of beauty and knowledge because he is terrified of losing his soul and dying—the soul, I remind the reader, is immortal, the antonym of death—an expression of the drive to survive that from the perspective of comparison psychology leads to the sacrifice of integrity and the employment of open-ended metaphors.

Despite his great gambit—to gain necromantic powers and live forever, to outwit Lucifer, and become a god; to dedicate his life to the pursuit of truth and beauty—he failed because his fear of death (his lack of courage, i.e. integrity) opened the floodgates of doubt and insecurity. His resolve, first weakened and then destroyed, he succumbs to death.

(The reader is reminded that from the viewpoint of comparison psychology, it is our fear of death [of the body and of the self] that drives us to manufacture survival devices—ungrounded metaphors—that undermine integrity and cause us to "lose the name of action."

Furthermore, comparison psychology holds that we consign our bodies to death—the literal metaphor of hell—through neglect of our bodies, through conscious acts of lying to ourselves, and from the stress consequences that ensue as a consequence of the denial of integrity.)

As Faustus's dream of living without fear and gaining immortality—and his goal of becoming the equivalent of a mighty god—was devoured by his fear of death, so, from the perspective of this argument, could heaven on earth be realized by humanity's committing itself to beauty as expressed in the wonders of the natural world, in creating the metaphorical products of the liberated human mind, and by abjuring the destructive consequences of fear-based reflexive thinking.

Through the agency of comparison psychology, it is proposed, the Renaissance dream might become a human actuality!

This possibility is aimed for by Faustus's gamble (Marlowe's ploy) that surviving our fear of death (twenty-four years of immortality) could make possible an untrammeled celebration of all the wonders that life has to offer.

Based, then, on my self-serving interpretation of the play, the concepts of heaven and hell (even the stereotypical morality-play characters), should be seen as metaphorical figures representing either a celebratory act of human freedom or the damning fact of cowardly submission.

From this view, Faustus's damnation derives not from pride and debauchery, typical personifications in morality plays, but from the reversal of physical survival needs against the self. He sacrificed mystery and magic for the sake of a shriveled physical self, enslaved (hypocritically) to its hopes of escaping death. And, ironically, he still went to hell!

Had Faustus, according to this thesis, been able to bear the pain (pursue beauty despite the exhortations of *both* angel and devil to conquer death by selling self) he would have escaped the Luciferian mandate. He could have confirmed his own prediction that "a sound magician [a great artist] is a mighty god" (I, i, 1. 61), and, just maybe, have outwitted in the process both Lucifer and death.

Like the psychosomatics who sell (consciously or not) their souls for sickness, like the victims of autonomic mirroring who sacrifice their bodies to an unnamed psychic emptiness, like the cannibalistic schizophrenics who devour their concepts of self in a vain effort to save them—

Faustus denied himself (through his fear of death) the gift of spirituality offered him and everyman, free and for the taking.

The soul he sought to save by selling he sold by selling out.

It is the act of Eden recapitulated: the act of murder, rape, of racial bigotry, of every act of evil done to ecology, to every woman, man, or child on this splendid planet.

Faustus said it all—in one fatal act of capitulation:

> Oh God,
> If thou wilt not have mercy on my soul
> Yet for Christ's sake, whose blood hath ransomed me,
> Impose some end to my incessant pain.

In a cowardly defense of self—a recapitulation of Faustus's fate—we do those things that undermine the very thing we seek to save. We sell our souls in the name of saving them.

The reversal of self-survival needs against the self is the origin of sickness in the world.

(For reasons of editorial convenience, Decalogue number X will be reserved as heading for the next chapter.)

CHAPTER EIGHT

Uncontaminated Metaphors

X. The path to freedom lies in the conscious creation of liberating metaphors.

Survival drive is not an evil thing. It is, in fact, not a thing at all. It is a set of functions, a law of systems, whereby energy and matter are created and sustained. More precisely, it is that force behind art, language, and all forms of human metaphor—existing, ideally, under the exegesis of self-concept, as opposed to instinct.

(This point of seeing survival drive as metaphor deserves emphasis, for if we accept metaphor as defined in this work, we must recognize the role it plays in even our most routine acts of survival.

(There is literally nothing we perceive—no action we can take, no event [human or not] transpiring on this planet or in the known universe—that does not derive from metaphor. That our very concept of self is a metaphor should, then, be no surprise.)

Whether this drive to survive is the breath of God or the creation of circumstance—whether it is mind or mindless—is of little relevance to this study.

What is relevant, however, is that in its function as metaphor survival drive is sublimated and invisible. Its operations, its way of expressing itself—through atoms, molecules, quarks, and solar systems—is primarily accomplished through that management system hypothesized in the science of quantum mechanics.

It does not take us aback, then, when a rock does not speak, when stars sparkle but do not sing, when oceans rise to the gravity of moons. We may marvel at the way the swallows return to Capistrano, that buzzards frequent Hinkley, and at the alacrity of kudzu, but we do not question the fact of motive, that, beneath the skin of things, explicable forces are at work. These forces—variously described in the metaphors of physics, chemistry, geology, astronomy, gravity, ornithology, or botany—are assumed to be subject to the law of systems. This assumption makes human functioning possible.

Certain species, however, while subject to the same law of systems, have acquired the ability to override unconscious motivations and take control of their actions. This ability has become so enhanced in humans that we are capable of both self-direction and self-analysis.

We not only ask questions, we seek answers. In our anxiety to survive, we invent systems, develop vaccines, and ride rockets to the stars. We build monuments, write masterpieces, explore the cracks and crevices of the planet, investigate the universe, and presume, through the use of metaphors, to capture and manipulate God.

Passionate as we are to know and understand the law of systems, we have understood—at least since Sigmund Freud—that we, too, are subject to hidden urges and that by taking thought we can understand these urges and assume some measure of control over their operations.

We have become students of what Freud called the unconscious—here termed survival drive—but we remain woefully ignorant, really, of the system of laws that govern us.

For more than 21,000 years, the self-concept has been aware of itself and, from the perspective of comparison psychology, humans have possessed—but not recognized—the tool they need to escape the unconscious tyranny of reflexive survival drive.

The reasons they have not done so are largely two: we have failed to use the tool that is self-concept responsibly, and we have preferred to live glibly—to function lazily on the rim of consciousness.

The plain truth is that our understanding of the law of systems, in so far as it relates to human psychology, is inadequate to the task of self-actualization. Because of this, and because of our willing submission to the subliminal promptings of the drive to survive, we have remained more satyr than human.

As a race, we have settled for dimly perceived metaphors called deities, for acquiescence to power, and for general feelings of impotence. The result has been social systems riddled by violence and a dangerously pillaged and dying planet.

We have failed to learn the lessons of survival:

> I watch a finger of flame stretch toward tinder. It
> flutters, flickers, knows success and blossoms into a
> ruddy, exuberant expression of life; or, tinder denied,
> its motion falters; it gasps, turns blue, and dies. Are
> its motives or its fate so vastly different from our own?

Life, it can be seen, is a gratuitous experience, and our efforts to expand it beyond the limits of available fuel and the efficiency of the machine are not only futile and foolish: they squander the energy allotted us on self-pitying enterprises. More tragically, we squander the energy that is ours to use on fantasies—ungrounded metaphors whose final end is ashes.

We must learn how not to be vassals of those subliminal forces concerned with mechanical survival only.

The mere fact of liberating ourselves from subliminal systems, however, will not solve our problems as spiritual beings. We must learn to take conscious control of the very energies of survival drive itself.

The initial step on this path of freedom, as affirmed in my first "decalogue," is acceptance of the fact that the seeds of our mortality were planted at the moment of inception, and they will come to harvest.

(The reader is reminded, in this context, that the fear of insanity is the metaphorical equivalence of the fear of death.)

Acceptance of this fact, it has been proposed, will liberate us to create synthetic metaphors uncontaminated by our fear of death. We need to recognize, in other words, that our fear of death is the "big-lie" imperative that starts us on the path of defensiveness, dependency, denial, and, ultimately, our loss of integrity.

Recognition of this reality, and a commitment to the principles of responsible self-sufficiency, will not only contribute to freedom in our physical lives but in our minds as well.

Once, while an associate professor of English, I wrote an explication of William Blake's "The Tyger" which was rejected by **The Spectator** for reasons of an angry tone—a subliminal absorption by me of Blake's understandable anger at rejection by his contemporaries.

I believe, today, that the poem—if not the essay that sought to free it from the baggage encumbering it—is an example of how a liberating metaphor, a poem, can tell us how it is possible to be free.

In any event, and at the risk of boring the reader with scholastic pedantry, I would like to recopy that essay here, slightly amended. But, first, the poem itself:

(This and all other references to the poems of Blake are taken from **British Literature: from Blake to the Present Day,** (*op. cit.*, pp. 16-21.)

The Tyger

Tyger! Tyger! burning bright
In the forests of the night,
What immortal hand or eye
Could frame thy fearful symmetry?
In what distant deeps or skies
Burnt the fire of thine eyes?
On what wings dare he aspire?
What the hand dare seize the fire?
And what shoulder, and what art,
Could twist the sinews of thy heart?
And when thy heart began to beat,
What dread hand? and what dread feet?
What the hammer? What the chain?
In what furnace was thy brain?
What the arm? What dread grasp
Dare its deadly terrors clasp?
When the stars threw down their spears,
And water'd heaven with their tears,
Did he smile his work to see?
Did he who made the Lamb make thee?
Tyger! Tyger! burning bright
In the forests of the night,
What immortal hand or eye
Dare frame thy fearful symmetry?

In the Forests of the Night

To Catch a Tyger

After reading the lyrics and running afoul of Blake's ambiguous symbolism, I turned to the criticism for guidance. I found myself, however, reacting much like the mythical critic who, upon examining Robert Browning's **Sordello** *from his sickbed ex-claimed, "My God! I've recovered in body but not in mind. I can't understand a single line of British poetry."*

In the case of Blake's poetry, I continued to feel that I understood (albeit, intuitively,) the poetry better than I did the criticism.

I studied on, feeling stupid, and pounding my head against what I perceived as a wall of erudite discussion about Orc, Urizen, and Los, until one day I stumbled on a statement of Aristotle's that Blake himself had made note of:

The wisest of the Ancients considered what is not too Explicit as the fittest for Instruction, because it rouses the faculties to act.

(This, as I understand its use in Blake's practice, does not mean that theme and motive are not present—that one is entitled to misguide the reader, or that one can use what I call elsewhere open-ended metaphors that can mean what the reader wishes them to. In my opinion, Blake wants and expects us to work to "get" his meanings.)

If Blake's gambit were to avoid being too explicit, I concluded, he would be beside himself with glee; for he has our critics whirling like the proverbial spinning jinny—a backyard twirling-construction popular in my days of summer dalliance back on the farm in southwest Georgia.

What bothered me, though, was my conviction that convolute criticism transforms that which is imaginatively alive into a frozen absolute so rigid as to be incapable of "instructing" the reader.

That criticism which crusts over the vital power of the imagination to move us would, I suspect, have been anathema to Blake.

And if I am correct in my conviction that good poetry moves us in ways that mere words cannot define, then anyone who deliberately sets out to translate Blake's poetry into prose counterparts has fallen victim to his gambit of deliberate ambiguity—a game whose very purpose is to prevent the crusting over of imagination.

This is not to say that Blake's poetry is without meaning or that explication is a tour de force. As this paper will attempt to show, Blake's poetry can profit from careful study; but the approach that succeeds best is imaginative rather than scholarly, intuitive rather than pedantic.

It is for this reason I abandoned much of the criticism as obscureantism—unintentional or otherwise.

*I rejected, for instance, Hazard Adams's contention in "Reading Blake's Lyrics: 'The Tyger'" (**Texas Studies in Literature and Language, II,** Spring 1960, reprinted in **Discussions of William Blake**, John E. Grant, ed., Boston 1961, p. 50, 1I)..."...that in effect Blake's early poems strive to express the same system that the later prophetic books approach." as showing little understanding of the way poetry works.*

The "system" of the mature poet (in my experience) derives from trying to interpret the emotional "truths" the early efforts reveal.

I see poetry as an effort to arrive at a "system" or, better yet, a synthesis that obviates the need for system; and to assume that philosophical concepts spring full blown into life contradicts everything I know and have experienced about the way poetry works.

Poems like "The Tyger" are sufficient unto themselves, and an understanding needs not be predicated upon a lot of critical obfuscation.

The first (and most telling) stumbling block to understanding "The Tyger," I believe, derives from the critical insistence upon dichotomy in the question "Did he who made the lamb make thee?"

To argue that God made the tiger and the tiger is either good or bad is to indulge in the sort of reasoning that angered Blake into declaring Satan good and God evil.

(And, as will be shown, such an interpretation turns the poem into a cramped theological exercise— light years distant—as I see it—from Blake's intent.)

The fact is that the answer to the rhetorical question is so obvious that only a school of obscurantism could have muffed it.

Yes, the same being made both tiger and lamb, and to those who have read **The Songs of Innocence** *and* **The Songs of Experience** *it will be obvious that this being is William Blake.*

This interpretation of the rhetorical question (which by the way, is more exclamation than question) opens up possibilities for interpretation I encountered in none of my reading.

For instance, when David Erdman suggests ("Blake: The Historical Approach," taken from **English Institute Essays**, *1950, ed. Alan S. Downer, New York, 1951, and reprinted in* **Discussion of William Blake**, *op. cit.., p. 23) that we look at some passages "in which Blake is looking at himself working" he suggests a possibility he does not pursue.*

I would like to propose that in "The Tyger" Blake is indeed discussing himself as creator and asking a question about the creation of art and the nature of the poet-creator. In point of fact, the actual processes involved in engraving is suggested in the poem.

This possibility is supported, I believe, by an examination of Blake's engraving that accompanied the original publication of "The Tyger."

Examination of this engraving reveals that the tree limbs on the plate divide the poem into four distinct parts, the first and last stanzas commenting wonderingly on poetic power.

The second and third stanzas raise the question (and it should be noted that the entire poem is a question) of where the poet-creator gets the inspiration (in what "distant deeps or skies?") for the beauty he/she recreates.

This point of inquiry is driven home by the question about the mortal daring involved in coming to grips with this kind of fundamental (and terrifying) creativity.

The third stanza describes the coming alive of the poetic vision ("And when thy heart began to beat") and makes the point that the hands and feet of poets are objects of dread because of the awfulness and awesomeness of the task undertaken by them, the heavenly material they have handled, and the terrifying terrain they have trod. The poet, it appears, works with the same "matter" as the Creator Himself.

The fourth stanza (the beginning of part three) deals with the metaphorical tools of the artist's trade: the hammer and chain (line 13) represent more than apparatus of the artisan's trade; they "metaphorize" the actual work of creating—including our meanings and our linking them together in a poem.

(Note, as well, how "hammer" and "chain" evoke the extended metaphors of "work-process" and "free-ing-from, amplifying the richness of synthetic metaphor.)

The furnace is explicitly identified with brain and emphasizes intensity and fusion. The last two lines of this stanza refer to the hands of the "dread" artist that dares "grasp" the white-hot conception, burning with the energy of godly creativity.

The first two lines of stanza 5 have never, to my knowledge, been interpreted for what they are: very nearly the most beautiful description of the effect of imagination in English poetry. At the moment the conception is successfully realized (when the metaphor comes alive), the stars indeed throw down their spears and water heaven with their tears.

It is a miracle of the highest order, and there is poignant awe and wonderment in the interrogative, "Did he smile his work to see? Did he who made the Lamb make thee?" The fact that the same poet can envision such disparate truths metaphors! As lamb and tyger and both be "true" is reason enough for wonderment and awe.

(At this point, I cannot resist discussing the stupid look on the tiger's face in Blake's engraving as an ironic comment on the disparity between the artist's vision and his achievement. Perhaps, too, Blake wishes to empha-size that it is the metaphorical rather than the physical tiger he is discussing.)

The concluding stanza which repeats the first, except for substituting dare for could, makes the point that the poet is daring indeed who will presume to fas-cimilate either the fiery force and ferocity that is the tyger's symmetry (and synthesis) or the milky meekness and mildness that is the discoverable essence (and symmetry) of the lamb.

From here on, though there is no literal evidence in the poem for doing so, and it is a leap I would not approve of, the reader may philosophize about the creative force behind a poem or engraving being of like quality to the creative powers of God that brought the universe to be.

Certainly Blake rejected dichotomies (as he did generalized visions of God as mass energy), and he apparently believed in the concept of God-germ in man. And there is no more telling attack on humanity's penchant for dichotomy than the opposites of lamb and tyger!

William Blake regarded as humanity's greatest heresy its tendency to formalize and "staticize" intuitive recognitions into dicta and dogmas, systems and denominations. On its primary level, "The Tyger" is an exhortation made in the name of poetic license—the right to create freely.

I suspect he would agree with the counting rhyme hinted at in the title of this paper:

Eenie meenie, miney moe. Catch a Tyger by his toe. If he hollers, let him go. Eenie meenie, miney moe.

The End

From the perspective of what I hope is a matured understanding of metaphor, there are things I could have said in the essay that were not said, Especially the anti-scholarship rant!... But I am pleased with the comments about an intuitive rather than scholarly approach to poetry, the objection to critical insistence on dichotomies, and the description of the act of imagination in the lines "When the stars threw down their spears, / And water'd heaven with their tears" pleases me still.

I would like, now, to expand upon the comments of the earlier essay:

There is virtue in a scholarship that generates metaphor, that brings to life that thing grown stale and staticized, that brings light where once there was darkness.

There is, however, little virtue in scholars writing for scholars, particularly when scholarship becomes a parasitic exercise—feeding off itself, and written in an esoteric jargon about as lively as a mud-stuck stick. This is subliminal survival drive, expressed very nearly in its worst possible form.

(This criticism of criticism is directed toward the "scholastic" principle of documentation—a kind of Silas Marner protectiveness equating ideas with money or genius—and refers only to synthetic metaphors, which by the very nature of their origin cannot by "owned." Hylozoic metaphors, however, since they contribute to physical survival, should be "bought and paid for.")

1. Blake disregarded much of the thought of his day and launched out into exploration of life based on his own views of human experience. He would have hated a footnote as intensely as he despised those dogmatic truths he called "mind-forged manacles."

2. The fact is: Giving people credit for their supposed ideas (the entire idea of plagiarism!) is a perversion of the unquestioned drive to survive. The object of life is not to accumulate credits; and if knowledge is truly pleasure (as it would be in a bonafide "Garden of Love"), it should be freely given.

3. And it should be understood, as well, that the human penchant for dichotomies is an expression of the drive for easy security.

Life is not a matter of blacks and whites, rights and wrongs, and "thou-shalt-nots."

4. Life is complex, confusing, and (like the flashing of fireflies or "a tyger burning bright in the forest of the night") is a searching process made up of momentary insights and temporary conquests.

5. Nothing under the sun is permanent, not even, ultimately, the sun itself.

More may be said of that act of imagination depicted in the stars throwing "down their spears" and watering "heaven with their tears." Like most effective figures, the metaphor is incongruous. The stars do not literally have spears or throw them, and starlight is neither liquid nor made up of tears.

Faced with these contradictions, we are forced to look elsewhere for commensurate meaning and find it in this search that indescribable moment of understanding when two conflicting concepts are melded into a spontaneous exclamation of "Ah, yes!," and a metaphor is born.

"Did he smile his work to see? Did he who made the lamb make thee?" Ah, yes, indeed!

This is the "peak" experience; this is the primal moment of creativity—dare I say orgasm?—and this, once it has been experienced in all its power, with nothing else on earth compares.

Finally, I would like to attempt here what I did not try in the essay. I would like to show that in the creation of metaphor we experience the ultimate act of freedom.

"The Tyger" is much more than a description of a tiger. Indeed, the tyger described here is like no tiger ever seen.

Like the metaphor for imagination, the poem requires that we look behind the tyger and beyond him.

We not only have to free ourselves from dichotomous thinking, we have to wrestle with questions (and the reader is reminded, again, that the entire poem is a question) of how and where metaphors are generated ("In what distant deeps or skies") and of what kind of courage it takes to launch ourselves ("On what wings dare he aspire?") without tethers of rope and oxygen into the alien regions of unchartered space—risking, yes, the death that is insanity.

And the ultimate question—even at the risk of heresy—of whether the kind of creativity involved in creating a poem is not (and I happen to believe it *is*) the same kind of creative frenzy involved in the making of this planet and of solar systems yet uncounted and unmade?

The creation of metaphor is an act of daring because it involves setting in motion a set of circumstances the outcome of which cannot be known.

Our only guidance is our determination to be honest with ourselves and our materials (and what an act of vulnerability is that!), our only hope that we are up to the task we have set for ourselves.

In our creation of metaphors, we experience the only kind of freedom we can ever really know. This is because terrestrial freedom is impossible, given the pragmatic fact that our minds require our bodies as means of transporttation. And bodies decay and die.

More significantly, we find our freedom in metaphors because it is through their use that we can transform the pragmatic fact of survival into what we, in the wisdom of ownership, can make truly our own—an object of artistic self-sufficiency, our self-created (recreated) work of art.

In so doing, we free ourselves from bondage to survival drive; we empower ourselves to become engineers of our own destiny; and as examples of a new approach to living we may discover possibilities for a verdant and luxuriant Eden where unimaginable transformations of the human spirit await our entry, long delayed.

A poem (like the metaphor of self-concept) is a risky enterprise. We undertake it at the risk of consummate failure, recognizing that not to risk is to concede failure before the fact.

At the same time, we can allow ourselves to write haphazard poems—jotting down random thoughts and calling them poetry—or we can mass-produce unanimity by proselytizing for universal standards devoid of standards altogether.

Blake's "The Tyger" is more than a poem about creativity. It is a metaphor illustrating that human freedom is a human possibility. Its operant is poem, freedom its epiphanant.

Conclusion:
The Gordian Knot Untangled

This work has proposed that the miracles of art, music, science, and literature are living examples of what is possible through the willed transmutation of primitive survival drive into synthetic, self-concept metaphors.

It has been implied (if not said) that our survival as a species depends upon our assuming responsibility for the still-evolving metaphor that is self-concept.

One perturbing question remains: What is there in us that compels us to kill and eat our gods?

It is a question, apparently, that bothered Sir James Frazer as well. In his prodigious catalog of survival metaphors, ***The Golden Bough*** (*op. cit.*) he proposed at least three answers:

1. Common sense decreed the god had to be killed before he became old and feeble. (Pragmatism asserts our primal detective is physical survival.)
2. Survival-of-the-fittest contests assured the survival of the spirit of vegetation in a "less delapidated tabernacle"; (Staying physically fit assures survival of the carriers of survival drive.")
3. The primitive mind conceived of holiness as a "sort of deadly virus" the prudent man would do all he could to avoid. (Departure from the primal mandate of physical survival [using synthetic metaphors] muddies the water.)

In addition to these hypotheses, Sir James discusses the paradoxical "crowning and killing" of the "final harvester"—the least-swift reaper of the grain—as a more humane way of sacrificing the god.

Each of his possibilities, the reader will note, can be specifically related to the metaphor stressed here of physical survival.

These explanations leave me unsatisfied—because, perhaps, they leave human beings in the same sad state he found us at the beginning of his work.

Even so, it is with thanks to Sir Frazer's artful identification of Aeneas's golden bough as mistletoe that I would like to propose an answer more compatible with my thesis of synthetic survival.

It has been stated that everything on this planet feeds off everything else—it is the method of comparison—and schizophrenia was presented as a radical instance of this in the realm of self-concept.

This inherent cannibalism—the fact that in order to live we must eat, to survive we must kill—may even have, it has been suggested, something to say about that universal contaminant, guilt.

Is it possible that to the primitive mind mistletoe served as evidence of something that survived without feeding off something else? It was, after all, found on the tree of the gods (the oak), it was rootless, and it stayed forever green.

(It has only been in modern times that we have found out its parasitic secret, and even so its hold on us remains so powerful that we continue to kiss [a prelude to coition and physical survival?] our lovers under it!)

The oak is wounded by the bolt of lightning, the Yule log burns that we may enjoy warmth and good fortune, the virgin bleeds that humans may be born, the corn god dies that we may feed, and we still devour the Eucharist.

If, indeed, it should be this survival paradox that governs so much of our unconscious lives—that gives lie to our most deeply revered pretensions, that forces the recognition (and the sublimation thereof) of our innate cannibalism, then it becomes understandable why we persecute the final harvester and why the scapegoat market flourishes even today.

It is at once the curse of life (was Abel such a sacrifice?), a symptom (if not the cause) of eating disorders and schizophrenia, and the origin of guilt. Is it true, we kill and eat our gods that we may live?

In a proposed solution to the problem suggested in these questions, I would like to suggest that in the sought-for perfection of self-concept humans may find the psychological equivalent of mistletoe—something that needs not eat its god, a non-carnivorous construction built on the sound foundation of taking responsibility for one's own synthetic self.

(That, even under this scenario we must eat to survive physically, is mitigated in the hope of future scientific discoveries. Soon, very soon, we will make our food from unbleeding particles snatched from the air and combined [through the act of metaphor] into whatever kind of food we desire!)

It is an audacious thing I am proposing, but should there be value in it, one small thread shall have been unraveled from the cord that binds us all, living and bleeding sacrifices on the altars of our own careless construction.

Freed from the serpentine embrace of our fear of death (and its psychological twins, insanity and guilt), we just might empower ourselves to brush aside the forfending scimitars at the gates of Eden and reenter—as titans at last!—the symbolic lands of our ancient origins.

Consummatum est!

APPENDIX I

The Evolution of Metaphor

(IN A NUTSHELL)

A metaphor is a perceived coherence. It may be found in the mind that is nature or in the mind of a sentient being. It may be reflexive, hylozoic, or synthetic, but it is always based on the drive to survive.

The syntax of metaphor is neuronal, though not necessarily linguistic. Implemented through the use of brain modules (physical metaphors perfected, through reiteration, in nature's search search for efficiency) these physical structures are conduits constructed for the purpose of directing the energy that is survival drive.

As long as physical survival was the *raison d'etre* for being, the rules of pragmatism worked well; however, when the fact of psychological survival appeared on the scene, the rules changed.

Now the construction of—and survival of—a non-physical sense of self required readjustment to the survival agenda, a readjustment objectified in the form of organ adaptation, as brain structures —like the hypothalamus and the angular gyrus—originally evolved to promulgate physical survival were adapted to expression of a new form of survival energy, the psychological.

But I get ahead of myself.

Over time, and doubtlessly contributory to creation of a functional brain, the fore-mentioned physical structures had the effect of establishing a basis for order in the midst of chaos; and, given the urgency of finding survival through the discovery of affinity, it was but a matter of time—of which there was an inexhaustible supply!—until Lorenz's butterfly took shape and, like the forces in a forest fire or thunderstorm, survival drive developed its own principles (laws) of survival.

From this point on, what had been an anarchy of particles hell-bent for some version of momentum decay, became instead a field of possibilities—an unending supply of potential affinity particles, since—as Internet dating services endlessly proclaim—there is a match out there for everyone!

The force that is survival drive—the monomaniacal pursuit of affinity particles—did not, of course, exist until that first accidental act of fusion; but after that the game was on, driven by the pleasure found in the *aha!* response, and the drive to survive quickly became the dominant force for order in the universe.

This first act of accidental fusion was, as previously stated, the first metaphor, and the subsequent thirst for fusion—even though reflexive—was sufficient to the task of creating energy, gas, matter, water, carbon, and eventually those metaphorical physical systems we name physics, chemistry, and biology. It is an interesting variation on the metaphor motif that the brain works in the exact same fashion as nature.

That massive contribution of Charles Darwin—the metaphor of evolution— provides compelling documentation for the progress of protoplasm up to the point of Homo sapiens, but the exploratory nature of metaphor—its compulsive search for survival—could not and has not remained static, and the laws of progression (the search for survival efficiency) eventually extended survival drive beyond the point of the reflexive creation of matter to the creation of metaphorical formulas designed to facilitate the business of survival.

So it was that as the brain—a physical structure (a metaphor, mind you) that, like nature, employed physical properties in the interests of survival—continued to evolve. (Using the same method of metaphor employed in reflexive metaphor, nature hit upon the strategy of hylozoic metaphor.)

The hylozoic metaphor—its function now almost certainly residing in the left parietal lobe of the brain, especially, perhaps, in the so-called left supramarginal gyrus (see Ramachandran, *op. cit.*, p. 26)—made possible the use of pragmatic design skills needed for the making of weapons and tools, all conscious metaphors owing their existence to this newly evolved diversification of survival drive.

Thereafter, much of the business of biological survival was in the hands of living creatures with at least minimal capacities to manage their own survival.

No longer limited to the reflexive gambit of biological trial and error, this new brand of metaphor gave the brain the wherewithal to conceive of community living, animal husbandry, and agriculture—all expressions of the drive to survive physically—and to set the stage ultimately for the evolution from the physical manipulation of matter to the imaginative wielding of idea.

This next step—synthetic metaphor—was driven, as all metaphors are, by survival drive. It continued the established precedent of finding grounding in matter, but now the mind was liberated to discover relationships between natural objects and ideas, to practice seductions, accumulate wampum, name chieftains, and fashion governments. Since then, the world has not been the same.

As is true with all manifestations of survival drive, synthetic metaphors did not spring full blown into existence but evolved over time—maintaining, of course, their emphasis upon survival. Nowhere is this evolution more apparent than in the arrival of the metaphor of self-concept where survival became bicameral—both physical and psychological, metaphorical and mortal.

Now, instead of counting with sticks or communicating with grunt and gesture—actions grounded in nature—humans could see sticks as numbers and use sounds as syllables and eventually as words.

Over time, and primarily as a consequence of human self-concept, the art of writing—the shaping of sounds into letters—made possible the recording of legends, family histories, recipes, calendars, literature, scientific theories, and music—including, of course, the tactile art forms of painting and sculpture.

As the metaphor of self continued its search for greater survival efficiency, the primary concern of Homo sapiens came to be survival of the psychological self, as configured in issues of internal security, along with the need for love, admiration, and the approval of others. In modern times, this process has reached the point where we recognize the importance of feeding self-concept with self-enhancing actions, such as systems of analysis—not only of mind states and their aberrations, but of medicine and medical practices, astronomy, physics, chemistry, biology, and botany. All of these concentrations are conscious manifestations of survival drive applied to self-concept.

While it might appear that with the metaphor of self-concept metaphors moved farther away from their material beginnings, becoming more and more abstract, this is not a conclusion one should embrace too quickly.

This is because self-concept is traceable to its matrix in the physical world, a fact made apparent in Dr. Ramachandran's reference to the image of self deriving from its image of the physical body (*op. cit.*, p. 256). As has often been said, nothing (and that includes metaphor) comes from nothing!

Furthermore, as will be shown below, the responsible construction of self-concept is dependent upon physical actions taken in a physical world; moreover, self-concept metaphors are grounded in ways that liberate them to perform survival functions more efficiently than when affinities were directly dependent upon correspondences found only in nature.

Thanks, then, to the evolution of self-concept, it became possible for humans to see the world in terms of self—as separate from nature—a perception that empowered them to name circumstances apart from themselves, to imagine abstract qualities, and to attend to matters in their own best survival interests.

Ultimately, this led to the option of filling the slots of operant with abstract constituents in the place of concrete nouns and noun clauses, thereby making metaphors the "food" of metaphors—a process that allowed for the survival of self-concept through self-directed choices.

This transition—having the effect of making metaphor the "food" of metaphor—made possible the grounding of metaphor in the dual worlds of actions performed and actions named. Both of these uses carried the advantage of taking place in a real world, where actions and their consequences can be consciously evaluated (and modified) in the best interest of present and future self-concept survival.

More importantly, this evolution made it possible for individuals to consciously select those actions that best contribute to an abiding sense of integrity—the element in self-concept against which all actions must be measured if self-concept is to be saved from the curse of being ungrounded and inefficient.

Needless to say, the placement of abstract constituents in spots once reserved for concrete objects had giant ramifications for the progress of humanity, with humans now empowered to make creative decisions in the interests of self-concept survival.

Among elements traceable to it are the digital revolution, the invention of computers, the birth of new industries and their related economies, and scientific inventions and algorithms. Writers seek greatness through it.

It was only a matter of time before the accumulation of property and wealth, the practice of warfare, congressional log jams, and behaviors based on bias and prejudice come to be used—the predatory survival metaphors they are—for purposes counterproductive to the positive construction of self-concept.

It never seems to occur to its pursuers—the followers of ISIS (the Post-Islamic State in Iraq and Syria) would have been as well advised to recognize—that the possession of power, similar to the amassing of wealth, is an ungrounded version of the reflexive hunger for physical survival—a metaphor not based on reality.

Even as the metaphor of self-concept has liberated humans to pursue more creative endeavors, so has it opened greater opportunities for the use of open-ended metaphors like videotaped beheadings.

(Open-ended metaphors, the reader will recall, are viewed as those figures in which no apparent relationship exists between operant and epiphanant, where readers can dogmatically assign the meanings they choose—regardless of writer intent, evidence-based reading, responsible scholarship, or reality-based observations.

Those individuals still among us who bury their being in philosophies based on the primitive impulses of physical survival drive—who have relinquished self-concept to tyrants, philosophies, or governments—should weigh very carefully the consequences of psychological security easily or carelessly bought.)

The opportunity for profligate use of open-ended metaphors has many consequences (the verbal ones having been discussed already, not the least of which are political systems based on the notion of divine right, power through regency, theocracy, or blood-line primogeniture.

Religions, as metaphorical systems designed to conceal or ameliorate the fact of death, are particularly subject to the use of open-ended metaphors.

Thus the concept of faith, the *sine qua non* of ungrounded metaphor, often requires such practices as believing in healing through prayer (the parents of a diabetic daughter were recently charged with murder because they saw the calling of a doctor as an act of idolatry!), in the handling of venomous snakes, and in the drinking of poisons, etc.

A similar evoking of faith is seen in obituaries and funeral services, with promises being made of reunions in the hereafter. Such protestations obviously console the bereaved and provide a way of coping with loss, but the proof of efficacy goes unreported, thus suggesting open-endedness. (Such metaphors, of course, are inimical to integrity.)

That people intent on evidencing the power of faith should die as a consequence of snake venom or poison, and then be accused by fellow practitioners as lacking faith, is one of the unobserved ironies of faith-based (ungrounded) metaphors.

(That such life-risking tactics are based on the reading of the Bible as the unexpurgated word of God is but another example of the lengths to which the use of ungrounded metaphors may drive their practitioners.)

When Saint Paul avers that faith without works is dead, he is (without his knowledge) affirming the danger of ungrounded metaphor.

It follows logically that open-ended metaphors play important roles in political philosophies—oftentimes nothing but reflexive responses to unexamined survival urge.

It never seems to occur to practitioners of these philosophies (metaphors) that opinions based on stereotypes and anecdotal experience serve as fodder for prejudice and reflexive living—a damming commentary on life quality and compelling evidence of the self-concept consequence born of an un-thinking reliance on reflexive metaphor.

(The feel-good certainty that accompanies an assertion of bias is never recognized for what it is—the satisfaction of survival (security being realized in survival-certainty)—in these cases, fraudulently derived from the use of ungrounded metaphors.)

Women are subjected to restrictive laws opposing abortion in Texas (and other states) on the basis of reflexive (unexamined and instinctive) metaphors insisting that life begins either at inception or at the end of twenty weeks.

The notion that women should be in charge of their bodies—a grounded metaphor if ever there was one!—is disregarded or viewed as absurd by legislatures made up predominantly of men.

In a letter to the editor, written (interestingly) by a woman (*Asheville Citizen-Times*, 7/27/2013, A6) Tammy Gorman writes:

> Also, some women have written in that they should have power over their own body. I agree since their body is separate from their mother's but if you're pregnant, the body inside you is not your body, and, no, you do not have the right to end your baby's life, period…If you take away someone's life, then you should forfeit your right to live.

The absurdity (and viciousness) of logic displayed here—apparently derived from the reflexive-based premise of the sacredness of life— is not the point of the citation.

The point is that life is here viewed as circumstantial since the life of the mother is coldly dispensed with in obedience to the Old Testament dictum of "an eye for an eye"—an absolutism based on biblical authority, an ungrounded metaphor with roots directly traceable to reflexive metaphor and its emphasis on physical survival at any cost.

Comparison psychology seeks to provide a solution to the dilemma of ungrounded metaphors by proposing that it is possible to choose our metaphors—be they actions or ideas—and that we owe it to our sense of self (and our sense of integrity) to select those metaphors that contribute best to the survival of self-concept—the empowering force in our universe and the one available path to real and lasting freedom.

One should not leave behind the subject of the evolution of metaphor without emphasizing the aforementioned importance of physical action to a consolidated sense of self.

Actions are, in point of fact, self-concept's operant, its metaphorical equivalent of the material grounding found in pre-synthetic metaphors, and it is through real actions in a real world—actions modifiable by grounding and integrity—that the survival and strengthening of self-concept is made possible.

Thus, the metaphor that is self-concept is grounded in actions, is measurable by consequences in the real world, and is empowered by integrity earned from a job done well and done consciously. It is the mechanism whereby meaningful change in the world is made possible.

With the wistful hope that the owners of lives spent enslaved to the government of reflexive and ungrounded metaphors may someday be rendered conscious, let me end this dissertation on the origin of metaphor with this stab at a poetic, albeit satiric, metaphor (apologies to William Shakespeare):

> All the world's a stage, and the mass of men
> Are actors speaking out the lines assigned
> To us. Survival-driven beings, we
> Spin out our lives in senseless paradigms—
> Pathetic, sad, and wasted metaphors
> Grounded in ungrounded emptiness:
> "Sans teeth, sans eyes, sans taste, sans everything."

APPENDIX II

A Lexicon of Metaphor

(With apologies to Ambrose Bierce, and to my editor, who sees my utilization of **The Devil's Dictionary** as irrelevant, if not distracting, and to my readers for my stubborn insistence on including my expurgated version of the document anyway, I justify my recalcitrance as follows: Many readers will see it as the work of the devil, regardless of what I say—which from Bierce's perspective it probably would be!—and because I use the conceit of Bierce's dictionary (following the precedent of Shakespeare's use of the **Holinshed Chronicles**) as a way of grounding my own "lexicon," the grounding concept being a significant and necessary aspect of my theory of metaphor.)

A

Abdomen: Defined by Bierce as "The temple of the god Stomach," the abdomen is the warehouse where the food that feeds survival drive is stored. It is the furnace that demands food the way a stove requires wood. Its "hunger" is a metaphorical description for the drive to survive.

Physical survival drive serves as the imprimatur on which the metaphor that is self-concept is painted and whose fuel is actions taken in the interest of survival.

As with the physical abdomen, the choice of "food" for the metaphorical self is up to its consumer and can be bad for the body or bad for the soul. Taking responsibility for one's thoughts and acting upon them is mandatory to the conscious creation of a viable self-concept.

Abortion: An action not surgically feasible in Bierce's day, the term does not appear in his dictionary. This said, associated as it is with politics and religion, and applicable as it is to the argument of metaphor presented here, it is a word of considerable moment in the lexicon of metaphor.

To that end, it is important to stipulate that the drive to survive—expressed through the postulated metaphors of reflexive, hylozoic, and synthetic—can be shown to have relevance to the issue of abortion, which is literally a negation (an abrogation of) the physical drive to survive.

The fact of reflexive metaphors is confirmed by the primal metaphors employed by anti-abortionists—their lurid depictions of aborted fetuses, repeated references to abortion being murder, assertions about life being sacred, begining at inception, and speculations about the degree of pain inflicted on the aborted fetus—metaphorical assertions tinged with primitive impulse and subject, in many cases, to the charge of being ungrounded.

Additionally, religious arguments—often reflexive and open-ended—are sometimes brought to bear on anti-abortion arguments, along with guilt-producing moral accusations.

Providing further evidence of reflexive involvement in anti-abortion arguments is the well-documented willingness of extremists to resort to the bombing of clinics and assassinations, acts suggesting, again, the involvement of primitive emotions associated by MacLean with the visceral brain, that region where unreformed violent tendencies reside.

Hylozoic metaphors may also have relevance to abortion on both levels of their expression—the practical and the instrumental. By reason of their being perceived as an important interim step on the path to synthetic metaphor, hylozoic metaphors also have important implications for the decision to induce or not induce abortion in the first place.

The hylozoic metaphor, is mainly concerned with those surgical and chemical interventions decided upon after the decision to abort has been made.

And while the interventions chosen are obviously hylozoic, in the sense of instrumentation, it is important to point out that they are also hylozoic in the sense of practicality. Sometimes, at the risk of offending people committed to the sacredness of life, decisions about the birth of a baby may present intolerable challenges to the welbeing of both mother and infant.

Furthermore, hylozoic metaphors may play important roles in case of pregnancies resulting from incest or rape, or when perceived as neces-sitated by fetal defects with crippling societal implications. As stated earlier, hylozoic metaphors represent an important interim step on the path to synthetic metaphor, their effects having easy access to reflexive feelings—feelings that unquestioned may have significant effects on self-concept.

But it is to synthetic metaphor, the parent of self-concept, that I now turn in the interests of shedding light on this most controversial and perplexing of issues. A mother's election of abortion is rarely reflexive, although reactions to it often are.

Self-concept, the reader will recall, is viewed here as the metaphorical agency responsible for psychological survival. All human accomplishments, from the invention of language to the engineering marvels of space travel, may be traced to it; nothing worthwhile takes place in the world of modern humans that is not traceable to this arbiter of human reality.

Abortion, as stated, is an abrogation of physical survival drive, and any interruption of so primal a metaphor cannot but instigate consequences ranging from the disruption of physical functions in a body primed for maternal function to the activation of powerful chemical and hormonal reactions.

There are physical healing issues to be dealt with as well, to say nothing of emotional consequences.

Small wonder, then, that the mere broaching of the subject of abortion arouses the most powerful of instinctual responses in significant portions of the population—responses harking back through the semaphore of metaphor, perhaps, to the very moments of cosmic creation.

It is, however, in the realm of the psychological that the synthetic metaphor of self-concept plays its most pivotal role, for it has access to all levels of metaphor, and the act of abortion (whether spontaneous or induced) is an operant (see below) with great evocative power, striking as it does at the very roots of physical survival.

Metaphor, being the source and implementer of survival drive, is capable of evoking the *aha!* response of certainty (a synonym for survival accomplished) on all its levels.

This is why it is imperative that those individuals intent on responsible construction of self-concept develop the skill of subjecting their metaphors to critical examination for ascertaining dominant metaphors, an action necessary to the responsible (that is, conscious) construction of self.

As stated repeatedly, individuals committed to the survival of their consolidated, and empowering sense of self, will take those actions conducive to their feeling good (secure) in their self-estimates.

Reflexive metaphors, deriving from primitive survival impulses, tend to emphasize survival of the physical self; and self-concept, the reader is reminded, is a synthetic metaphor—concerned with survival of the psychological self.

It is here that the decision to abort becomes a matter of great moment, one not to be entered into lightly. This is also the point when hylozoic metaphors come into play, when options must be carefully examined and practical consequences weighed.

Needless to say, it is important that those people involved take especial care that they choose their metaphors carefully, abjuring (as the death to integrity it is) the ungrounded metaphor (see *Open-ended Metaphors, pp. 311 ff above.*) Guilt should not be a factor.

Actions energized by fear, embarrassment, external pressures —whether brought by peers, parent, or community—are expressive of a poorly constructed sense of self and are, as all reflexive metaphors tend to be, destructive to a personal sense of integrity.

The fact is, although some metaphors are clearly more efficient than others—and careful attention must be paid to metaphors grounded in medical research, scholarship, and practical considerations—that the question of abortion is not subject to winning or losing arguments, there being no such thing as absolute truth, particularly in the realm of self-concept.

The decision as to what action is best (with regard to abortion or any other conscious action) must be the sole responsibility of the individual most involved, and that person, if confident in her ability to make decisions, will know with certainty the action that is in her own best interest. An action consciously taken should have no deleterious impact on one's sense of self.

First there was pregnancy, and then there was abortion. Pregnancy is, of course, a reflexive consequence—the result of a sperm cell gaining access to a receptive ovum—and, as such, an instance of survival drive seeking out and finding an affinity, making, in other words, a metaphor. The production of a fetus is survival drive made physical.

In addition to reflexive machinery, the fact that couples may utilize reflexive metaphor without consideration of consequences confirms that pregnancy can be a consequence of reflexive metaphor. While the conscious decision to make a baby makes it a hylozoic metaphor, the decision to rear the child responsibly makes it a synthetic one.

(It is often reported that this reflexive merger of sperm and egg is an example of the Darwinian concept of survival of the fittest—the fastest gamete getting there "firstest with the mostest."

(As persuasive a metaphor as this is, it ignores the factor of proximity. The fact is that the closest sperm cell [the one with a head start] gets there first, and the fact of proximity is purely a matter of propulsive force and quantum probability.

(Like all metaphors in nature, this discovery of affinity is a random outcome produced by that compulsive search for unity, here called survival drive. If the hand of God is involved, he is a very busy God.)

As with everything on the planet, including abortion, it all comes down to this: Will we assume responsibility for choosing those actions most conducive to the creation of a positive sense of self, or will we circle blindly, subject to the controlling winds of circumstance and ungrounded metaphors?

Carelessness is no excuse, and parentage is not a one-way street; an unplanned baby is a human consequence; and being wanted is a basic human right.

While abortion used for birth control is a sacrilege, carelessness is a curse, and not being enslaved to survival drive is the essence of humanness.

These days, with the unapproved release of the proposed brief by Justice Samuel Alito and the subsequent abrogation of "Roe vs. Wade," the issue of abortion has assumed epic electorial proportions. Conservatives are celebrating the preservation of innocent lives while liberala lament the loss of individual rights necessary to the survival of a constitutional democracy.

Analysis of the metaphors employed in this discussion reveal a preponderance of reflexive survival metaphors in the conservative arguments, as contrasted with those of the liberal one. In other words, the anti-abortion metaphors can all be traced to the physical survival impulse, while the liberal arguments are all traceable to psychological (self-concept survival) synthetic metaphors. This book exists, it should be noted, to celebrate the evolutionary triumph of the miracle that is synthetic metaphor.

Absolutes: This is not a term Bierce addresses directly, limiting him-self, instead, to a discussion of governmental powers.

It is proposed here that absolutes occur rarely in nature (mortality is the only certain one) and, as used by humans, they constitute an equivo-cation made in the interest of psychological survival.

The term, absolute, refers here to those set-in-concrete, black-and-white answers certain ones of us cling to as though they were written in stone and hand-delivered by God.

It was to absolutes that William Blake was referring in "The Garden of Love" when he wrote that priests are "binding with briars my joys and desires." Bierce had absolutes in mind when he defined, metaphorically, an adage as "boned wisdom for weak teeth." The one viable absolute is that there are no synthetic absolutes.

Allusion: A term not considered by Bierce, and one generally not thought to belong in the dramaturgy that is metaphor; it is one, nonetheless, of great importance in the view of metaphor proposed here.

A metaphor capable of reaching roots down to any event—historical, personal, or literary—and enshrouding any topic with powerful associations and reverberations, allusion makes all experience its territory and, as a literary device, its efficacy is only limited by ignorance.

Anxiety is not an issue addressed by Bierce (though, given his forte for irony and sarcasm, perhaps it should have been). This said, anxi-ety—that scourge of modern times, has roots, according to Scott Stossell (*The Atlantic*, January/February 2014, 87), stretching as far back in his-tory as Demosthenes and Cicero—is deserving of inclusion here. (For a discussion of its consequences seen from the perspective of comparison psychology, see p.320 on anxiety.)

Of anxiety this may be safely said: unlike schizophrenia, in which the essence of the illness may be characterized as a double-bind struggle between competing versions of reality, or drug addiction, in which the impetus for survival involves a desperate need to escape life stress of the present, anxiety's prevailing temper seems to be a dogged determination to preserve self-concept regardless of cost or consequence.

Survival, it should be noted, is at issue in all three modes of coping. With schizophrenics, the issue is sanity; with drug addiction (including alcoholism), the prevailing impetus is escape from life circumstances seen as insufferable; and with anxiety the issue is survival of self-concept—at any cost, including frantic therapy-hopping, hospitalization, and pharmacological over-dosing.

With anxiety, as with addiction, the only real solution is self-concept reconstruction.

Art: Bierce's definition is primarily facetious, if not dismissive, but as viewed here art is the only form of metaphor not tainted by greed and cannibalism.

Art, in all of its manifestations, expresses the drive to survive through the miracle of synthetic metaphor.

The sculpture does not persist, save in the emotion it evokes; the artist's painting freezes in time an ineffable human experience; a musician captures in sound the unknowableness of knowing, the wordlessness of feeling. Josh Blake, a thoughtful contemporary musician, says of it: "Music is love through vibration...a pure expression of life force." And the poet celebrates the tragic, and sometimes heroic, essence of our humanness.

The arts, when they are real—that is grounded in the integrity of their metaphors—survive our dying and preserve for all time insights into the meaning of what it is to be human.

When created solely for monetary gain—and those creators of greeting-card art know who I mean!—such creators are parvenus as guilty of sin as the moneylenders in the temple!

Bodies rot, and heaven is a lie. The arts—our dream of freedom from dying utterly—capture essences, outlive us all, and constitute our only hope, excepting history, for transcending mortality.

B

Baby: According to Bierce, a baby is "A misshapen creature of no particular age, sex, or condition, chiefly remarkable for the violence of the sympathies and antipathies it excites in others, itself without sentiment or emotion."

Bierce is a cynic and takes pleasure in bitterness, but certain aspects of his description ring true. For instance, almost all of the force of survival drive is directed in the newborn to satisfying hunger. In fact, scientists inform us that the inutero infant, denied sustenance, lives off the mother and the detritus of discarded cells. Even the sex of the infant is de-emphasized, except in the minds of parents—and China!—to the point of irrelevance.

Bierce is correct, as well, in his assessment of "sympathies" aroused in crib visitations. Without even knowing it, viewers respond reflexively to survival drive's implanted imperative, as is confirmed by their gooing and cooing without conscious thought and without any concern for foolishness. The newborn babe, of course, is oblivious to everything but nutrient and discomfort.

All this said, it is important to realize that the newborn is little more than a portmanteau for the energy that is survival drive and is unaware, even, of its separateness (its identity), carrying no innate sense of self.

The exact chronology of self-concept development has been carefully studied, and the consensus seems to be that self-concept begins with the infant's discovery of separateness from its mother. Though reflexively instilled from birth, it is then the babe learns the effectiveness of consciously looking cute, smiling and, if necessary, screaming the heavens down.

Interestingly, once awareness of its singularity becomes known, the child blames itself, not the parent, for its failure to secure survival needs.

This is a source of guilt born of a frustrated survival drive ("Why am I so incompetent?"). The destructiveness of this conclusion should establish, for once and all, the importance of parental responsibility—before and after insemination—as well as their ownership of the consequences of neglect or abuse.

Right-to-life adherents might be well advised to examine their metaphors for reflexiveness in light of the implications of ungrounded opinions based on absolutes such as all life being sacred—even that engendered by rape—and that life begins at conception or upon the detection of a heartbeat.

The physiological processes of parturition proceed without regard for social or political considerations, decisions made on the basis of unthought-out metaphors do not exist in a void, and they are not without life-shaping consequences.

The making of babies should adduce from a responsibly constructed sense of self, not from the urgings of a drive neither recognized nor understood.

Beauty: The result of metaphors finding kinship (and pleasure) in other metaphors, it is the *aha!* response evoked by discovery of unthought-of relationships found in natural objects, in hylozoic discoveries, and in works of art. It is the intuitive recognition of symmetry realized—in the worlds of matter and of art.

(On my morning constitutional, two winters ago, I had occasion to examine the waves and coils and peninsulas etched atop the frozen, water-filled mud holes along my path. Some of these designs were beautiful and possessed of that kind of magical symmetry often found in modern art.

More recently, the observation was refreshed by another frozen mud hole, this time with lines etched on the frozen surface into what resembled the stylized shape of the human heart. I found myself thinking:

these shapes are metaphors, products of natural processes [engrained laws] following the mandates of physical survival—in these cases, perchance, indebted to the presence of roadside pollutants such as tar or motor oils.

As it would be the height of stupidity not to heed the imbedded laws of nature that fashioned these designs and learn from them, so would it be insane to jump to the conclusion that lines producing the shape of the human heart somehow establish the existence of love in the universe, engrained in and demonstrated by a loving nature.

Such a conclusion—observable in the philosophies of Romanticism, pantheism, and certain religious doctrines—might well serve my personal need for order, structure, and meaning [survival!], but it would also illustrate the inherent danger of ungrounded metaphors—in art, in mud holes, and in life.)

It is no coincidence that the youth among us are endowed with those desirable characteristics most conducive to pregnancy—as it is no coincidence that young women seem to be experiencing puberty much earlier these days than they did before.

(In this phenomenon, it occurs to me we may be seeing survival drive at work—nature adjusting to consequences born of birth control and assuring its survival by the art of circumvention.)

It is no accident, either, that the physical qualities of beauty disappear (autophagy takes hold) when survival drive has no further use for the worn-out vehicles of its energy—the budding signs of virility no longer wanted or required.

Beauty may be in the eye of the beholder when it comes to art and nature, but some beholders behold better than others.

Bigot: "One who is obstinately and zealously attached to an opinion that you do not entertain," is Bierce's definition, which, despite the sarcasm, is one with elements of merit.

Seen from the perspective of comparison psychology, the bigot is the inheritor (and initiator) of historical prejudices, is oblivious to the importance of personal integrity in construction of the metaphor that is self-concept, and is so consumed by the need to preserve his physical and psychological self that this obsession is subsumed into his view of the world.

Blind to his inner motives, and convinced by anecdotal experiences confirming his prejudices, the bigot is ignorant of and impervious to the possibility of empathy for people not endowed with his properties.

A bigot is a blind man walking.

Brain: Of the brain, Bierce writes, "An apparatus with which we think that we think," a nod to Descartes. He would agree, I think, with the assertion that in all too many human beings, the brain is the house of robotic behaviorism.

Seen from the view of metaphor proposed here, the brain is first and foremost the organ of physical survival. It evolved over eons to facilitate the transfer of genes in the most efficient way possible, foregoing, thereby, the need for engineering more reflexive—conceivably clumsy—engrams of survival.

It can now be said that the brain, especially the human version, is a metaphor of the brain that is nature, even possessing, as the metaphor of science matures, the ability—using nature's methods—to create matter.

This modern brain put thinking humans in charge of survival through the invention—unintentional and self-servingly utilitarian—of the metaphor of self-concept. That humans might elect to put it to the purposes of psychological survival was not, of course, an issue of concern in the original design.

This said, it can be further said: in its creation of self-concept (making a metaphor of herself, at root, an act of survival) nature provided the precedent for transferring the drive for physical survival into its metaphorical equivalent—the drive for survival of the psychological self.

From this point on, the world would never be the same.

ESTON ROBERTS

C

Comparison psychology: Bierce makes no reference to psychology in his dictionary; nevertheless, it is a science that since his day has come to have enormous relevance—not only to scientists and former professors but to the general populace.

The concept of comparison psychology championed here is based upon the primacy of metaphor in all permutations of matter and idea; and metaphor, it is argued, is responsible, even, for consciousness itself.

Consciousness is a primary issue in all brands of psychology, and this is the case with comparison psychology as well. However, unlike other approaches, the proposal advanced here is based on survival and its opposite number, the fear of death.

Coming under its purview are all the stratagems humans employ in trying to avoid the anathema that is dying.

Survival drive (see definition below) is the engine behind every form of creation, and metaphor is its tool of actualization. Metaphor is not only the language of physical matter, but it also speaks in science, religion, all forms of literature, and in language itself.

In comparison psychology, the most important manifestation of metaphor is found in the concept of self—a metaphor based, as all metaphors are, on the drive to survive.

Self-concept, it is argued, is the metaphorical counterpart of the physical body, and it exists for the same purposes as does physical survival drive—to assure physical survival, yes, but survival of the metaphorical self as well.

Self-concept, then, is the engine of survival in physical and phenomenal worlds. It is the agent of consciousness (see definition below), the arbitrator of psychological health, and the empowering force behind all human endeavors.

Basic to the concept of comparison psychology is the assertion that each individual is capable (through the conscious choice of action and idea) of constructing a concept of self for which he is solely responsible, a construction for which she feels justifiably proud, and one which serves as foundation for feelings of competency and self-worth—necessary constituents of a grounded sense of integrity.

All psychological imbalances not traceable to physiological dysfunction may, according to the precepts of comparison psychology, be traced to avoidance of those actions and ideas necessary to the construction of a strong and self-sufficient concept of self.

Comparison psychology, then, is an approach to living that can be taught and consciously applied to daily living. Seeing that this is done is the responsibility of public education, parenting, and every cognizant human being on the planet.

Consciousness, a life-force traceable to self-concept and discernible in all advanced life forms—from dolphins to canines, from cats to simians, from whales to Homo sapiens—evolved from that most basic reflexive drive to stay alive. Found in organisms as primal as the living cell it reached its apex in the human animal who finds itself, nowadays, threatened by advancements in artificial intelligence.

The quality of consciousness exists in exact proportion to the character of self-concept.

Deepak Chopra, Donald D. Hoffman, and Zen Buddhists everywhere are correct when they assert that consciousness is fundamental to the existence of the universe—what we do not see does not exist for us. Where they err is in their failure to recognize that consciousness originated as a reflexive act—a reflexive metaphor born of accident and at the behest of survival drive. It possesses no consciousness of itself except through the agency of self-concept.

Consciousness is an evolutionary consequence of survival drive reaching its peak in the conscious use of metaphor as mirrored in self-concept. Those employers of reflexive metaphors are, without knowing it, denying their hopes of freedom in the phenomenal world. Only the realized concept of self is capable of full consciousness.

Cowardice: Bierce describes the practitioner of this art of equivocation as "one who in a perilous emergency thinks with his legs."

Cowards follow the pack, support the bully, and care more for the opinions of others than they do their opinions of themselves.

From the perspective of this writer, cowardice is a product of laxity, a willing acquiescence to the reflexive impulse rather than to the con-scious one.

Cowards "run" from their responsibility to choose wisely, to act courageously, to never act (or tolerate thoughts) that damage the con-scious construction that is self-concept, or to abandon the mandate of humanness: To be—in the words of the Army commercial—the best that they can be.

Legs are not the issue—character is.

D

Death is not a subject broached by Bierce, but it is a subject important to the philosophy undergirding comparison psychology.

First, death is defined here as the senescence of cells, a physical consequence born of the natural expenditure of energy in a physical world. Given the current state of medical science, and the dubious possibility of perfect health, death is a fact we would be wise to accept as our inevitable lot, a wisdom that liberates us to get on with the business of responsible living.

With respect to senescence, it is interesting to note that elephants possess advanced survival instincts—even mourning the death of a member of their herd, and—according to Graeme Shannon ("Proceedings of the National Academy of Sciences," *USA Today*, 3/16/14/ 6B—possess the ability to tell people of different ethnic groups apart after their speaking a few sentences, and capable of using vocal information "to discern threat." Still, it must be said, they lack the prescience to foresee their own death.

The same seems to apply to all life forms save Homo sapiens, this ignorance being a consequence of non-humans not possessing a knowledge of history, a human proclivity made possible by spoken language and writing—developments effectuated by the evolution of self-concept and the drive for its survival.

Thus, thanks to a highly developed (and still evolving) sense of self, humans are aware of their mortality and expend enormous stores of energy and capital trying to avoid it. This is indicated by the pervasiveness of religions and, peraventure, the instances of many wealthy humanitarians doing good in hopes of society's forgiving them for the methods they employed in amassing their riches.

Poets, novelists, and scholars of all ilk fight death by seeking that immortality that comes from meaningful accomplishment, from their hopes of surviving death in history and the memories of their readers.

And now we have cryonics!

It is to our fear of death that most psychological problems may be traced. It follows, therefore, that solutions to these problems begins with an acceptance of death's inevitability and the application of our best efforts to the responsible construction of a positive, non-defensive sense of self.

The most compelling evidence of the human problem with death is the extremes to which humans go to avoid it.

Dictionary: Bierce defines the dictionary as "a malevolent literary device for cramping the growth of a language and making it hard and inelastic." This dictionary, however, is a most useful work. Enough said.

E

Eating is defined by Bierce under the heading of "Eat," and of it he writes: "To perform successively (and successfully) the functions of mastication, humectation, and deglutition"—words that exist in my *Websters* but add little to their assigned meanings.

Of Edible, he writes: "Good to eat, and wholesome to digest, as a worm to a toad, a toad to a snake, a snake to a pig, a pig to a man, and a man to a worm."

He would have written (had I my way): "That which adduces to survival of the physical and non-physical self—metaphors responsibly chosen that contribute to the wholesome survival of both forms (physical and metaphorical) of self."

From the view taken in this document, eating food is a process made mandatory by the comparison-based survival mandate: either a thing is edible or it is poisonous.

Beginning with this initial comparison—an early physical survival metaphor—the survival mandate evolved (through the natural process of comparison) into concepts like "useful" and "threatening," to survival enhancements found in warmth and shelter, animal husbandry, farms and pastures, to precious metals and jewelry, to money and, ultimately, to consciousness of self—the "poison" of which is doubt.

The mandate that we must eat to survive (a precedent engrained in the earliest microbe) is onerous to me because, in essence, it is a form of coercion—our being required to kill in order to survive.

Although we may choose to lie and plagiarize, it is not necessary in the world of metaphor that we kill in order to write, and I am hopeful for that day when science will make it possible for humans to survive without feeding off the innocent.

As for those vegetarians who argue that plants are not conscious and it's all right to eat them, allow me to refer them to Percy Bysshe Shelley's comment that those who eat plants (and he was a vegetarian!) partake only of the dumb.

Like humans, all plants and animals compare to survive, and—going all the way back to the interstellar marriage of cosmic particles—the evolving metaphor that is comparison is the ultimate source of an evolving consciousness.

It is, therefore, a matter of faith to me—no matter what you cannibals say—that the giant oak across the highway from me whose roots, some springs ago, were undercut by the hungry lust of the flooding river, possessed some form of consciousness—albeit of the tongueless kind.

Anything that old, with such accumulated mass, must have acquired some form of consciousness. It made acorns to survive, and, though now buried in the river, continues to send out green shoots (evidence of a form of consciousness) in springtime. To argue that the tree is insensate and therefore fair game to marauding humans is for me the epitome of arrogance and the true cost of pragmatism.

To kill with malice or without taking thought are acts with consequence, and no possessor of a responsibly constructed sense of self should ever kill—without taking conscious and regretful thought—another living thing. The assertion that this is nature's way brings no absolution.

Education, Bierce writes, is "that which discloses to the wise and disguises from the foolish their lack of understanding."

From the viewpoint of metaphor as defined here, education is the process (beginning with parenting) of teaching the young how to assume responsibility for a conscious sense of self. Ideally, parents are qualified based on experience and by their possession of a responsibly constructed sense of self.

This instruction—delegated, eventually, to the public school system—should be grounded on the mastery of languages, mathematics, history, science, and human relationships, but directed always toward the end point of students feeling good about the consequences of their efforts, of their having made conscious contributions to the survival of their positive concepts of self.

The accumulation of knowledge is necessary to the controlled function of metaphor, meaning that no student should be allowed to fail—ever. The notion that our best lessons are taught by failure is self-forgiving and chauvinistic.

It is not the responsibility of education to prepare our progeny for citizenship, for good work ethic, or for patriotism. Done rightly, education would exist to provide society's children with the opportunity and incentive to think, and to think independently—without conditioning or the penalties of social prejudice.

The end of education is self-sufficiency based on an earned sense of competence, not the creation of carbon copies of ourselves. It is one of the most important sources of grounding in the metaphor that is self-concept.

Ego: A term not addressed, if known, to Bierce and, these days, one associated with vanity. Ego is a Freudian term most at home in psychoanalysis. Comparison psychology prefers the self-concept usage.

The ego is the one structure known to humans that—because it is made by them, consciously or reflexively—is subject to modification based on its drive to survive psychologically. Individuals can purposefully choose those thoughts and actions best designed to strengthen and enhance the survival of their sense of self.

Feeling good about one's ego is the metaphorical equivalent of successful survival in the physical world.

Epiphanant: A coinage meant to describe the second term in this writer's definition of metaphor. It is the emotional awareness of that *aha!* moment when an affinity is found, is a consequence of that ongoing search for survival responsible for creating everything in the two worlds of human experience, and is the stimulus for the animal search for pleasure.

While always abstract in their initial manifestations, the evolution of the self-concept metaphor made epiphanants amenable to placement as operants (see below). This necessitates the conscious recognition (or selection) of affinities, else metaphors are ungrounded and ineffective.

Evil (interestingly and ironically) is not an entrant addressed by Bierce in *The Devil's Dictionary*, but its manifestation is one integral to the concept of metaphor.

Evil is defined here as an unconscious perversion of the metaphor that is survival drive—an assertion of the primacy of physical survival at any cost: ego gone berserk, the ultimate apostasy, and the willing erasure of self-concept responsibility in the interest, only, of physical survival.

While there is no such thing as evil personified, a bully is always evil.

F

Freedom: Bierce defines freedom as "exemption from the stress of authority," and it is a common definition in terms of general practice.

People (especially politicians) make a big to-do about freedom, saying they will make it the touchstone of their term(s); and our constitution makes much of individual freedom, especially from tyrants; but— no matter the hopeful grandiloquence brought to it—freedom is never experienced in the real world.

People can vote for (or give money to) politicians and get laws passed that forward their personal agendas; they can make money, save money, and build towering financial empires; but despite their best efforts they will get sick, age, and die. From the perspective of comparison psychology, the realization of a consolidated sense of self is the only path to freedom.

Capitalism—that red-in-tooth-and-claw, physical survival metaphor that promises freedom—can only provide money, and money like flesh is friable.

Our only hope for freedom lies in the world of mind, specifically in the world of self-concept.

It is only in this realm that humans have control, where they can determine input and condition results, where they can construct a sense of self impregnable to (capable of withstanding) life's inevitable slings and arrows, self-pity, and attempts of the callous to demean or destroy.

An empowered self-concept—one not driven by fear of dying and all its attendant survival stratagems—can free the individual from the constraints of fear, permit conscious decisions and actions chosen for their efficacy in a willed construction of self, and make possible the kind of courage needed to undertake actions of great and lasting moment.

Humans are not the inventors of their bodies, nature is; and bodies will develop arthritis, age, and decay. In the realm of self-concept, though, humans can be the architects of their intellectual beings and leave behind them, thereby, objects, actions, and ideas that will benefit humanity and long outlive their passing.

Freedom is for the free.

G & H
(Omitted for Irrelevance)

I

I is facetiously defined by Bierce as "the first word of the alphabet, the first word of the language, the first thought of the mind, the first object of affecttion." He is not far off the mark, for the first metaphor the human infant is capable of is the awareness of self as a separate entity, separate from the mother's breast.

All too often, though—from the perspective of this philologist of metaphor—the concept that is "I" is not loved enough in the right sense of the word, "rightness" to be defined later.

The Christian church, and many Asian philosophies known to me, are quick to denounce self-love as anathema to everything. This is by no means a coincidence, for the above-mentioned theorists see ego as antithetical to their perceptions of the purposes for existence.

Buddhists that I know, for example, see the ego as an expression of self-absorption, a kind of constipation of the mind that stands in the way of the perfect serenity. Admittedly, that aptly describes certain self-absorbed individuals consumed with the objective declension of the word "me"—the planet whose only sun is self. Inner peace, however, is not the reason for existence.

The Christian church, on the other hand, seems to see the emphasis upon "I" as evil and averse to its objective of heaven attained by immersing one's sense of self in unquestioning obedience to dogma.

This abnegation of ego amounts, nonetheless, to an erasure of self—the one entity in the universe susceptible of self-service in its most positive sense.

These forms of ego denial not only have the effect of enhancing the coffers of churches—churchgoers sacrificing 10 percent of their income to grease the skids to heaven by virtue of self-abnegation (a small price to pay for eternal life spent in a heavenly condominium minus maintenance fees)—but it also sets up priests and preachers as God-informed adjudicators of rightness and wrongness.

It is a form of power whereby the adjudicators derive dual benefits—fiscal means of survival, and ego support (self-righteous feelings of piety) obtained by steering people in the "right" direction.

The mind recognizes (and self-concept welcomes) that rightness born of integrity.

The point has been made already that the sense of self mirrored in the pronoun *I* is a metaphor whose construction is the consequence of choices (conscious or unconscious) made by the individual. Since it is a self-made metaphor (ignorance of the law is no excuse), it follows that it is possible to abjure those kinds of "evils" that do not contribute to a positive sense of self.

Imagination is defined by Bierce as "a warehouse of facts, with poet and liar in joint ownership." Viewed from the perspective of comparison psychology, this is a useless and humorless definition.

Imagination is the essence of metaphor. It is the consequence of discovered similarities (and differences) found in objects and ideas. Some minds seem better at finding unexpected congruities than others, but metaphors are the engines that make imagination possible.

William Blake illustrated that *aha!* moment that is imagination in the following lines from "The Tyger": "When the stars threw down their spears, /And watered heaven with their tears."

It is in the act of imagination—the same act of survival recognized by two particles discovering homogeneity in space, magnified millions of times in the evolved human brain—to which Blake speaks. It is the ecstasy every artist lives for—a "high" that surpasses any potion invented by nature or the engines of man!

The work of the artist is to use imagination to create things (discover connections) that have not existed before.

Immorality: Bierce defines the adjectival form (immoral) as *inexpedient* and goes on to argue that morality derives from the fear of conse-quences. My definition is more succinct: men are guilty of immorality when they allow primitive survival drive to condition their responses.

Immortality: As he is prone to do, Bierce resorts to poetry for definition:

> A toy which people cry for,
> And on their knees apply for,
> Dispute, contend and lie for,
> And if allowed
> Would be right proud
> Eternally to die for.

It is a definition that, with the exception of "toy," I heartily applaud. If I would add one proviso, it is this: immortality is the perceived antidote to dying, the unacknowledged terror that animates much of humanity's planetary actions and leads to the obfuscation of which it dedicates 90 percent of its efforts.

The human animal resorts to the accumulation of wealth on the grounds that if money keeps us fed and warm and sheltered (and psychologically secure) in this life, then it will surely keep us safe in the hereafter. This subliminal, osmotic motive is a prime example of the way the unexamined metaphor that is physical survival drive actuates human behavior and turns life into wasted effort.

Shakespeare's immortality is the only kind I know.

Integrity: This is not a word selected by Bierce for inclusion in his dictionary, but it is the lodestone of the metaphor that is comparison psychology.

As every metaphor in nature owes its existence to a predecessor, so is it in the world of idea that every metaphor owes a debt of gratitude to a version of metaphor found in the natural world. This is true of autonomic mirroring, of eating disorders, and the movement of metaphor from physical to psychological survival.

This "truth of origin"—this naturally based integrity owing its existence to the metaphorical method engrained from the beginning of metaphor—may be seen as an instance of an "idea" in nature being assimilated (carried forward) into a new and advanced variation on survival efficiency—this time the true-to-one's self metaphor here called integrity.

As grounding has been shown to be necessary to effectiveness in metaphors, so may it be said of the metaphor that is self-concept. Its grounding is found in the conscious measurement of all thought and action against the standards of a self-constructed sense of integrity.

As previously discussed, the metaphor of self-concept is an evolutionary product of synthetic metaphor, a development allowing for the substitution of abstract operants to places once restricted to objects only found in nature.

Because of this newfound subjectivity, integrity mandates that self-concept be a conscious construction measured against the criterion of chosen actions contributing to the survival of a positive sense of self.

The obverse side to this kind of consciousness is the possibility that the image of self be based on those practices driven by the same impulses that motivate survival in the physical world—among them, primitive fears, reflexive racism, and the use of force in resolving conflicts—the consequences of which the human race has come to know all too well!

Integrity, then, is the conscious selection of those actions and ideas best suited to constructing a responsible sense of self. Without it, people become sounding cymbals, Calibans devoid of sense or imagination, servants to unguided impulse. With it integrity becomes the grounding in our oath to be true to ourselves—in so far as it is possible to never lie to ourselves or others.

Irony: Not addressed by Bierce, the term is included here as an instance of metaphorical practice based not on logically evident affinities but on their opposites. In other words, the reader is required to read into the ideas expressed the opposite of what is apparent. Irony is a subterfuge requiring reader input; and may be used as an instrument of veiled hostility.

In my novel, *White in the Moon*, I have attempted to turn irony against itself by having my characters (in "A Hagsipian Fable") utter absurdities without awareness of their inanities—a version of dramatic irony meant to display villainous cupidity (and stupidity) and allowing intelligent readers to experience the irony (and anger) directly; it evokes the ironic shift by the readers' recognition of obtuseness, eliminating, thereby, one step on the stairway to irony.

Death is the ultimate irony because it confirms the frailty of the human hope for eternal happiness.

J

Justice: According to Bierce this quality is "a commodity which in a more or less adulterated condition the State sells to the citizen as a reward for his allegiance, taxes, and personal service."

From this writer's perspective, justice is one of the many positive consequences growing out of a person's commitment to construction of a consolidated sense of self. Injustice that damages person or property should be adjudicated in a court of law.

No people committed to building a sense of self derived from conscious investments in feeling good about themselves would ever (could ever) condone an act of aggression (physical or psychological) against another person; any acts predicated upon bigotry; unwarranted arrest or imprisonment; the theft of personal property; rapacious commerce; or enslavement of another human being.

Justice—except in the case of court adjudication—is not a state responsibility. In fact, when it becomes necessary for institutions to enforce self-concept investments, such actions are rendered meaningless. A coerced virtue is no virtue at all.

K
(Omitted for Irrelevance)

L

Language is defined by Bierce as the music with which we charm the serpents guarding another's treasure. While it is recognized that it is possible to "steal" through language, I must insist on a more universal usage.

Language, one of metaphor's greatest divarications, originated initially from issues related to physical survival. It was, after all, necessary to sound the alarm when the lion approached; it was important to count the cattle; and chant the songs that gratified the gods; and to woo the reluctant maiden to the cave.

However, under the impress of metaphor and the evolution of self-concept, language quickly evolved (through letters representing sounds—an obvious act of metaphor) into writing; and writing evolved into ledgers, scriptures, legal documents, patents, and histories—recordings of significant human accomplishments, poems, biographies of heroes, and to the writing down of musical notes and mathematical formulas.

Based, once, on the drive to feed the body and secure survival through magic and spirituality, language came to concern itself with that other vision of survival—that which involved self-concept and inven-tions, the sciences, and the arts—even novels and poetry.

Language is metaphor incarnate and, like all metaphors, is based on survival. In an ideal world its use would be grounded by integrity, not salesmanship.

Logic: Defined by Bierce as "the art of thinking and reasoning in strict accordance with the limitations and incapacities of human under-standing." He goes on to trace its basis to syllogism.

From the perspective of the theory of metaphor, logic is that metaphor born of the desire to develop systems useful to surviving physically. It was utilized in warfare, in hunting for food, in securing property, in argument, and finally in the creation of mathematics and the sciences—metaphors that became edifices to the capacity for greatness in the human mind, a capacity far excelling in importance its rudimentary save-my-life origins.

Logic survives today because of its great efficiency in fabricating things helpful to physical survival and, when applied to survival of the ego, creates, mainly, automatons.

Its use in mathematics and the sciences is gratefully excepted.

Love: Forever the cynical humorist, Bierce defines love as "a temporary insanity curable by marriage." To this lexicographer of metaphor (and the discussion is here restricted to romantic love), it is a metaphor traceable to the physical act of sex.

Once the metaphor that is self-concept came into being, it became necessary (for obvious reasons) to rid sex of its bestiality and its associated feelings.

This was attempted, once, by the invention of courtly love—an ungrounded metaphor of idealized conduct that ran its course due to its numerous violations by lords and ladies. Later on, a similar "purification" was taken on by romance novels, soap operas, and Hollywood—relegating the dream to fantasy once and for all. Christianity seeks to pen it up in commandments.

In modern days, romantic love's imprimatur of choice is marriage, a legal contract stipulating fidelity and requiring enormous stores of willpower to sustain.

It is viewed by some men of my acquaintance as a small price to pay for regular sex. However, given the high frequency of infidelities, it is a contract of limited efficacy. When institutionalized by law, its greatest virtue exists in its provision for the welfare of children. Laws, it must be said, are poor enforcers of fidelity.

Humans prefer that love be a transcendent virtue brought into being by divine intervention, but to me it seems to be a consequence of emotion-inducing peptides designed to facilitate the making of babies and the perpetuation of survival drive.

These chemical influences lack permanence, however, and (minus a commitment to preserving one's positive sense of self) primal impulses often take precedence.

(Nature is without morals, and human attempts to assign them [witness the Romantics!] are destined to fail.)

So long as we allow self-concept to be a reflexive creation, so long will romantic love remain a vision of "want to be," a dream with only one correlative in the physical world, that being lust.

My one-time definition of love as "the deep-down knowledge of the total worth of another human soul" proved invalid when the object of this definition proved it wrong. Still, should such a love prove practical, it would forgive human frailty and focus, instead, on the inherent goodness possessed by humans not obsessed with the savagery of survival at any cost.

It is not possible, comparison psychology holds, to love a thing incapable of loving you back; hence, love is a synthetic metaphor capable of grounding in willing sacrifices made in the best interests of oneself and others.

When corrupted by self-doubt or suspicion, love can be seen as reflexively self-serving and undeserving of the name.

M

Metaphor: For reasons unknowable, Bierce did not include this term in his dictionary. A concept well known to Aristotle, and doubtlessly known to Bierce, it is a term deserving of definition and one that would have profited from his gimlet wisdom.

Speaking of Aristotle: through no fault of his own, he is responsible for the foisting of an incomplete treatment of metaphor upon humankind, one responsible for much of the error in the world.

Metaphor, as this work seeks to demonstrate, is a phenomenon with applications to far more than just rhetoric. In fact, many studies of metaphor as a rhetorical device can be kindly characterized as orgiastic exercises in the use of ungrounded metaphor, approaches that severely limit the scope of this most powerful of instruments.

As quantum physics (a metaphor unavailable to Aristotle) has made evident, metaphor underlies all energy and matter and is, in fact, responsible for the creation of both.

It is no coincidence, then, that those rhetorical metaphors are best (most effective) that contain close connections to the physical world from which they originate.

Because it is inherent in the method of nature, metaphor cannot be restricted to linear figures of speech. It can, in the world of literature, range in dimension from a single expression in a sentence—and all figures of speech are metaphors—to an entire poem, a work of art, a volume of works, and even to works of fiction and nonfiction.

This said, language is not the *sine qua non* of metaphor. All science, for instance, is metaphor based on the grounding that is matter. (Mathematics, being based on digital metaphors, is dependent—like self-concept—upon results for its grounding.)

Christianity, for instance, is a powerful metaphor, its roots spiraling down through the annals of modern history. A massive effort at human conditioning (and mostly an honorable one), the metaphor that is Christianity has been touched by the greatest minds in human history.

Dante and Milton have left their tracks there, as have Rembrandt and Bach, Aquinas and the Venerable Bede, Tillich and Bonhoeffer, Kierkegaard, Niebuhr, C. S. Lewis, and many others.

In no other human enterprise has greater energy been expended— no greater monuments built—than in religious extrapolations, a telling commentary on the transcendent importance of survival in the human way of thinking.

One of the main weaknesses of Christianity, as I see it, is, like all metaphors ungrounded in matter or consequence, it is based on a wish rather than reality. C.S. Lewis recognized this weakness and argued insistently (and unconvincingly) for the materiality of God.

The metaphor that is Christianity derives from the recognition of human mortality and the understandable need for its antonym—for some alternative to its inevitability, a way of surviving beyond an existence where matter decays and death is certain.

In his important work referred to often in this document, V.S. Ramachandran writes: "You can't get very far in science by trying to explain one mystery with another mystery."

And, though not a science, this is the basic problem with the metaphor of Christianity.

It bases itself on the mystery of Christ's resurrection—an inexplicable and undocumented miracle—and then requires an act of faith in that resurrection to assure survival beyond the grave—faith being the very essence of ungrounded metaphor, survival drive applied to mythology.

This book, then, grounded—as it seeks to be on quantum mechanics, brain study, and a commitment to integrity—may be seen as a metaphor of the philosophy of metaphor, a concept derived from (and grounded in) the method (and solidity) of nature herself.

From the perspective of this self-assigned lexicographer, all forms of matter and energy (and Einstein established they are the same) were created from that survival force generated when two random cosmic particles collided, discovered affinity, and liked it.

Not only was this the first metaphor, it was the first instance of consciousness—since the very act of recognizing affinity requires some capacity for seeing sameness in similarity or difference—two perceived differences or similarities constituting an affinity.

This first instance of metaphor is here called survival drive, for it was from that moment of recognition—this *aha!* response codified as pleasure—that the need to seek out and find other partners derives.

(Back in those years, before shade overtook my garden spot, I planted a variety of vegetables each spring; but it is to my success in growing green beans that I direct this discussion.

I discovered, early on, that if I kept the beans picked—a deliberate exploitation of survival drive I heartlessly pursued—they would continue to produce throughout the summer.

As humans, past and present had done before me, I was consciously harnessing survival drive to my own selfish needs, using the cosmic compulsion to reproduce to my own survival purposes.

This same survival drive, the earliest form of metaphor, permeates the universe (it created it, after all!) and is remarkable for the way it continues to evolve, even to the present day.)

By its nature, metaphor is exploitative and investigative, and Charles Darwin was speaking of this search for workable combinations in his use of the term *evolution,* itself a metaphor suggesting the ways biological matter transforms itself over time and in the interests of greater survival efficiency.

Evolution is a descriptor equally applicable to all forms of mass, including the geological, the cosmological, and even metaphor itself.

Given the exploratory nature of metaphor, it is not surprising that it evolved from the strict business of physical creation to a more sophisticated level of survival—a level that applied the underlying mechanism of metaphor to metaphor itself. The metaphor in this case was synthetic, the ultimate source of the metaphor that is self-concept.

The development of self-concept was itself a survival innovation that facilitated survival of the individual (eliminating the need for additional, and cumbersome, physiological reflexes); but it took on, in the way of metaphor everywhere, the unexpected property of a concern for survival of a non-physical self—a metaphorical self, ideally grounded in conscious and responsible actions.

(Self-concept, unlike metaphors grounded in physical stuff, must seek its grounding in actions, actions consciously selected and acted upon.)

To feel good about one's self, comparison psychology holds, one must take responsibility for construction of self-concept, and this is done by living up to self-made standards of behavior and thinking, not those of a self-satisfied and gluttonous world.

Returning now to self-concept and the transformation allowing for use of nonphysical constituents in the formula that is metaphor, it is safe to say that since this "unexpected" turn of events, the world has not been the same.

Survival as facilitated through language can be traced to it, as can all forms of religion, the social sciences, and the arts. Even engineering, mathematics, and the physical sciences can be shown to find their roots of origin there.

(For a more detailed analysis of the evolution of the metaphor that is self-concept, consult Appendix I.)

A metaphor, then, is more than a pretty picture. To paraphrase a famous metaphorist, all the world is *not* a stage: It's a metaphor!

Mind: Of mind, Bierce opines as follows: "A mysterious form of matter secreted by the brain. Its chief activity consists in the endeavor to ascertain its own nature, the futility of the attempt being due to the fact that it has nothing but itself to know itself with."

While this writer greatly enjoys Bierce's wit and irony, he feels compelled to stipulate the following:

Mind is hardly a form of *matter*, though the brain is, and the word *secrete* does not describe its process; mind is an evanescent form of energy—resident, perhaps, in self-concept—that animates the brain; it is electrochemical, it exists as a consequence of connections made between synapses, and is omnipresent.

1. All its energies (save for inadvertent flashings) are initiated by survival issues, either of the body or of self-concept. The brain is a survival organ; the mind (self-concept?) directs its function.

2. The *chief activity* Bierce refers to is an expression of the desire to define reality, a necessary antecedent to survival. This desire to survive physically led—through metaphorical processes—to the desire to survive psychologically.

3. The mind *knows itself* through the agency of self-concept—a notion not available to Bierce—and it evolved (and continues to evolve) as a result of the forementioned metaphorical shift from physical to psychological survival.

Scientists may well someday succeed in mapping out the regions of the brain that, when stimulated, occasion certain responses, but they will never pin down or isolate the emotions their probings initiate.

Neuroscientists and psychologists who seek to "know" the brain are themselves servants of mind; and all their discoveries, I predict, will be traceable to metaphor.

Along this line, readers are directed to the ***Scientific American*** article, "The Language of the Brain"(10/2012/, 54-59.) The "spikes" Messers Sejnowski and Dellbruck emphasize are *aha!* responses.

N
(Omitted for Irrelevance)

O

Operant: A word not represented in Bierce's dictionary, and one adapted by this writer to the description of one aspect of the anatomy of metaphor. As defined here, an operant is the object (or idea) that functions as base—that is traceable to the fundamental source (the grounding material) from which metaphor germinates.

When Alfred Noyes states in "The Highwayman" that the *road* was a *ribbon* of moonlight, "road" should be seen as operant—the real object from which the epiphanant (see **E** above) "ribbon" and its qualifying epiphanant "of moonlight," derives.

The prepositional phrase, then, functions as modifier and enhances the picture. As all modifiers, it would be meaningless except for the metaphor to which it is attached.

Operants, it should be noted, may turn epiphanant when made abstract—that is, when they are divorced from nature, as in "the road to nowhere"—and it is difficult, sometimes, to retrace the transformed operant to its map of origin—as indicated in the world of chemistry where "the interaction of small molecules with chiral biomolecules such as enzymes also depends on which enantiomer is used." (***Science***, September, 2011, 1831).

Additionally, operants may also be implied, necessitating the reversal of the metaphorical method—as in the case of "womb" on page 231.

Nevertheless, in defense of the philosophy that is comparison psychology, and as etymology's comparative method illustrates with respect to language, it must be said: All metaphors begin with a basis in the real world, and it is to that physical grounding that their integrity may be traced. Whether noun, action, or name of an action, an operant is to idea as germ is to germination.

Fidelity to operant is the foundation of integrity.

P & Q
(Omitted for Irrelevance)

R

Religion: Of this word Bierce writes, "A daughter of Hope and Fear, explaining to Ignorance the nature of the Unknowable."

To this writer, religion is a survival metaphor through which humans seek continued existence in the face of their inevitable (and fear-inducing) mortality. In all its varieties (and there are thousands of them), most religions promise resurrection, reincarnation, or some other form of continued existence beyond the grave.

Since no one has confirmed survival in the hereafter—one reason for the prominent role played by Jesus Christ in Christianity, that Romanized version of the Judaism metaphor—theologians have come up with the concept of faith, an ungrounded metaphor (see *self-concept* below) where logic and evidence play no role and where the need to believe (survive) is so strong that even the possibility for doubt is negated.

To the extent that religions are (at base) a product of the drive to survive our dying, to that extent are they a threat to the development of a solid sense of self based on integrity.

Reparte is defined by Bierce as "prudent insult in retort. Practiced by gentlemen with a constitutional aversion to violence, but a strong disposition to offend."

When indulged in as a form of wit, jousting with one's friends as harmless one-upmanship, reparte is one thing. When engaged in as an expression of hostility, seeking to render nonphysical harm to a nonphysical entity, it is an act of cowardice invoked, at least in part, by a sense of inadequacy on the part of the person leveling it. Based on the desire to dominate, it is an unconscious expression of the drive to survive at the expense of humanness.

It is included in this dictionary as an instance—one of many!—of the way survival drive can take on multiple manifestations, many to destructive ends.

Responsibility: Of this concept Bierce writes, "A detachable burden easily shifted to the shoulders of God, Fate, Fortune, Luck or one's neighbor. In the days of astrology, it was customary to unload it upon a star."

In the version of metaphor proposed here, responsibility is more than an exercise in transference. It is the lens through which individuals attempt to examine every thought and action for their contribution to the positive construction of a positive sense of self.

The first mandate of the metaphor that is self-concept is the stipulation that individuals must assume responsibility for the creation of self-concept, else it will develop reflexively—according to haphazard events and environmental factors.

People who take on parenting responsibilities—and for the sake of self-concept their doing so should be a conscious choice—must assume responsibility for educating their children to self-concept construction as their prime human responsibility, as their one path to self-sufficiency.

At a certain point—probably in early adolescence—parents should allow the child—short of exposure to life-threatening or illegal activities—to deal with consequences of irresponsibility. The parent, whose job, ideally, has been done by then, is expected under the theory of comparison psychology to eschew all forms of criticism, reminding the child, only when necessary, of the importance of self-governance to the development of an independent sense of self.

(The powerplay, "So long as you live under my roof…" should not be used to coerce behavior. The child, after all, did not ask to be born, and coercion is anathema to self-government.)

(Guilt is acid to self-concept and should never be employed by people in positions of authority.)

All educational institutions—public or private—will profit from programs centered on the concept of self-constructed self-concepts and, under this approach, mastery in every field of learning would be presented as opportunities for affirmation to that end.

Self-concept construction is not a parental responsibility, though their acceptance of parental obligations requires that they do all they can to remove natural impediments to their child's right to acquire one.

(By natural impediments is meant the absence or inadequacy of food, shelter, and necessary medical attention. Children gain strength from facing and triumphing over obstacles and, aside from educating them to this, parents should not intervene in social or academic situations.)

Responsibility is a big word in self-concept theory!

S

Self-concept, a synthetic metaphor created through the process of comparison in the realm of ego, is self-conscious.

This term is not addressed directly by Bierce, but of self-esteem he writes, "An erroneous appraisement." Needless to say, he does not conceive of self-esteem as a property of that separate metaphorical entity defined here as self-concept.

Like all metaphors, self-concept is an object, but one made not of matter but of idea. Like any object, it affects its environment, but in this case its effects are metaphorical with physical consequences.

In fact, the role of self-concept has advanced to the point now, as the seat of consciousness and arbiter of reality, that a healthy, self-constructed self-concept is the adjudicator of success in all realms of survival—physical and psychological—and including academics, finances, and even (evidence suggests) the mental and physical wellbeing of our bodies.

Even as positive self-concepts foster rewards in the physical world, so do they enhance those human qualities of high seriousness, a confidence-based willingness to take risks in human relationships, and an intensification of the powers of human empathy.

As an artifact of synthetic metaphor's continuing evolution, the metaphor of self-concept is a synthetic metaphor, but a synthetic metaphor with a difference.

This difference—and it is a very important one!—lies in the fact of a newly evolved faculty for dual abstraction—an evolutionary advancement allowing self-concept to see itself as separate from the natural environment, empowered to see objects as objects, as actions, and as the name of actions.

This faculty, in other words, was a metaphorical adjustment that made possible the placement of metaphorical constituents in any position on the subject-verb-object equation—making, in other words, metaphor of metaphor.

Self-concept—itself a metaphorical abstraction derived originally from the physical body upon which it was based—evolved to the point where, freed from its umbilical attachment to the physical, it could now facsimilate the very process of nature and create its own objects—objects made of idea and, in a manner of speaking, copies of itself.

Endowed with the creative powers of nature whereby ideas of objects could be made objects and vice versa, self-concept was now liberated to create a new world, a world made not of matter but of idea.

Like all metaphors, this new metaphor was a manifestation of the drive to survive, but in this case survival drive was metaphorically translated into the desire to feel safe, competent, and admired—to feel secure in one's estimate of self.

This evolution, while the most significant in the history of the planet—in fact all the advancements of society and civilization may be traced to it!—brought with it some disquieting issues for explication.

The first of these issues—since humans were now empowered to employ metaphors in any way they chose—was that the grounding element present in synthetic metaphors limited to objects in nature no longer applied.

In earlier metaphors, every metaphor could be traced to an origin in its predecessor—a premise that provided the foundation for natural integrity, for grounding as an important element in metaphorical effectiveness (see discussion of verbal metaphors).

This elimination of grounding, however, was only apparent, and grounding had, instead, been rendered metaphorical. Grounding was no less required for metaphorical effectiveness, but now it had to be consciously created; it had to be optional, based on conscious action, and it had to be pertinent to survival of the newly evolved psychological self.

The need for grounding, then—along with the motive for object-based integrity—was transmuted into metaphorical groundedness, corresponding to that quality of object-based metaphor responsible for its effectiveness in earlier manifestations. Grounding had to be deliberate, based on actions consciously chosen, had to demonstrate logical, survival-based connections, and (if needed) utilize the employment of knowledge-based research and scholarship.

Along with the metaphorical transmission of the conscious facts of grounding came an important attribute of earlier forms of metaphor deserving of greater emphasis, and this was the forementioned fact of grounding in action.

Whether reflexive, hylozoic, or synthetic, survival has always been predicated upon action—actions taken in the best interest of physical survival—and this predication was readily inculcated into the metaphor of self-concept.

This transmission made it possible for individuals to select those actions (and thoughts and ideas are actions) that were in the best interests of self-concept survival. Humans could make conscious investments in self-concept survival and ground self-concept in actions with consciously anticipated (hoped for) consequences.

In the newly made Eden-world, survival became a product of choice (conscious or reflexive), a matter of personal integrity (the metaphorical counterpart of successful physical survival), and a willed consequence of actions consciously chosen for their contribution to a confident sense of self.

Thanks to this concept of self, the possibility exists for freedom born of psychological well-being, the existence of genuine creativity, and the disappearance of those reflexive responses most responsible for the evils that threaten the survival of planet Earth.

There is more to be said about the importance of grounding in the construction of self-concept, but suffice it to say now that it is only through fidelity to grounding—not falling victim to open-ended metaphor—that self-concept integrity is possible.

Finally, from the perspective of self-concept theory, self-esteem is a quality that may be earned or unearned, a mind state in which people may feel good about themselves as a consequence of conscious actions, or one in which the individual boasts of a sense of worth developed gratuitously—as a result of living a reflexive, unchallenged existence.

In that individual whose life has been insulated from stress by wealth or patronage, for instance, a sense of specialness or superiority may ensue, and this individual may know great success in a world that functions at the behest of physical survival. After all, it is instinctive survival drive that built that world!

Even so, there are consequences to a reflexively constructed sense of self.

For instance, those individuals whose concept of self is developed reflexively—unburdened by the day-to-day conflicts required for physical and emotional survival—may find themselves subject to the control of primitive impulses, those properties of a reflexive mind that lead to jealousy, hostility, and prejudice against people different from themselves.

Also, their sense of *noblesse oblige* may come from a position of condescension.

The publicized practice of the rich doing good after their physical survival is assured might be traced to the fact of an unearned (reflexively developed) sense of self and to a guilty desire to compensate for survival purchased at the expense of others. (Guilt, the reader is reminded, is to self-concept as acid is to flesh.)

Moreover—and most tragically—such individuals can never know that freedom made possible by a consciously constructed sense of self. (See *freedom* above.)

On the other hand, a feeling of self-esteem garnered from a consciously constructed self-concept will be spared the acidic consequences of guilt and the other automatic indemnities (think defensiveness and greed) that plague the world.

The quality of self-esteem growing out of a responsibly constructed self-concept is a source of empowerment for good—of the planet, its biota (including people), and the individual.

Selfish: Of this word Bierce writes, "Devoid of consideration for the selfishness of others," a typically sardonic comment with shades of kinship to Ayn Rand's infamous "virtue of selfishness." Even the theory of self-concept treated here has been accused by some of being grounded in selfishness.

The fact is, dedicating oneself to construction of a consolidated sense of self is anything but selfish. All of evolution points to the importance of the individual—survival of the fittest being a case in point—and the evolutionary development that is self-concept has liberated life force in ways yet to be fully understood.

Furthermore, there is nothing intrinsically wrong with being the best (most confident) person one can possibly be—all religious strictures negating ego aside. Renouncing self in the interests of conglomerates and of those institutions that profit from the fear of dying and the promise of life after death, has never been in the best interests of the individual.

In any event, developing responsibly one's sense of self is an act of empowerment that costs no other person anything.

A liberated individual—coming from a position of strength based on earned self-confidence—is much more capable of generosity than a defensive soul bound up in the self-protective business of saving a threatened self.

That person who does good as an investment in the approbation of others or of survival beyond the grave is the epitome of selfishness.

Survival Drive: While not an issue of concern to Bierce, the force is evident to all who have chosen to look. The changing of the seasons is evidence of it, as is the impulse of the seed to germinate, the oak tree to make acorns, and the need of humans to reproduce themselves in the form of offspring. It is also made evident in those strategies we employ to avoid injury or disease, as it is in the compulsion of parents to protect their offspring.

(The oft-repeated hypothesis—that nothing comes from nothing—is useful when speaking of the importance of natural grounding in metaphor, but when presented as evidence for the need of a deity, it owes too much to physical survival drive to be countenanced—the metaphor being traceable to the fact that the human brain, as a reflexive product of survival drive, has no alternative to seeing everything linearly—as either good for physical survival or not.

(Given the advent of self-concept, humans need not be—indeed should not be!—so limited.

(This black-or-white monomania—either it is good for physical survival or it isn't—is the source of the human habit of pragmatism so omni-evident in the minds of reflexive thinkers everywhere.

(As quantum mechanics has made clear in its rejection of exactitude in favor of probability, nature does not operate on black or white dicta.

(Furthermore, the concept of metaphor presented here [in the opinion of this writer] provides a theory of origins supported by the discoveries of science and is not reliant on magic or divine intervention.)

As used here, the term survival drive is meant to represent that pervasive quality in the universe whereby all forms of matter are driven to bind—in the parlance of metaphor, to survive—conception meaning, here, to give birth to or to ideate. Survival drive (as stated before) was the first metaphor.

As for the impetus behind survival drive, its driving force is found in what humans identify as pleasure—a survival impulse geared into the system (see "The Joyful Mind," M. L. Kringelbach and K.C. Berridge, *Scientific American*, [40-45, 10/2012]) that found the *aha!* expression in the act of fusion characterized in physics by the behavior of merging particles and in biology by the fact of orgasm.

As an instinctive engineering force, survival drive did not initially require cognition to evolve—it only had to recognize affinities reflexively. Self-concept, on the other hand, is the one coinage on the planet subject to human control, and this is accomplished through the conscious selection of those actions and ideas meant to enhance it. (See *self-concept* above.)

The earliest surviving expression of the drive to survive in humans is traceable to the appearance of tools and weapons—utilitarian objects made from the shaping of stone implements—and, later on, by the shaping of arrows, other forms of weaponry, and cave paintings, as well as the manufacture (coming later) of utensils born of smelting sciences.

Of course, there were always rocks and clubs, and it is interesting to speculate as to which came first—weaponry or the tools of hunting and agriculture. For what it's worth, my vote is for weaponry!

One of the most intriguing expressions of survival drive is found in the cave paintings referred to earlier, said to have been dated to the Upper Paleolithic Epoch, around 33,000 BCE. These remarkably beautiful (and often expressionist) depictions are especially interesting because of the portrayal in them of humans as diminutive stick figures dominated by vividly drawn pictures of aurochs and bison, often portrayed as larger than life.

This paradox is seen as evidence that the metaphor of self-concept—survival drive's most powerful creation—had not yet been fully realized, meaning the cave paintings are seen here as a kind of production, a mystical spell meant to facilitate the killing and trapping of prey, an application of reflexive metaphor directly traceable to the need for food and physical survival.

That art should arrive before a consciously developed self-concept should not surprise, for art at its most basic level deals with creation, and when addressed today (say in poetry, my personal area of interest) artists may elect to avail themselves of the energies inherent in reflexive metaphor—an option leading to the conscious shadowing metaphors with primeval energies.

Art (a form of surviving) needs not always be a product of instinct or insanity!

Art of every kind and age is traceable to survival drive, and, thanks to an evolving self-concept, it has grown ever more conscious and sophisticated.

The appearance of synthetic metaphors and the deliberate use of self-concept for reasons of psychological survival had to wait the coming of medicine men and priests—self-assigned official overseers of survival, physical and spiritual.

T, U, V, W, X & Y
(Omitted for Irrelevance)

Z

Zero: The mathematical equivalent of nothing, an empty space hospitable to invaders—digital or imaginary—where, with the introduction of plus or minus signs, a mirror universe—a kind of welcome-to-all-comers force field—springs magically into existence. Therein, figures (opposite-number functionaries) dance out miracles of obverse or inverse functions possessed of magical properties.

Confirmation of the possibility that every particle—in addition to its negative and positive numbers—has an invisible twin orbiting in ghostly unison—the zero is testament to the creative power of metaphor. Zero is the gateway to metaphor—the quantum equivalent of eternity.

Each of us begins at zero, possessing, notwithstanding, a force field of positive or negative energy, the nature of which is determined by the side of zero we choose to occupy.

Index

willed consciousness 290, 359
Williams 85, 147
Williams, Redford 83, 84, 86
Williams, Tennessee 33
willpower 134
wit 378
witchcraft 42, 43, 45
Wolff, H.G. 73
Wolf, Stewart 93
word salads 202, 203
Wordsworth, William 273

X

Xanadu 37

Y

Yarboroughs 267

Z

Zen Buddhists 45
zero 391

www.ingramcontent.com/pod-product-compliance
Lightning Source LLC
Chambersburg PA
CBHW020915140626
46545CB00015B/54